THE RIDDLE OF EXISTENCE SOLVED; OR, AN ANTIDOTE TO INFIDELITY. BEING AN ANSWER TO PROFESSOR GOLDWIN SMITH'S "GUESSES AT THE RIDDLE OF EXISTENCE"

Published @ 2017 Trieste Publishing Pty Ltd

ISBN 9780649693610

The Riddle of Existence Solved; Or, an Antidote to Infidelity. Being an Answer to Professor Goldwin Smith's "Guesses at the Riddle of Existence" by W. J. Fenton

Edited by Trieste Publishing Pty Ltd.
Cover @ 2017

www.triestepublishing.com

W. J. FENTON

THE RIDDLE OF EXISTENCE SOLVED; OR, AN ANTIDOTE TO INFIDELITY. BEING AN ANSWER TO PROFESSOR GOLDWIN SMITH'S "GUESSES AT THE RIDDLE OF EXISTENCE"

 Trieste

THE
RIDDLE OF EXISTENCE SOLVED

OR

AN ANTIDOTE TO INFIDELITY

Being an Answer to Professor Goldwin Smith's
"Guesses at the Riddle of Existence."

By W. J. FENTON.

AUTHOR OF

"The Unity of the Spirit"; or, "Failure of Brethrenism as a
United Testimony."

God, who at sundry times and in divers manners spake in time past
unto the fathers by the prophets, hath in these last days spoken unto us by
His Son, whom He hath appointed heir of all things, by whom also He
made the worlds.—HEB. 1 : 1, 2.

TORONTO:
HENDERSON & CO., 8 AND 10 LOMBARD STREET.
1898.

PREFACE.

THE apparent confidence with which Professor Goldwin Smith, in his Preface to "Guesses at the Riddle of Existence," takes it for granted that "liberal theologians have at least half resigned the belief in miracles" and "given up the authenticity and authority of Genesis," and that "with these they must apparently give up the Fall, the Redemption and the Incarnation," are well adapted to shake the nerves of any unsophisticated enquirer after truth. But when such an enquirer sits down to read the book itself without a dictionary by his side, and comes across such words and expressions as these: "Anti-Malthusian," "Strangely anthropomorphic," the "Mosaic Cosmogony," "Vitality of protoplasm," the "Cosmogonical and historical foundations of traditional belief have been sapped by science and criticism," "The hypostatic union of the Pope and the Holy Ghost," "Dogmatic religion is geocentric," "Such a cataclysm," "This altruism," "Transcendental solipsism," "Physic thaumaturgy," etc., with frequent references to the great discoveries of science, it is little wonder if he begins to fancy that the very foundations of faith are giving way, and to feel as if nothing is before him in the future but a great blank void, into which a host of learned professors, scientists and "liberal theologians" are peering with troubled faces, guessing at what they had been evoluted from; and wondering whither they are going after this brief span of existence is over.

In the oldest book of the Bible we find Elihu saying as he speaks on behalf of God, "But there is a spirit in man, and the inspiration of the Almighty giveth them understanding. Great men are not always wise; neither do the aged understand judgment" (Job 32 : 8, 9). And in the New Testament we read, "But God hath chosen

the foolish things of the world to confound the wise, and
God hath chosen the weak things of the world to confound the things that are mighty; and base things of the
world, and things which are despised, hath God chosen;
yea, and things which are not, to bring to nought things
that are, that no flesh should glory in His presence"
(1 Cor. 1 : 27-29). And again we read, " But the natural
man receiveth not the things of the Spirit of God, for
they are foolishness unto him, neither can he know them,
because they are spiritually discerned" (1 Cor. 2 : 14).

The book which Professor Goldwin Smith has published under the general title of " Guesses at the Riddle
of Existence" is really a collection of five essays, not
connected with each other in any 'other sense than that
they are all infidel writings. The separate titles given
to them are : (1) Guesses at the Riddle of Existence,
(2) The Church and the Old Testament, (3) Is there
Another Life ? (4) The Miraculous Element in Christianity, (5) Morality and Theism. The first, third and
fifth of these are mainly composed of abstract specula-
tions and metaphysical reasonings, not likely to do much
harm, and certainly no good, of themselves to any intelligent reader. It would, therefore, be a waste of time to
reply to them separately. But the real venom of the
book is contained in the second and fourth essays, which
are sandwiched in between the other three, apparently
to make them more palatable to the tastes of readers
who may not think there is anything very dangerous in
his other productions.

The first of these essays, which gives the title to the
book, comprises only about forty-five pages, and, instead
of being his own guesses, it is almost exclusively devoted
to his remarks upon the guesses of other people, including Professor Drummond and Messrs. Kidd and
Balfour, all of which guesses, together with his remarks
upon them, really amount to nothing worthy of serious
notice. The writing of this comparatively harmless
essay, seems to have been simply taken advantage of by
the learned professor for the purpose of putting all his

infidel writings before the public, in one volume, under a new title.

In his second and fourth essays his chief aim has been to disprove, if possible, the inspiration and authenticity of the Old Testament Scriptures, and especially of the Book of Genesis, against which he seems to have a special antipathy; and to deny the truth of miracles recorded in both Old and New Testament Scriptures, with the expectation, doubtless, that if he succeeds in these objects there will be nothing left in support of Christianity as a supernatural religion, whose faith, as he admits, is still that of those who are the "salt of the earth."

The writer's main object in the following pages is to show, chiefly from the Word of God itself, how frivolous are the arguments used by infidel writers against the inspiration and authenticity of the Scriptures as compared with the overwhelming weight of evidence of the most positive kind, by which they are proved to be a Divine revelation from God to man. Instead of replying, therefore, to the separate essays as such, he decided to treat them as a whole, and reply to the arguments and assertions contained in them in the way that seems to him best suited to bring the general subject of infidelity, with its pretensions and fallacies most clearly before the minds of those who might possibly be led astray by the plausible theories of modern skepticism.

It is quite possible that he has, without knowing it, advanced arguments that have been already used by other and abler writers, and that he has also, through ignorance of their writings, omitted many weightier arguments which they have used. However this may be, it is hoped that some things written herein, if not quite new to persons exercised on the subject, may at least be so arranged as to prove helpful to those, and especially to young people, who are in danger of being misled by the confident assertions, vague generalities and plausible sophistries so insiduously presented by Professor Goldwin Smith, who is all the more dangerous because of the refinement of his style, and his apparent candour in some respects, which prevent him from indulging in vulgar blasphemies in the same manner as Voltaire, Paine and Ingersoll, whose very coarseness has often doubtless proved an antidote to the poison they tried to instil into the minds of others.

It is really sad to see this learned and eminent professor, in company with his friends, the "liberal theologians," floundering about in nature's darkness, like the ancient philosophers whom they quote so frequently; and trying to weave out of their own fertile brains some philosophical theories to take the place of that Divine Revelation of Himself and His purposes which God has given, and the faith in which they are taking so much pains, if possible, to destroy.

CONTENTS.

CHAPTER I.

CHAPTER II.

Chapter III.—*Continued.*

CHAPTER IV.

CHAPTER V.

CHAPTER VI.

APPENDIX A.

APPENDIX B.

EXPLANATORY NOTE.

THIS book, except the Conclusion and Appendices, was hurriedly written nearly two years ago, within a few weeks after the first appearance of Professor Goldwin Smith's "Guesses at the Riddle of Existence." It was not published before for various reasons, amongst which was the fact that the writer was so busily engaged with other and necessary work that he had not time even to look over the manuscript more than once since it was written. It is, perhaps, unnecessary for him to say, what must be self-evident to any reader, that he cannot make any pretensions to either scholarship or literary skill, in this simple endeavour to show from the Word of God itself, that the Bible is what it professes to be, a Divine revelation from God to man. If the Scriptures quoted have been so arranged as to let that Word, as the Sword of the Spirit, speak for itself in defense of its own Inspiration and Authenticity, he will be better satisfied, and the book itself will be more profitable reading, than if, by any arguments or theories he might use, he were to obtain credit from avowed infidels and "liberal theologians" for erudite scholarship and scientific knowledge, in meeting their attacks upon revealed truth with their own weapons.

Toronto, December, 1898.

ERRATA.

Page 52. In sub-heading read "fittest" instead of "fitted."

Page 65. In ninth line from foot insert "will of the" between "the" and "flesh."

Page 105. In first line of second paragraph insert the words "among critics" between the words "opinion" and "as."

Page 109. In fifth line of second paragraph read "messenger" instead of "messengers."

Page 236. In sub-heading read "Reverse" instead of "Result."

CHAPTER I.

THE MODE OF DIVINE REVELATION.

THE Bible proves itself to be a Divine Revelation from God to man by its own internal evidence; and the Gospel which it unfolds is always the power of God unto salvation without the help of human science or learning of any kind. They do not require a certificate of character from ungodly men to make them worthy of belief; and the facts still remain as they were when Christianity was first established, " To the poor the Gospel is preached, and not many mighty, not many noble are called."

In the first chapter of Hebrews we are informed of the mode of this Divine Revelation, "God, who at sundry times and in divers manners spake in times past unto the fathers by the prophets, hath in these last days spoken unto us by His Son, whom He hath appointed heir of all things, by whom also He made the worlds" (Heb. 1 : 1, 2).

This is in striking contrast with the methods of Revelation claimed by the founders of many false religions, who profess to be themselves the sole recipients of spiritual communications from the Divine Being, at least for the purpose of founding their systems.

No Other Mode Suggested by Skeptics as more Reliable.

Those who try so hard to find discrepancies in the statements of Scripture, and on this ground to deny their inspiration or authenticity, do not even suggest any other mode of Divine Revelation with which they would have been satisfied. In reference to God's revealing Himself in human form to Abraham, Professor Goldwin Smith quotes approvingly from some unknown writer in *Lux*

Mundi as follows : " Why should we force ourselves to believe that a Being who fills eternity and infinity became the guest of a Hebrew sheik ?" To which it may be answered that no one is forced to believe anything that God has revealed, but if He is known to be the speaker through any channel, the refusal to believe His Word is the most presumptuous sin of which any mortal can be guilty. The first question to be settled is, Has God really spoken ?

He strongly objects to the reception of traditional evidence from the time of Adam to Noah, which had been handed down from father to son before being incorporated in the sacred writings by Moses, but he does not state any other reasonable way in which the same narrative could have been supplied, without a direct revelation of all the facts from the Holy Spirit, to the writer; and he calls such traditional evidence an Assyrian legend (see Appendix A) without furnishing a particle of proof that his assertion is correct. Regarding the first five books he says that " Documentary analysis and the philosophy of history combined have made it highly *probable* that writings ascribed by our Bible to Moses not only were not his, but were of a date as late as the captivity. It is *likely* that the schools of the prophets played a great part, as did the monasteries of the Middle Ages, in composing the chronicles of the nation "; and for these assertions of mere probabilities no evidence whatever is produced. In reference to the Psalms he says that " the pensiveness of the Captivity *seems* to pervade the Psalms," thus suggesting the shadow of a doubt, without the slightest reasonable probability as to David having not really been their author. With respect to the books of the Old Testament generally, and notably the historical books, he says they " are for the most part by unknown authors, and of unknown dates," but he has not informed his readers what that has to do with the question of their inspiration. After complaining, as we have seen, of the lack of direct revelation instead of traditional evidence, he says that " all seers, as their name imports, have

visions. Primitive law-givers speak by Divine command. In no other way apparently is inspiration claimed
by the authors of the Old Testament." It does seem that
in this quotation the professor makes a distinction without a difference so far as the question of inspiration is
concerned, for if the instrument God uses is really
inspired, it matters not whether the revelation has been
made to him by a vision, by an audible voice, or by the
silent guidance of his thoughts by the Holy Spirit as he
writes what God has commanded. Nor is it of any consequence whether or not the writers themselves put
forward any claim to inspiration, or whether or not they
cite elder authorities, such as the Book of Jasher, to
which Professor Smith refers, so long as the mind of God
is spoken and the truth declared. As a case in point,
see the course taken by Paul, the inspired apostle to the
Gentiles, when he was preaching to the Athenians, and
quoted what their own poets had said.

The Book of Hebrews declares that God "at sundry
times and in divers manners spake in times past unto
the fathers by the prophets," and we have seen that the
learned professor has taken exception to every method
by which the great Author of the universe has thus
deigned to reveal Himself and His thoughts to human
beings on this terrestrial sphere, but he has not even
suggested any other mode of revelation which would
have been satisfactory to himself and his friends, the
liberal theologians or "higher critics."

It is certain that if one book had been found like the
Book of Mormon, claiming to have come direct from
heaven, it would at once have been pronounced a forgery
by the very parties who now try so hard to throw doubts
upon the authenticity and inspiration of the Old Testament Scriptures.

God's Mode the Best Safeguard Against Imposture.

In speaking to men "at sundry times and in divers
manners," God has provided the best safeguards against
fraud and imposture that could be supplied according to

the circumstances of the various ages when He has thus spoken. An infinitely wise Being, the Creator of the universe and the Author of all of nature's laws could have endowed mankind since the Fall supernaturally with a perfect knowledge of all scientific problems which have since by patient research been discovered; but instead of doing this He provided him with intellectual faculties capable of investigating the wonders of nature and of Nature's laws. The curse which came upon man for his disobedience declared " cursed is the ground for thy sake; in sorrow shalt thou eat of it all the days of thy life; thorns and thistles shall it bring forth to thee; and thou shalt eat of the herb of the field; in the sweat of thy face shalt thou eat bread till thou return into the ground; for out of it wast thou taken : for dust thou art, and unto dust shalt thou return." Before the Fall, in a condition of spotless purity, in the very likeness of God Himself, he needed not to work for a living; all nature was subject to his will, and, as the viceroy upon earth of the great Creator, Adam gave their names to every living creature. The earth yielded its increase without any manual toil, and man only required to take and eat that which it provided for his support. And just so, had he continued in a state of primeval innocence, we know not how rapidly his intellectual powers might have grasped far more knowledge of science and Nature's laws than has yet been attained through the laborious process of study by men, who have been evoluting downwards instead of upwards, through the debasing effects of sinful propensities and habits upon the higher faculties of their nature. This much is certain, on the unfailing testimony of the Word of God, which is our only possible source of knowledge on the subject, that men before the Flood and after the Fall must have been both physically and intellectually far superior to any uneducated men that have ever been heard of since. Even Cain, the murderer, built a city and called it after the name of his son. Jubal was the father of all such as handle the harp and organ; and Tubal Cain was the instructor of every artificer in brass and iron, showing the possession of a wonderful amount of knowledge of science and art in antediluvian days. And this corresponds with what we read later on in Gen. 6 : 4. "There were giants in the earth in those days; and also after that, when the sons of God came in unto the daughters of men, and they bare children to them; the same became mighty men, which were of old, men of renown." This does not read much like a description of men evoluted from monkeys, as Professor Darwin and his scientific friends would have us believe that all the human race have been.

But the discoveries of archaeological science have brought to light much collateral evidence in support of the positive testimony of Scripture as to the knowledge of some branches of science and art which prevailed in, or very shortly after, antediluvian days, and the remains of buried cities that have been unearthed have proved beyond a doubt the existence of a high degree of civilization, such as would be indicated by the quotations from Genesis which have been given above. And in this connection it may be as well to remark, that Professor Goldwin Smith and other infidel writers are in the habit of assuming that all scientific men are agreed in thinking that the discoveries of science have contradicted the testimony of the Scriptures, in such a manner as to destroy faith in their inspiration and authenticity. But this is not the case. Many of the most eminent scientists are devout Christians, and boldly maintain that all the great discoveries of science, when fairly considered, are calculated to strengthen faith in the unerring truth of the Word of God. Take, for example, our own most eminent geologist, Sir William Dawson, who is at the same time a most earnest and devout Christian worker.

Reliable Traditions Contrasted with Legends.

Supposing, then, that in the antediluvian ages the art of writing was unknown, whilst only one language and a very high degree of intelligence prevailed, the only means of preserving history would be by tradition, and

as a general rule, the reliability of this tradition would
depend upon the number of persons through whom it
had been transmitted to the one who first commits it to
writing, and thus makes the tradition become history.
If a man tells us something that he has himself seen, we
are bound to receive his testimony, if his character is
unimpeachable, and if what he says is not contradicted
by equally reliable evidence. If his testimony is not published until after his death, we must weigh well the character of any one who professes to have heard his statements before we attach much importance to them, but
if there are a dozen intelligent and reputable persons,
who all declare positively to having heard him make the
same statements, we rely upon their evidence as fully as
if we had heard the evidence of the first witness with our
own ears; and if these persons, before their death, again
hand down the same story to other equally intelligent
and reputable witnesses, their testimony to the facts
related is received with confidence. In this manner statements of certain facts have in early ages and in many
countries been handed down from father to son through
succeeding generations as tradition, until they were at
length committed to writing, and thus became embodied
in history. It is evident, however, that the more frequently verbal traditions are handed down from one
generation to another, the greater liability there is for
error to creep into the narrative without any intention
on the part of the narrators to state what is untrue. And
just here it would be well to clearly mark the distinction
between reliable tradition and legends which have been
handed down in the same manner from one generation
to another. This is necessary, because Professor Goldwin Smith alludes (page 73) to the story of Creation given
in Genesis as only an Assyrian legend (see Appendix A),
without producing a particle of evidence in support of
his assertion. Reliable tradition might, perhaps, be
described as statements of important facts by many competent witnesses, handed down from one generation to
another, without being impeached by any other reliable

testimony until it is committed to writing. A legend, on the other hand, is a fanciful story by unknown authors, founded, it may be, originally on certain facts, but enlarged by poetic license till it has become more in the nature of romance than any statement of actual events which have occurred. In the handing down of reliable tradition by competent persons, where care is taken to state only what is correct, there is a tendency to stick closely to the material facts and omit many details that may seem unimportant. With legends, on the other hand, upon a very slight substratum of fact, there is generally a great superstructure of poetic fictions, which have been added by unknown contributors as the stories increased in age, and were frequently intended to celebrate the praises of some real or imaginary hero.

Applying these tests to the first eleven chapters of Genesis, which Professor Smith characterizes as an Assyrian legend (see Appendix A), especially that portion of the history of the human race which is prior to the Flood, to what conclusions are we forced? Here are facts of the most stupendous importance to the whole human race, simply stated, without any redundancy of detail or appearance of poetic imagery. Here is the genealogy from Adam to Noah, giving the age of each individual in that line of descent, and making special mention, in very brief terms, of one man, Enoch, who, after he had attained the age of sixty-five years, walked with God for three hundred years, and was not, for God took him. Here we have the story in few words of deep disgrace and humbling failure on the part of Adam and Cain, and at length of the whole human race (Noah only excepted), which ends in their destruction by the Deluge, without a single attempt to indulge in poetic imagery or to exalt any man as a hero. And then again, the story of the race, from Noah to the Tower of Babel, is another sad history of failure on the part of all mankind, ending with the dispersion of the race and the confusion of tongues, and including long genealogies from Noah down to Abraham, with no attempt whatever to sing the praises of any hero. For what purpose, it may be asked, were these genealogical tables preserved and the names of cities given to us in these chapters whose ruins have been discovered in recent years, and thus confirmed the correctness of the Scripture narrative ?

Great Ages Ensured Correctness of Earliest Traditions.

But one of the surest guarantees that we have of the correctness of the traditional history of our race before the Deluge is the great age to which men then lived, as well as their great intelligence, which at last developed into open infidelity, as it is fast doing at the present time. Adam lived 930 years, and when he died, Lamech, the father of Noah, was fifty-six years old, and Lamech died only five years before the Deluge, when Shem, Noah's son, was about one hundred years old. Noah lived 950 years, and when he died Abram was sixty-three years old; and Shem lived 600 years, and survived Abram about eight years.

Here we find that besides the father of Noah, many thousands of other intelligent and reputable persons (including Lamech's grandfather, Enoch, who walked with God three hundred years), all lived for hundreds of years contemporaneously with Adam, the first progenitor of the human race, from whose own lips they had doubtless often heard the story of the Creation as it had probably been revealed to him by Jehovah in the Garden of Eden, and also the sad story of the Fall, which brought about such a terrible change in the condition of himself and all his posterity. And Abram, and many thousands of their other descendants, had doubtless often heard from the lips of both Noah and Shem all that Noah's father had learned from the lips of Adam respecting Creation, as well as the more recent history of the Deluge, by which the whole human race had been destroyed except themselves and their few relatives who were saved in the ark. Is it possible that any traditional testimony could be more direct and trustworthy than this ? And is it at all probable that the testimony thus transmitted to Abram, Isaac and Jacob, with each of whom God held personal converse, would be by them corrupted, or that up to the time of Moses the brief narrative of such important facts would be altered materially in any respect whilst the Israelites still adhered to the worship of the one living and true God ?

Moses Best Qualified to Commit Traditions to Writing.

Moses was, by his early education in the house of Pharaoh, skilled in all the learning of the Egyptians, and through the careful training of his own mother we may also be assured that he, as the great grandson of Levi, the son of Jacob, was thoroughly conversant with all the records and traditions of the Hebrews. There was, therefore, no one who was so well qualified as he to embody in permanent history the various revelations that God had given in speaking with audible voice to Adam, to Cain, to Noah, and to Abraham, Isaac and Jacob, as well as the authentic histories and genealogies which had been handed down through such direct and trustworthy channels.

"But," says the Professor (page 78), "Abram's ancestors served other gods" (Joshua 24 : 2). Quite true, and this just accords with the whole testimony of Scripture that fallen man is ever prone to depart from the true God and lapse into idolatry. The same thing happened again and again with the Israelites after they had entered the promised land. But if it is intended by this remark to impeach the trustworthiness of the testimony of Abraham as one of the channels through which such important Divine revelations had been handed down, there is no force whatever in such a suggestion as Abram was called out from his father's house, and himself made the recipient of direct revelations from God. And besides this, as we have seen, he was sixty-three years old when Noah died, and Shem outlived him by about eight years, so that he was by no means dependent upon his own immediate ancestors for the knowledge he possessed of the previous part of human history, which is all compressed into a very brief summary.

Apart, then, altogether from the question of the inspiration of Moses as the author of the Book of Genesis, we find that God's manner of revealing Himself and His will to the human race was by speaking to certain men, who, taught by the Spirit, recognized His voice as the voice of God, and that at various times he appeared to them in the form of a man, and these revelations, with the concurrent history and genealogy, have been handed down through the most trustworthy channels as reliable traditions until they were embodied by Moses in the form of history.

God's Direct Revelations to Moses as His Prophet.

As to the inspiration of Moses, however, no reasonable man can have any doubt. The manner of God's revelations to him was different from that of any former revelations to the human race. First, He spoke to him out of a bush, which was burning but not consumed; commanded him to put his shoes from off his feet, for the place whereon he stood was holy ground; and then told him of His purpose to use him for the delivery of the children of Israel, and revealed Himself as the I AM THAT I AM, a name indicating, as Dr. Young says, rather the *unsearchableness* of God than His *existence*, as is commonly supposed (Ex. 3 : 2, 14). In this case there is the Shekinah flame, always indicative of Jehovah's presence, which also appeared. And in Ex. 6 : 3, He explained to Moses the difference in the manner of His revelation of Himself, saying, "And I appeared unto Abraham, unto Isaac, and unto Jacob by the names of God Almighty, but by my name, JEHOVAH was I not known to them," this word meaning *the existing one*, and being the incommunicable name of the God of Israel.

And again on Mount Sinai there was the Shekinah fire, indicating the presence of Jehovah, when "the Lord descended upon it in fire; and the smoke thereof ascended as the smoke of a furnace, and the whole mount quaked greatly. And when the voice of the trumpet sounded long, and waxed louder and louder, Moses spake, and God answered him by a voice, and the Lord came down upon Mount Sinai, on the top of the mount; and the Lord called Moses up to the top of the mount, and Moses went up" (Ex. 19 : 18-20). And there Moses received from God Himself the Ten Commandments and other laws for the children of Israel.

And upon another occasion Moses was called to come up unto the Lord in Mount Sinai with Aaron, Nadab and Abihu and seventy of the elders of Israel. And it is said " they saw the God of Israel, and there was under his feet, as it were, a paved work of a sapphire stone, and as it were the body of heaven in its clearness " (Ex. 24 : 10). And the Lord said unto Moses, " Come up to Me into the mount, and be there, and I will give thee tables of stone, and a law and commandments which I have written, that thou mayest teach them. And Moses went up and his servant, Joshua; and Moses went up into the Mount of God " (vs. 12, 13). And further on we read, "And Moses went up into the mount, and a cloud covered the mount. And the glory of the Lord abode upon Mount Sinai, and the cloud covered it six days, and the seventh day He called Moses out of the midst of the cloud. And the sight of the glory of the Lord was like devouring fire on the top of the mount in the eyes of the children of Israel; and Moses went into the midst of the cloud, and gat him up into the mount; and Moses was in the mount forty days and forty nights" (Ex. 24: 16-18).

Could anything be more imposing and solemn in the presence of a whole nation than what is stated in Ex. 20 : 18, 19, when immediately after the giving of the Ten Commandments we read that " all the people saw the thunderings, and the lightnings, and the noise of the trumpet, and the mountain smoking; and when the people saw it they removed and stood afar off. And they said unto Moses, " Speak thou with us, and we will hear; but let not God speak with us lest we die." And in v. 21 we read, "And the people stood afar off, and Moses drew near unto the thick darkness where God was." Here again is the Shekinah fire, betokening the presence of Jehovah.

These things were not done in a corner by a few imposters to be palmed off upon credulous dupes in future ages. These revelations of God's majesty were made in the presence of a vast multitude, and have never been questioned until a few modern infidels favour us with their opinions that it is *not probable* that such a manifest revelation of God's presence ever took place; and perhaps they will *guess* that it was volcanic fire coupled with a severe thunderstorm at the same time that caused the phenomena which took place on Mount Sinai. Well might Abraham say (as the Lord Jesus Christ declares that He said) to the rich man in Hades, " If they hear not Moses and the prophets, neither will they be persuaded though one rose from the dead " (Luke 16 : 31).

Public Manifestation of God's Presence to a Whole Nation.

Before these revelations were given to Moses the Israelites were familiar with the presence of the Lord, who in their journeys went before them in a pillar of cloud by day and a pillar of fire by night (Ex. 13 : 21), and Moses was frequently receiving communications from God, who desired to enter into a more intimate relationship with men by *dwelling* in the tabernacle which He commanded them to build, and where He promised to meet with Moses and speak to him (Ex. 29 : 42-45). So after the tabernacle had been set up " it came to pass, when Moses went out unto the tabernacle that all the people rose up, and stood every man at his tent door, and looked after Moses until he was gone into the tabernacle. And it came to pass as Moses entered into the tabernacle the cloudy pillar descended, and stood at the door of the tabernacle. And the LORD talked with Moses, and all the people saw the cloudy pillar stand at the tabernacle door; and all the people rose up and worshipped, every man in his tent door. And the Lord spake unto Moses face to face, as a man speaketh unto his friend" (Ex. 33 : 8-11). Here again we have the presence of Jehovah manifested by the Shekinah fire. Moses on this occasion asked to be shown God's way, that he might know Him and find peace in His sight, and the Lord answered, " My presence (or Shekinah) shall go with thee, and I will give thee rest" (Ex. 33: 15). And when Moses came down from the mount his face shone, and he wist it not; but the people were afraid to go nigh him, and when he was speaking unto them he had to put a veil over his face, which was taken off again when he went into the presence of the Lord, and this was witnessed by all the children of Israel (Ex. 34 : 29-35). After the tabernacle had been dedicated the Shekinah fire was always between the cherubim above the mercy-seat of the ark until the destruction of the temple of Solomon ; and thus through all those years that unearthly flame was a constant reminder of Jehovah's presence in their midst. But enough has been stated to show the remarkable and public manner in which the Divine Revelations were given to Moses. It is no wonder that Professor Smith and other infidel writers would like to wipe out such testimony as this and try to persuade us on their simple assertions that it is *probable* the Pentateuch was written many centuries afterwards during the Captivity in Babylon, an assertion which is not supported by any evidence whatever.

Professor Smith's Attack Upon the Book of Genesis, Etc.

So far as the Book of Genesis is concerned it is evident that reliable traditions and records were handed down through the most trustworthy channels to the man who, of all others, was best fitted by his education and early Hebrew training to embody them in permanent history—to Moses, the inspired prophet, unto whom the Lord spoke "face to face as a man speaketh unto his friend"; and who was, therefore, doubtless commissioned by Him to do this very work, and made the recipient also by special revelation of all the information contained in the first chapters of this book regarding Creation and the Fall. At all events, it is only reasonable to believe that in the familiar personal intercourse to which he was admitted by Jehovah he would ask for information concerning those most important facts in connection with the world and the human race, and would thus be enabled to commit to writing what God had specially revealed to him.

But Professor Goldwin Smith questions the fact of any sojourn of the Hebrews in Egypt at all (page 65), because, forsooth, " nothing certainly Egyptian seems to be traceable in Hebrew beliefs or institutions !" Why, this is one of the very strongest proofs that Moses was the author of the Pentateuch. Is it at all likely that he, as God's inspired prophet, who was divinely appointed to lead His chosen people out of Egypt, and write down laws for their future guidance, which Jehovah Himself communicated to him, would incorporate with these anything that pertained to the idolatrous institutions of Egypt ? The mere suggestion of such a flimsy basis on which to found a doubt of the truth of Scripture ought surely to be beneath the dignity of anyone who desires to get credit for candour in the investigation of historical facts.

The Professor also, on pages 57 and 58, makes the following objections to the narratives in the Pentateuch and to the authorship of Moses:—

First—That the alleged record is of a date posterior by many centuries to the events, and, therefore, no record at all, plainly appears from the mention of Kings in Genesis 36 : 31.

Second—The words of Genesis 12 : 6—" the Canaanite

was then in the land "—shew that the book was written
when the Canaanite had long disappeared.

Third—Moreover, the writer always speaks of Moses
in the third person.

Fourth—The words of Deut. 34: 10—"there arose not
a prophet since like unto Moses"—imply that the book
was written after the rise " of a line of other prophets."

And he adds, " These things were noticed by critics
long ago, but the eyes of faith in England and America
at least have been shut."

His Objections Easily Answered.

In reply to these objections, it may seem superfluous
to state that every one of them is susceptible of the most
easy and natural explanation. Those who maintain the
Divine inspiration and authenticity of Scripture as it
came from the pens of inspired writers, do not for a
moment contend that copyists and printers have by
miraculous power been kept from making mistakes, in
reproducing copies of the Sacred Writings, or that some
interpolations have not been inserted in these copies
during the many ages that have elapsed since they were
first written. It is the part of true criticism to discover
and explain these errors and interpolations made by
copyists; and the result of such work in the past has
always been to bring out into fuller and brighter light
all those glorious truths that God has revealed through
His Word.

But there is another kind of criticism by avowed infidels and unconverted professors who call themselves "liberal theologians," or " higher critics," and who seize with
avidity every pretext to attack the authority of the Scriptures, which bring before their minds doctrines so repug-
nant to their natures as the Fall of Man, with its fearful
consequences here and hereafter, and God's only remedy
for Sin by the Atoning Sacrifice of His own dear Son;
and these persons are ever ready to avail themselves of
any excuse, however trivial, for raising doubt as to the
divine authority of the Word of God.

A little calm reflection upon the actual circumstances of the case will enable anyone to see a reasonable explanation for each of the four apparent discrepancies to which Professor Smith has referred. Taking for granted what is really the fact, that the first five books in the Bible, known as the Pentateuch, were divinely inspired when they came from the pens of Moses and various amenuensis whom he may have employed in actually commiting them to writing, it must be borne in mind that before the art of printing was discovered there were many centuries during which the only means of reproducing copies of ancient documents was by the slow and laborious process of writing by hand upon parchment, and that no claim for the inspiration of the copyists employed to do this work has ever been set up by anyone, so far as the writer is aware. It is altogether likely that during the Mosaic dispensation, extending over many centuries, this work was performed in the schools of the prophets by men liable to err like men at the present day, and some of whom, with the best intentions, might think proper to insert a marginal note occasionally, truthful in itself, and explanatory of some fact then present to the mind of the copyist. Supposing that such marginal notes were made by a copyist as are referred to in the first and second of the Professor's objections quoted above, they would be simple statements of facts to which no one could take exception so long as they remained in the shape of marginal notes. Supposing, again, that centuries afterwards some other copyist were to incorporate these truthful marginal notes with the original text, the whole difficulty is explained, and any candid searcher after truth would say that in the very nature of things these must be interpolations by copyists employed throughout many ages in transcribing again and again, first from the original text and afterwards from other copies of the inspired writings. But it would be absurd to maintain that the insertion of such interpolations was any proof that the original document was not written at the time when all other reasonable evidence showed

that it must have been written. And more absurd still
would it be to maintain that the original documents could
not have been inspired because the copyists had inserted
these interpolations. It was, doubtless, amongst other
things, to guard against just such tampering with the
written Word by copyists that such a solemn warning
as this is given, " Every word of God is pure; He is a
shield to them that put their trust in Him. Add thou not
unto His words, lest He reprove thee and thou be found
a liar " (Prov. 30 : 5, 6). See also Rev. 22 : 18, 19.

Just as in the case of the Revised Version of the Scriptures, every error that has been discovered in the translation has only brought out more clearly the fundamental
truths revealed in them, so it will also be found that every
interpolation by copyists, which by fair processes of
analysis and deduction are discovered in the Sacred
Writings, and either explained or expunged, will only
bring out more fully the inerrant character of the inspired
Word as it was originally given by God through the
prophets. Those two probable interpolations to which
Professor Smith takes exception, are all statements of
actual facts which may have been inserted by copyists
as explanatory notes centuries after the books of Genesis
and Deuteronomy were committed to writing by Moses,
and it is, to say the least, extremely unfair to argue that
because of these interpolations he could not have been
the author, and the books were not inspired. There
would be just as much reason for denying the inspiration
and authenticity of the Psalms because in the Authorized
Version certain words have been inserted in italics which
totally destroy the sense, as the translator may have
thought he improved the reading of the passage by such
interpolation. Look, for instance, at Psalm 84 : 3, where
the translator has completely spoiled the sense of a beautiful passage by inserting the word " even " in italics.
The absurdity of making it appear that the sparrow built
a nest for itself on God's altar is self-evident. But this is
not the fault of the inspired Word which compares the
swallow's nest to God's house, where His altars are, and

His people may dwell. Christians have nothing to fear
from candid and thorough criticism of the Scriptures by
those who are alone qualified to engage in this work,
namely, men who have been trained for it in God's own
school, and who, being filled with the Spirit themselves,
are thus enabled to " compare spiritual things with
spiritual," and arrive at correct conclusions upon every
point that may be raised.

The second objection to the statement, " The Canaanite was then in the land," apart from the probability of
interpolation, really amounts to nothing, as no one con-
tends that the book of Genesis was written in the time of
Abraham. It was, on the contrary, written centuries
afterwards by Moses, by whom such a statement might
be made, but it would not follow as a matter of course
that the Canaanites were not still in the land at the time
he as a historian wrote of that fact.

The third objection which Professor Smith makes to
the authenticity of the Pentateuch is, if possible, much
weaker than the first and second. He says, " Moreover
the writer always speaks of Moses in the third person,"
and from this he would have us infer that Moses was
not the author of the Pentateuch. Surely, as a professor
of history, he must be aware that this objection really
amounts to nothing, as the same thing has been done by
other authors in both ancient and modern times, and the
authenticity of their works has never been questioned on
that account. Take, for instance, that very able history
of the Red River Expedition to quell Riel's rebellion,
which was written by Lord Wolseley, then Colonel
Wolseley, in which he constantly speaks of himself in
the third person as Colonel Wolseley, but no one has
ever pretended to say that he is not the author of the
book which, on the title page, declares that it was
written by him. If, however, after the lapse of some centuries, only one copy of this book could be found, and
the title page was missing, some critics would probably
be prepared to assert that he was not the author, and
even to deny that such a person as Colonel Wolseley

ever existed. But it is unnecessary to say more in answer to such a frivolous objection.

As to the fourth objection, it is conclusively shown a few pages further on that the last chapter (34th) in Deuteronomy was probably added by Joshua, the successor of Moses, and that his doing so does not affect the claims of Moses to the authorship of that book.

And with respect to the four objections which have just been considered, and shown to be unworthy of serious notice as arguments against the inspiration or authenticity of the Pentateuch, the professor gravely remarks, " These things were noticed by critics long ago, but the eyes of faith in England and America, at least, have been shut." How sad it must seem to him that Christians should believe God rather than the critics, who on such slight grounds try to make it appear that the Bible is not an inspired book!

Professor Smith's Mistake About the Church.

Professor Goldwin Smith (page 59) speaks of Abraham as the founder of the Church. This is a mistake. He was the progenitor of the Hebrew race, and in him and his seed all nations were to be blessed. But the Church of God was not founded until Pentecost, when the Holy Spirit came down and baptized believers into the "one body," of which Christ is the head, and ever after the human race has in the sight of God been divided into three classes—the Jew, the Gentile and the Church of God (1 Cor. 10 : 32).

The building of the Church was yet future when Jesus said to Peter, " Thou art Peter, and upon this rock I *will* build my Church " (Matt. 16 : 18); and the Church of God is now built, not upon Abraham and the patriarchs of the Mosaic dispensation, but " upon the foundation of the apostles and prophets " of this more glorious dispensation in which we now live, "Jesus Christ Himself being the chief corner-stone " (Eph. 2 : 19-22). This, however, is a subject which cannot be rightly understood without the teaching of the Holy Spirit, who only dwells in the believer (1 Cor. 3 : 15; 6 : 19).

Insidious Surmises instead of Arguments.

Professor Goldwin Smith further says (page 65) : "The history of the Exodus is connected with the account of the institution of the Passover, and analogy may lead us to surmise that national imagination has been busy in explaining the origin of an immemorial rite." This suggestion might be dismissed with the simple statement that *surmises* are not *arguments*, and, therefore, such a remark is not worthy of notice. But it is not too much to say that on no other subject would he so trifle with the facts of history. Here is a solemn rite which he himself calls immemorial, observed by a whole nation yearly, in the manner prescribed by the sacred writings preserved by them; describing the first institution of the rite, and giving minute directions as to how it was to be observed : and throughout their whole history these writings are ascribed to Moses. What more positive evidence could be expected regarding the authorship of any writings than what was thus preserved throughout a nation's history in connection with a solemn rite, which the whole people observed every year in obedience to the instructions given in those writings ? How absolutely uncalled for is the *surmise* which this learned professor makes that possibly the *national imagination* has been busy in explaining the connection between the Passover and the Exodus and the Author of the Pentateuch!

God's Last Revelation of Himself to Moses.

The last revelation by God to Moses of His own presence accompanied by the Shekinah glory and the Shekinah fire, was peculiarly touching. On account of his presumptuous sin it had already been revealed to Moses that he must die before the children of Israel entered into the land of promise, to which he had been leading them for forty years, and, as his end drew near, we read in Deut. 31 : 14, "And the Lord said unto Moses, Behold, thy days approach that thou must die ; call

Joshua, and present yourselves in the tabernacle of the congregation that I may give him a charge. And Moses and Joshua went and presented themselves in the tabernacle of the congregation. And the Lord appeared in the tabernacle in a pillar of a cloud; and the pillar of the cloud stood over the door of the tabernacle. And the Lord said unto Moses, Behold, thou shalt sleep with thy fathers," etc. Then follows solemn warnings to the children of Israel as a nation; and in v. 22 we read, "Moses, therefore, wrote this song the same day, and taught it to the children of Israel"; and in v. 24 it is stated, "And it came to pass, when Moses had made an end of writing the words of this law in a book until they were finished, that Moses commanded the Levites, which bare the Ark of the Covenant of the Lord, saying, Take this book of the law, and put it in the side of the Ark of the Covenant of the Lord your God," etc. Then follows that wonderful song of Moses in Deut. 32, spoken by him in the ears of the congregation of Israel (Deut. 31 : 30), after which we read from v. 47 to the close of the chapter, "And the Lord spake unto Moses the self-same day, saying, 'Get thee up into this Mountain Abarim unto Mount Nebo, which is in the Land of Moab, that is over against Jericho; and behold the land of Canaan, which I give unto the children of Israel for a possession; and die in the mount whither thou goest up, and be gathered unto thy people; as Aaron, thy brother, died in Mount Hor, and was gathered unto his people; because ye trespassed against Me among the children of Israel at the waters of Meribah-Kedesh, in the wilderness of Zin, because ye sanctified me not in the midst of the children of Israel. Yet thou shalt see the land before thee, but thou shalt not go thither unto the land which I give the children of Israel." Then follows in Deut. 33 the blessing of "Moses, the man of God" upon the children of Israel, after which we have in Deut. 34 the account of his ascent into Mount Nebo to the top of Pisgah, where the Lord showed him the promised land, and from v. 4 we read, "So Moses, the servant of the Lord, died there in the land of Moab according to the word of the Lord, and He (God) buried him in a valley in the land of Moab, over against Beth-peor; but no man knoweth of his sepulchre unto this day. And Moses was an hundred and twenty years old when he died; his eye was not dim, nor his natural force abated; and the children of Israel wept for Moses in the plains of Moab thirty days; so the days of weeping and mourning for Moses were ended, and Joshua, the son of Nun, was full of the spirit of wisdom ; for Moses had laid his hands upon him; and the children of Israel hearkened unto him, and did as the Lord commanded Moses. And there arose not a prophet since in Israel like unto Moses whom the Lord knew face to face," etc.

What a wonderful death! What a grand funeral! and what a striking commentary is the judgment of God upon His chosen servant on the words, "If the righteous scarcely be saved, where shall the ungodly and the sinner appear" (1 Peter 4 : 18). This grand old man, who went alone to the top of that mountain to die, and to be buried by Jehovah, who had "talked with him face to face as a man talks with his friend," had commenced his great life work at eightly years of age. After spending forty years in the school of God in the wilderness, before he was fitted for his forty years of service as the leader of God's chosen people, moses, the inspired law-giver of Israel, who had failed and borne the judgment entailed by his failure; did not (with all his meekness) hesitate to proclaim himself an inspired prophet of Jehovah as he looked forward to the coming of that One in whom there would never be any failure, of whom he prophesied, "A prophet shall the Lord your God raise up unto you of your brethren like unto me; him shall ye hear" (Acts 7 : 37).

Attacks Upon the Book of Deuteronomy.

With special reference to the authorship of the Book of Deuteronomy, which infidels and "liberal theologians" are not willing to ascribe to Moses, let any candid en-

quirer look carefully at the statements just quoted from
the last four chapters of that book, and he will not have
much difficulty in arriving at a correct conclusion. Com-
paring the Song of Moses in Deut. 32 with that in
Ex. 15, there is no difficulty in deciding that they were
written by the same author. Then again in Deut. 31 : 22
it is stated, " Moses, therefore, wrote this song the same
day "; and in v. 24. "And it came to pass when Moses
had made an end of writing the words of this law in
a book until they were finished," etc. Do not these statements certainly prove that Moses was the author of the
book and of the song to which they refer ? " But," say
the critics, " the Song of Moses, and his blessing upon
the children of Israel, and the account of his death and
burial all appear in the last three chapters, and after the
statements which you have quoted from chap 31." Quite
true, but was that any evidence that Moses was not the
author of this book ? It is distinctly stated that he wrote
the song on the same day that Jehovah had last revealed
Himself to him in the pillar of cloud over the door of
the tabernacle. After Jehovah had given His charge
briefly to Joshua we read, " When Moses had made an
end of writing the words of this law in a book until they
were finished," etc. What does this imply ? Is it not
that after the song had been written the book of the
law was finished, so far as the work of Moses upon it
personally was concerned ? But the song written out by
him previously was afterwards spoken by him in the ears
of all the congregation of Israel; and, although it is not
stated, it is quite possible that his blessing upon the
children of Israel in chap. 33 may also have, like the
song, been committed to writing before it was pronounced by him. However that may be, there can be
no question from the evidence of the book itself as to
his authorship of chaps. 32 and 33. although these have
been added after the book of the law was said to have
been finished. Then as to chap. 34. The last in the book,
it would, of course, be absurd to contend that Moses
wrote the account of his own death and burial, nor is

it at all likely that any one ever set up such a contention.
How, then, does that affect the authorship of the book?
Suppose, for instance, that some uninspired writer in
modern times was engaged in a work which he was
unable to complete before death overtook him, but that
only a few pages remained to be added, including a poem
which he had written out and some other matter that he
had written, and that he desired his amanuensis to add
these things on the last pages, and to insert a closing
chapter, giving an account of his own death and burial;
and supposing these directions to be faithfully carried
out, would he thereby lose his claim to the authorship
of that book? The absurdity of such a suggestion is
self-evident, but not more so than the refusal to recognize Moses as the author of the Book of Deuteronomy
because certain matter was added after his death, which
in the very nature of things could not be inserted before.
But how does this affect the question of the inspiration
of the last chapter? We have seen that at that last
interview with Jehovah in the pillar of cloud at the door
of the tabernacle, both Moses and Joshua, his servant
and successor, were summoned to be present, and God
gave to Joshua the assurance, "I will be with thee";
and we read in chap. 34 : 9, "And Joshua, the son of
Nun, was full of the spirit of wisdom, for Moses had
laid his hands upon him." There is, therefore, no doubt
that God's inspired leader completed the work which
Moses left unfinished, but that did not affect either the
question of inspiration or the claim of Moses to be regarded as the author of the book.

After the death of Moses the Lord spoke to Joshua,
saying, "As I was with Moses, so will I be with thee: I
will not fail thee, nor forsake thee" (Josh. 1 : 5). And at
the siege of Jericho the Lord appeared to him as a man
with a drawn sword in his hand, and proclaimed himself
as "Captain (or Prince) of the host of the Lord," and told
him to loose his shoe from off his feet, for the place
whereon he stood was holy (Josh. 5 : 13-15), and on many
occasions afterwards the Lord spoke to Joshua; and in

his charge to the children of Israel he said, " Be ye, therefore, very courageous to keep and to do all that is written in the book of the law of Moses," etc., thus witnessing to the fact that Moses was the author of the books of the law. And if any further evidence on this point is required, we could give that of the Lord Jesus Christ Himself in Matt. 19 : 7, 8, referring to the passage in Deut. 24 : 1, " They say unto him, Why did Moses then command to give a writing of divorcement, and to put her away ? He saith unto them, Moses, because of the hardness of your hearts, suffered you to put away your wives, but from the beginning it was not so," and He thus recognized Moses as the author of the Book of Deuteronomy; and in replying to the temptations of Satan He quoted three times from that book.

God's Revelations Through Other Prophets.

In the time of the Judges there was generally departure from God, which is summed up in the last verse of the book in this way : " In those days there was no king in Israel, and every man did that which was right in his own eyes." And yet during those centuries of general lawlessness God spoke to His people repeatedly through various channels, and raised up instruments of deliverance from their adversaries at various times. The Lord appeared unto Gideon as an angel, and appointed him as the deliverer of His people from the Midianites, encouraging him with the assurance, " Surely I will be with thee," and deliverance was obtained (Judges 6 : 16). And an angel of the Lord appeared to the wife of Manoah, promising her a son, who should be a Nazarite from the womb; and Samson was born and used as an instrument in executing God's vengeance upon the Philistines.

In 1 Sam. 3 : 1 we read, " The word of the Lord was precious in those days; there was no open vision." And we read in v. 3 that when Samuel was laid down to sleep where the Ark of God was that the Lord called "Samuel"; and he answered, " Here am I," and he arose and went to Eli, thinking it was he that called him. This was repeated several times, and at length Eli perceived that it must be the Lord that had called the child, and told him the next time this happened to answer, " Speak, Lord, for Thy servant heareth." Then the Lord told him of the judgments that were to be executed upon Eli and his house for the wickedness of his sons, which were afterwards literally fulfilled; and after that we read in v. 21, "And the Lord appeared again in Shiloh : for the Lord revealed Himself to Samuel in Shiloh by the Word of the Lord," and " he was established as a prophet of the Lord," and the mind of the Lord was repeatedly made known through him to Saul and the people of Israel, and also to David before he came to the throne.

Through Nathan, the prophet, and Gad, the seer, the word of the Lord came repeatedly to David regarding His dealings with himself personally; but in the Psalms we have an inexhaustable fund of deep, spiritual teaching suited to the people of God in all ages, with prophetic forecasts of Christ and the future glory of the Messiah, which must have been the result of direct inspiration from God, as it was also recognized by the Lord Jesus Christ Himself after His resurrection, when He said to His disciples that " all things must be fulfilled which were written in the law of Moses, and in the prophets, and in the Psalms concerning Me."

During the reigns of the kings of Judah and Israel God raised up many prophets, to whom He revealed His will in various ways, and through them spoke to the kings and people of Israel. Some of the greatest of these prophets, such as Elijah and Elisha, have left no writings behind them, but their sayings and deeds and God's revelations to them are embodied in the historical records of Israel and Judah. Others again, such as Isaiah, Jeremiah, Ezekiel, Daniel, Zechariah and the minor prophets have left us their own records of God's revelations to them, made " at sundry times and in divers manners," but all revealing to us in one way or another the same Infinite Being who had first spoken to Adam,

and afterwards to Noah, to Abram, Isaac and Jacob, and
at length in the presence of the whole nation amidst the
thunderings and lightnings of Mount Sinai had revealed
to Moses the law which was ever since recognized as
coming direct from Jehovah to His chosen people.

God's Revelation By His Son.

God had revealed His will to men throughout many
ages; by appearing to them personally as a man; by sending angels to them in the forms of men; and by speaking
to them with audible voice, which they recognized as the
voice of God. He had spoken to them in dreams and
visions of the night, and in the thunders and lightnings
of Sinai; by the tables of stone and the statutes delivered
to Moses; by the pillar of cloud by day and the pillar
of fire by night, which accompanied them through all
their wilderness journeys, and afterwards by many other
prophets whom He had sent to them. Thus had He " at
sundry times and in divers manners spoken in times past
unto the fathers by the prophets." But at length, in the
fullness of time, He in these last days "spoke unto them
by His Son, whom He hath appointed heir of all things,
by whom also He made the worlds." What amazing
condescension! The Second Person in the Godhead, the
Creator of the universe comes from heaven to earth in
order to reveal to sinful men of Adam's race His Father's
will, and His Father's heart of love towards all mankind,
as expressed by Himself in John 3 : 16, " God so loved
the world that He gave His only begotten Son, that
whosoever believeth on Him should not perish, but have
everlasting life." What good news to come from the
lips of the Son of God! Surely no one ought to be so
foolish as to reject salvation on such easy terms. But
it seemed to be too good news to be true. A few poor
fishermen of Galilee heard His call, obeyed His word
and followed Him, leaving their nets, which were their
all, behind them. His conception in the Virgin's womb,
by the power of the Holy Spirit, had been announced by
an angel to His mother and His reputed father. Born

in a stable, cradled in a manger, an angelic host heralded His birth. Reared in a lowly station, until, at thirty years of age He entered upon His life work of three and a half years. The Jews, as a nation, refused to recognize or accept Him as their long-looked for Messiah. At His baptism by John in the Jordan the Holy Spirit, in bodily form, like a dove, descended upon Him, and a voice came from heaven which said, "Thou art My beloved Son; in Thee I am well pleased." Again, in the Mount of Transfiguration, with His face shining as the sun, and His raiment white as the light when He appeared with Moses and Elias in the presence of Peter and James and John, a bright cloud overshadowed them (indicating the Shekinah glory), and a voice out of the cloud said, "This is My beloved Son, in whom I am well pleased; hear ye Him." And in His temptation in the wilderness Satan said to Him, "If Thou be the Son of God, command that these stones be made bread," and "if Thou be the Son of God cast Thyself down." And the demons whom He was casting out addressed Him by the same title, saying, "What have we to do with Thee, Jesus, Thou Son of God ? Art Thou come hither to torment us before the time ?" And in Matt. 14 : 33 we read, "Then they that were in the ship came and worshipped Him, saying, Of a truth Thou art the Son of God." And when He asked His disciples, "But whom say ye that I am ?" and Simon Peter answered, "Thou art the Christ, the Son of the living God." What was the response of Jesus to this reply ? "Blessed art thou, Simon Bar-jona; for flesh and blood hath not revealed it unto thee, but My Father which is in heaven." That He had Himself claimed to be the Son of God is also proved by the taunts of His murderers as He hung upon the cross when they said, "If Thou be the Son of God come down from the cross"; and again, "He trusted in God; let Him deliver Him now, if He will have Him, for He said, I am the Son of God" (Matt. 27 : 40, 43). And in v. 54 of the same chapter we read, "Now when the centurion, and they that were with him watching

Jesus, saw the earthquake and those things that were done they feared greatly, saying, "Truly, this was the Son of God." Mark's gospel commences with these words, "The beginning of the Gospel of Jesus Christ, the Son of God." And in this gospel we read that before He was delivered to Pilate the high priest asked Him, "Art Thou the Christ, the Son of the Blessed?" and Jesus said, "I am." In Luke's gospel we read that at the annunciation the angel said to Mary, "Therefore also that holy thing which shall be born of thee shall be called the Son of God." In the Gospel of John we read, "No man hath seen God at any time; the only begotten Son, which is in the bosom of the Father, He hath declared Him" (John 1 : 18), and six times in the third chapter of John Jesus is referred to either by Himself or by John the Baptist as "the Son of God." In the fifth chapter of John Jesus speaks of Himself eight times as "the Son of God." In the ninth chapter (vs. 35-38) he asks the man who had been born blind, "Dost thou believe on the Son of God? and he answered and said, Who is He, Lord, that I might believe on Him? And Jesus said unto him, Thou hast both seen Him, and He it is that talketh with thee. And he said, Lord, I believe, and he worshipped Him." In John 10 : 35 He said to the Jews who were about to stone Him, "Say ye of Him whom the Father hath sanctified and sent into the world, Thou blasphemest, because I said I am the Son of God?" In John 11 : 4 Jesus said regarding the sickness of Lazarus, "This sickness is not unto death, but for the glory of God, that the Son of God might be glorified thereby"; and in v. 27, Martha, replying to a question which He had put to her, said, "Yea, Lord, I believe that Thou art the Christ, the Son of God, which should come into the world." In John 17 : 1 Jesus commences His prayer to the Father in these words, "Father, the hour is come : glorify Thy Son, that Thy Son also may glorify Thee." And in John 20 : 31 we read, "But these are written that ye might believe that Jesus is the Christ, the Son of God, and that, believing, ye might have life through His name."

The officers who were sent to arrest Jesus were constrained to say, " Never man spake like this man " (John 7 : 46); and He boldly threw down this challenge to His enemies, " Which of you convinceth Me of sin ?" and afterwards said, " Before Abraham was I am," upon hearing which they took up stones to cast at Him.

At His examination before the high priest He was condemned for blasphemy only because He claimed to be the Son of God. Judas hanged himself because he had " betrayed innocent blood." Pilate's wife sent word to her husband, saying, " Have thou nothing to do with that just man "; and Pilate himself washed his hands before the multitude, saying, "I am innocent of the blood of this just person."

Resurrection and Ascension of Jesus.

But in addition to His own testimony as a sinless man that He was also " the Son of God," the crowning proof was His resurrection from the dead, as we read in Rom. 1 : 2, 3, "Concerning His Son, Jesus Christ our Lord, which was made of the seed of David according to the flesh; and declared to be the Son of God with power, according to the Spirit of holiness, by the resurrection from the dead."

Each of the evangelists gives an independent record of the resurrection of the Lord Jesus Christ, naming certain reputable witnesses to whom He appeared, most of whom afterwards sealed their testimony with their blood; and the Apostle Paul gives a summary of the evidence upon this point, "For I delivered unto you first of all that which I also received, how that Christ died for our sins according to the Scriptures, and that He was buried, and that He rose again the third day according to the Scriptures, and that He was seen of Cephas (Peter), then of the twelve; after that He was seen of above five hundred brethren at once; of whom the greater part remain unto this present, but some are fallen asleep. After that He was seen of James, then of all the apostles. And last of all He was seen of me also as of one born out of due time" (1 Cor. 15 : 3-8). Again and again during His ministry had he foretold His death and His resurrection on the third day, but His disciples were slow to believe such a statement until the evidence of their own senses convinced them that it was an accomplished fact.

At the end of the Gospels of Mark and Luke and in the first chapter of Acts we have the account of His ascension to heaven from the presence of His disciples, and in Acts it is added, "And while they looked steadfastly toward heaven, as He went up, behold, two men stood by them in white apparel; which also said, Ye men of Galilee, why stand ye gazing up into heaven ? This same Jesus which is taken up from you into heaven shall so come in like manner as ye have seen Him go into heaven" (Acts 1 : 10, 11).

Against all this positive evidence of the resurrection of the Son of God is only that of the soldiers who were set as a watch at His tomb, and who were bribed by the priests to say that His disciples came and stole Him away while they slept! (Matt. 28 : 13).

Would the Lord Jesus Certify to an Imposture.

The law was given by Moses, but grace and truth came by Jesus Christ (John 1-17). The first promise of redemption for the fallen human race was given by God when addressing the Serpent. He said, "I will put enmity between thee and the woman, and between thy seed and her seed; it shall bruise thy head, and thou shalt bruise his heel" (Gen. 3 : 15). And so, in fulfilment of this promise we read of Christ, " Forasmuch, then, as the children are partakers of flesh and blood, He also Himself likewise took part of the same; that through death, He might destroy him that had the power of death, that is, the devil" (Heb. 2 : 14). Moses, as he looked forward with prophetic eye to the future, said, " The Lord thy God will raise up unto thee a prophet from the midst of thee of thy brethren like unto me; unto him shall ye hearken" (Deut. 18 : 15). Other prophets in succeeding ages had spoken of Christ as they by faith had looked forward to the coming Messiah. All these predictions were included in the Old Testament Scriptures, then in possession of the Jewish nation, and, referring to these, the Son of God said that Abraham replied to the rich man in Hades, " If they hear not Moses and the prophets, neither will they be persuaded though one rose from the dead " (Luke 16 : 31). The Lord Jesus Christ, as the Son of God, knew whether or not Moses and the prophets were really the authors of the books ascribed to them by the Jewish people. Is it possible that if they were not the authors He would try to perpetuate a wrong impression ?

Professor Smith's Denial of Jesus as the Son of God.

Professor Goldwin Smith speaks of Jesus only as "the great Teacher of humanity" (page 187), and on page 181 he also says, " In calling Himself the Son of Man Jesus might seem to identify Himself with a mystic figure in Daniel; but the Son of Man is not the Son of God, nor is it the son of a Jew; it is a title of humanity." On page 137 he says, " The effect produced by the teaching of Jesus and His disciples is beyond question the most momentous fact in history." On page 139 he quotes from the author of *Supernatural Religion* as follows : " The system of Jesus might not be new, but it was, in a high sense, the perfect development of natural morality, and that it confined itself to two fundamental principles, love to God and love to man."

On page 174 he says, " We cannot conceive of two natures, Divine and human, though we may mechanically repeat the form of words." And again he says, " The sayings of Christ would not be less true or applicable if they had been cast ashore by the tide of time without anything to designate their source "; and on page 176 he asks, " Did Jesus give Himself out or allow His followers to designate Him as the Messiah ? It is impossible to tell." From all these quotations it is evident that the learned professor only recognizes Jesus as a mere man whilst regarding him at the same time as a good man and " the great Teacher of humanity." But he must surely be prepared to admit that if the claims of the Lord Jesus Christ, quoted in the foregoing pages from the four gospels, are not correct He must have been one of the most infamous imposters that ever walked the face of this earth. If He was not the Son of God as well as the Son of Man, as He claimed to be, He must have been a bad man to assert what He knew to be false, and if He did not know that what He said was false, He was too ignorant to be regarded as " a great Teacher." The professor can choose which horn of the dilemma he pleases. But Christians will prefer to believe the record of the inspired Word that God has given of His Son, and to thank Him for having at " sundry times and in divers manners spoken in time past unto the fathers by the prophets, and that in these last days He has spoken unto us by His Son."

In the next chapter the writer proposes to notice some other objections which the Professor makes in his various essays, to the inspiration and authenticity of the Scriptures.

CHAPTER II.

THE CUSTODY AND CRITICISM OF DIVINE REVELATION.

IN considering at the beginning of the previous chapter the manner in which reliable tradition had probably been handed down from Adam to Moses through the most trustworthy channels, a good deal had to be stated which would, perhaps, more properly come under the heading of this chapter. It will not, of course, be necessary to repeat what has been already written respecting that portion of the inspired Word. But in referring to the custody of Divine revelation from Adam to Noah this matter might be put in a somewhat different form by stating that Enoch, who walked with God 300 years before he was taken to heaven without dying, was 308 years old when Adam died, and his son, Methuselah, was 243 years old when Adam died, and Noah was 600 years old when his grandfather, Methuselah, died in the year of the Flood. It would only be fair to conclude that a man like Enoch, who walked with God 300 years, and most of that time contemporaneously with Adam, would be sure to meet personally with the first progenitor of the human race, and obtain from his own lips the story of Creation as the Lord had revealed it to him; of the Fall and the curse entailed thereby, which brought so much misery to himself and his posterity; and of future redemption by the atoning sacrifice of Christ, in the Scripture narrative so dimly outlined. And it may also be taken for granted that such a godly man as Enoch would not fail to impress upon the mind of his son, Methuselah, the facts which he had learned from Adam, even if Methuselah himself had not learned them from Adam's own lips during the 243 years that he had lived contemporaneously

with him. And as Noah lived 600 years contemporaneously with his grandfather, Methuselah, he had ample
opportunities to obtain from the most trustworthy channel the fullest and most reliable information upon the
subjects referred to.

Another circumstance showing the reliability of the
traditions and genealogies handed down from Adam to
Noah is the remarkable fact that Adam himself and every
one of his descendants in the direct line to Noah were
alive when Noah's father, Lamech, was fifty-six years of
age, and that the last of them to die was Methuselah, in
the year of the Flood; and when Noah was eighty-four
years of age every one of his ancestors was alive except
Adam, Seth and Enoch.

Duration of Human Life in Primeval Ages.

Much speculation has been indulged in by skeptics
as to the duration of human life in primeval ages, and
many of them are disposed to question the correctness
of the Scripture narrative on this point without producing a particle of evidence to the contrary. All departure
from God has commenced with unbelief of His Word,
and Divine revelation has been so given and preserved
as to leave fallen men wholly without excuse if they
refuse to believe the records that He has caused to
be handed down to them in the Bible regarding Himself and His dealings with the human race. In His
infinite wisdom He so ordained that the great ages to
which men lived in antediluvian days should provide the
surest guarantee that the traditions handed down by
them were reliable; and the same method was continued
down to the time of Abram, who, as we have seen in
the former chapter, lived contemporaneously with both
Noah and Shem.

Up to this time God had been dealing with the whole
human race under various dispensations, with failure in
each case on the part of man as the inevitable result.
Created in the likeness of God Himself, in a state of

innocence, and endowed with freedom of will, he had failed and fallen. Left with the testimony of Adam, Enoch and Noah, and doubtless many other faithful witnesses to the consequences of the Fall, the whole earth became corrupt before God and was filled with violence (Gen. 6 : 11). Only one man (Noah) was at length found walking with God, and he was commanded to build the ark; and in it himself and his family were saved when all others were destroyed by the Deluge (Gen. 9 : 9). God entered into a covenant with Noah, and again dealt with the human race as a whole. After the terrible example of the destruction of all others by the Flood, his descendants soon departed from the knowledge and service of the true God, which they had received from Noah, and failure, almost universal, again took place, until men seemed to think only of how to escape the righteous judgment of God in event of another Deluge. The Tower of Babel (see Appendix A) was built, the confusion of tongues followed, and men were scattered upon the face of the earth. Before the Flood (Gen. 6 : 3) God had announced His intention of shortening human life to one hundred and twenty years on account of the general wickedness which then prevailed, but this purpose was only brought about gradually down to the time of Abram.

Abram the Fitted Custodian of Divine Revelations.

It is altogether likely that the long duration of life, which assured the correct handing down of Divine revelations and reliable traditional history, had at the same time a hardening effect upon the consciences of men. And when God shortened the span of human life He chose one man and his posterity to be henceforth the custodians of those most important and sacred revelations and traditions which He designed to be carefully preserved for future ages. In examining the genealogy in the direct line from Noah to Adam as the

duration of human life becomes gradually shortened
(Gen. 10 : 10-20) it is worthy of notice that Abram lived
contemporaneously with all his own ancestors since the
Flood, including Noah and Shem. It is morally certain
that, as the eldest son of his father, Terah, he held the
birthright in that illustrious family, who traced their
pedigree directly back to Adam, the first created man,
and that he would thus be the one who, as a matter of
right, according to patriarchal customs, would be entrusted with the custody of all the archives and traditional lore connected with such an ancestry. The call
of Abram by God was no hap-hazard matter. It was given
to the one who of all other men then living was best
qualified by his position to be the custodian of Divine
revelations already given, and of the reliable traditions
and genealogies received by him from his ancestors,
which he had the most abundant opportunities of veri-
fying, while they were all living who had existed since
the Flood. It is very likely that all his immediate ancestors had since the Deluge, as a pastoral people, occupied those parts of Armenia and Mesopotamia lying
between Mount Arrarat and Ur of the Chaldees where
the call of God came to him. As was usual in those
patriarchal days, it is also probable that, as no time had
been fixed for his departure, he, as a dutiful son had remained with his father at Haran until his death, and then
departed for Canaan as the Lord had spoken to him.

Professor Goldwin Smith thinks it very unlikely that
the great Being who inhabits eternity and infinity would
deign to be the guest of a Hebrew sheik; but has he ever
paused to consider that, even before the call of God came
to Abram, he was, according to his lineage, the representative man of the human race at that particular time,
and the probable custodian of its most important traditions ?

Abram's Faith in God.

In the call which God gave to Abram he commenced
to deal with one family upon the principle of grace.

leaving, as it were, all the rest of the human race in the meantime to their own devices. He commanded him to go to Canaan, which He promised to give to him and to his seed for an everlasting possession (Gen. 17 : 8). Abram built altars unto the Lord at Sichem, at Bethel, and in Hebron, and thus proved that he, as well as Noah, understood that it was only through the atoning sacrifice that fallen men could acceptably appear in the presence of God. And in his meeting with Melchizedek, the priest of the most high God, and giving tithes to him, we find that there were other worshippers of the true God in Canaan, who, like himself, had received the knowledge of Him through their ancestor, Noah, and his descendants. Since the Creation God had been looking for faith on the part of man, but finding very little. Now He promises to Abram an apparent impossibility : that he in his old age should have a son through his wife, Sarah, whose womb was dead. "And," we read in Gen. 15 : 6, " he believed in the Lord, and He counted it to him for righteousness." And after the great trial of his faith upon Mount Moriah God further covenanted with him thus : " By Myself have I sworn, saith the Lord; for because thou hast done this thing, and hast not withheld thy son, thine only son; that in blessing I will bless thee, and in multiplying I will multiply thy seed as the stars of heaven, and as the sand which is upon the sea shore; and thy seed shall possess the gate of his enemies; and in thy seed shall all nations of the earth be blessed, because thou hast obeyed my voice." God at length had found a man who would believe His simple word, contrary to all natural appearances, and who would obey Him under all circumstances ; and He revealed Himself and His purposes more fully to him than He had yet done to any human being; and the covenant of grace was repeatedly renewed, and the promise was further given, "And in thy seed shall all the nations of the earth be blessed" (Gen. 26 : 4). The meaning of this promise we find in Gal. 3 : 16, which reads thus : "Now to Abraham and his seed were the promises made. He saith

not, and to seeds as of many; but as of one. And to thy
seed, which is Christ." This is the sum and substance
of all revelation from God to man since Adam fell. The
seed of the woman, who was to bruise the serpent's head,
and the seed of Abraham, in whom all nations of the
earth were to be blessed, are one and the same person
the Messiah promised to Israel, the Redeemer of mankind, the Son of God Himself, of whom we read, " God
was manifest in the flesh, justified in the Spirit, seen of
angels, preached unto the Gentiles, believed on in the
world, received up into glory " (1 Tim. 3 : 16).

Abraham and His Descendants Specially Interested in the Custody and Criticism of Divine Revelations.

In order that there should be no reasonable obstacle
in the way of men exercising faith in those revelations
as the Word of the living God, it was most important
that the custodian of them should be deeply interested
in preserving them in their purity. The promises made
by God to Abraham, to Isaac, and to Jacob and their
posterity, were well calculated to make them most deeply
interested in preserving all that God had revealed to
their fathers respecting that glorious earthly heritage
that was in store for them as a people, through whom
all nations of the earth were to be blessed. As ancient
families in modern times have exercised great care in
the preservation of title deeds to estates now in their
possession; and even greater care with regard to documents showing their title to a much larger inheritance,
which they expect to receive and enjoy in the near future;
even so have the descendants of Abraham, Isaac, and
Jacob jealously guarded the sacred writings which told
them of their pedigree, extending backwards to Adam,
the first created man; of a noble ancestry, with whom
Jehovah held personal intercourse; of the promises
made by God to their fathers of earthly blessings above
those of every other people; of the coming of that won-

derful person, their Messiah, who was to reign over them gloriously, and in whom all nations of the earth would be blessed. These promises, at first in the form of reliable tradition, and afterwards perhaps partly or wholly committed to writing before the time of Moses, we may be sure were preserved by the children of Israel with the greatest care, until at length they were embodied in permanent form in the Book of Genesis by Moses, the inspired prophet of Jehovah. The custodians of Divine revelation before the days of Moses were the people most deeply interested in its preservation, and the inspired prophet who embodied those revelations in sacred history was the one with whom God talked " face to face as a man with his friend." Surely it must be admitted that down to the time of Moses the persons who had the custody of Divine revelations were the very best that could be found in the various ages in which they lived.

In confirmation of the writer's remarks regarding Abram on a previous page it may be added that Josephus states that Berossus mentions Abram without naming him when he says thus : " In the tenth generation after the Flood there was amongst the Chaldeans a man righteous and great, and skilful in the celestial science." Also, that Hecataeus does more than barely mention him, for he composed and left behind a book concerning him. He says also that Nicolaus, of Damascus, in the fourth book of his history writes thus concerning him : "Abram reigned at Damascus, being a foreigner, who came with an army out of the land above Babylon, called the land of the Chaldeans; but after a long time he got him up, and removed from that country also with his people, and went into the land then called the land of Canaan, but now the land of Judea, and this when his posterity were become a multitude; as to which posterity of his we relate their history in another work. Now the name of Abram is even still famous in the country of Damascus; and there is showed a village named after him, *The Habitation of Abram.*"

Custody of Divine Revelations by Jewish Sanhedrim and Priesthood.

After the giving of the Law by Moses and the appointment of the seventy elders to aid him in governing the people, these elders with himself formed the first Sanhedrim or Supreme Council of the nation, avowedly, at least, subject to the direct rule of Jehovah. This body of magistrates or councillors was, as well as the priests, directly interested in preserving the law by which they should be guided in the administration of justice, as it was delivered by God to Moses; and they would also, as representatives of the whole people, be intensely interested in the preservation of their genealogy from Adam to Abram, and of the promises to Abraham and his seed that had not yet been fulfilled. From the time of Moses, whether under the rule of Judges or Kings, they were organized as a nation, with the proper officers to look after the safe-keeping of their laws. But the priests also were most deeply interested in the preservation of the books given to them by Moses, in which alone were to be found all the details of the ceremonial law, by which they were to be guided in their sacrifices and other religious observances. It is hard to suppose the possibility of their not taking care of such important documents, however great might be their departure from the true worship and service of Jehovah at various stages of their history.

Thus there were provided the most effectual guarantees for the custody of the Pentateuch, or the first five books in the Bible, as they came from the hands of Moses to the Israelites, as a nation which regarded these books as containing their code of civil laws and religious ritual, to which reference had to be made continually.

The historical books, written after the Exodus, give in very brief terms the national history, and recount God's dealings with them as His chosen people; and many chapters are occupied with details as to the division of the land amongst the twelve tribes who came out of Egypt with Moses; with genealogical tables; with strange names of ancient cities and countries, all interwoven with records of failure and consequent judgment by Jehovah, which, taken all together, have not the slightest appearance of works of fiction or legendary lore. It is impossible to conceive of these books being aught else than what is claimed for them, a correct history of the nation which has preserved them with its other sacred writings received from Moses. But these historical books, as well as Genesis and other books of the Pentateuch, contain many additional revelations from Jehovah, which are incorporated with the history of the nation and the most important genealogies. Could any method have been devised which would have been better adapted for securing the custody of those additional revelations from God to man? The correctness of the history thus handed down is confirmed by other cotemporary history, and by the ruins of buried cities, which in recent years have been unearthed in various eastern countries.

With these historical books and the Pentateuch the Jewish nation has preserved and handed down to us the Book of Job, the Psalms of David, and the writings of Solomon, in all of which there is so much practical instruction for the regulation of daily life, and so much that is calculated to awaken devotional feeling of the highest character.

And in later ages to these have been added the books written by the various prophets foretelling, besides other events, the coming of their Messiah, His rejection, and death, and Second Advent and millennial glory, when all the promises given by God to Abraham, Isaac and Jacob will be literally fulfilled.

And all this mass of Divine revelations, from the time of Adam to the time of Christ, accumulating and expanding as the ages have rolled on, has thus been handed down to us and kept intact by the plan which God in His infinite wisdom devised, of first making one family, and afterwards one nation, deeply interested in its preservation.

Professor Smith Denies Inspiration of Old Testament Scriptures.

Professor Goldwin Smith (page 78) asks, "What is the Old Testament?" and himself answers the question thus, "It is the entire body of Hebrew literature, theology, philosophy, history, fiction, and poetry, including the poetry of love as well as that of religion, all bound in a single book. This statement is not correct. Surely he must be aware that no books of fiction are included in the Old Testament, although there is much sublime poetry, conveying spiritual lessons. And on page 94 he says: "The time has come when as a supernatural revelation the Hebrew books should be frankly, though reverently, laid aside, and no more allowed to cloud the vision of free enquiry," etc. Certainly a very cool proposition! But a very unwise course to take.

Necessity and Value of Honest Criticism.

These statements of the learned, but rash, Professor naturally bring us to the consideration of the criticism of Divine revelation, which is as important as its custody. There is a vast difference between honest criticism and infidel skepticism. The latter starts with the assumption, either that there is no God, or that He has never given a revelation of Himself to man. The former reverently acknowledges that a Divine revelation has been given, but recognizes at the same time the possibility of human failure in connection with its preservation as it first came from Jehovah, and the danger of imposture on the part of uninspired men. Frequent warnings are given in the Old Testament Scriptures against false prophets, as, for instance in Deut. 18 : 20-22, "But the prophet which shall presume to speak a word in my name which I have not commanded him to speak . . . even that prophet shall die, and if thou shalt say in thine heart, How shall we know the word that the Lord hath not spoken? When a prophet speaketh in the name of the Lord, if the thing follow not nor come to pass . . . the prophet hath spoken presumptuously; thou shalt not be afraid of him"; and in Jer. 23 : 28-32. " The prophet that hath a dream, let him tell a dream; and he that hath my word, let him speak my Word faithfully. What is the chaff to the wheat, saith the Lord ? Is not my Word like as a fire ? saith the Lord; and like a hammer that breaketh the rock in pieces ? Therefore I am against the prophets, saith the Lord, that steal my words, every one from his neighbour. Behold, I am against the prophets that use their tongues and say, He saith. Behold, I am against them that prophesy false dreams, saith the Lord, and do tell them, and cause my people to err by their lies, and by their lightness; yet I sent them not, nor commanded them; therefore, they shall not profit this people at all, saith the Lord." And again in Ezek. 13 : 1-3 we read, " And the word of the Lord came unto me, saying, Son of man, prophesy against the prophets of Israel that prophesy, and say unto them that prophesy out of their own hearts, Hear ye the word of the Lord. Thus saith the Lord God. Woe unto the foolish prophets that follow their own spirit and have seen nothing." In many other passages similar language is used.

As to the great care which was taken by the Jewish nation from the earliest ages to preserve their sacred writings in their purity and integrity, the best authority is Josephus, who says : " We, therefore, who are Jews, must yield to the Grecian writers as to language and eloquence of composition; but then we shall give them no such preference as to the verity of ancient history, and least of all as to that part which concerns the affairs of our several countries. As to the care of writing down the records from the earliest antiquity among the Egyptians and Babylonians, that the priests were entrusted therewith, and employed a philosophical concern about it; that they were the Chaldean priests that did so among the Babylonians; and that the Phoenicians, who were mingled among the Greeks, did especially make use of their letters both for the common affairs of life, and for the delivering down the history of common transactions. I think I may omit any proof, because all men allow it so to be. But now as to our forefathers, that they took no less care about writing such records (for I will not say they took greater care than the others I spoke of), and that they committed that matter to their high priests and to their prophets, and that these records have been written all along down to our own times with the utmost accuracy; nay, if it be not too bold for me to say it, our history will be so written hereafter. I shall endeavour briefly to inform you. For our forefathers did not only employ the best of these priests, and those that attended upon the Divine worship for that design from the beginning, but made provision that the stock of priests should continue unmixed and pure; . . . and this is justly or rather necessarily done, because every one is not permitted of his own accord to be a writer, nor is there any disagreement in what is written; they being only prophets that have written the original and earliest account of things, as they learned them of God Himself by inspiration; and others have written what hath happened in their own times, and that in a very distinct manner also. For we have not an innumerable number of books among us, disagreeing from and contradicting one another (as the Greeks have), but only twenty-two books, which contain the records of all past times, which are justly believed to be Divine. And of them five belong to Moses, which contain his laws, and the traditions of the origin of mankind till his death. This interval of time was little short of three thousand years; but as to the time from the death of Moses till the reign of Artaxerxes, King of Persia, who reigned after Xerxes; the prophets who were after Moses wrote down what was done in their time in thirteen books. The remaining four books contain hymns to God and precepts for the conduct of human life. It is true our history hath been written since Artaxerxes very particularly, but hath not been esteemed of the like authority with the former by our forefathers, because there hath not been an exact

succession of prophets since that time; and how firmly
we have given credit to these books of our own nation
is evident by what we do; for during so many ages as
have already passed, no one hath been so bold as either
to add anything to them, to take anything from them,
or to make any change in them; but it is become natural
to all Jews, immediately and from their very birth, to
esteem those books to contain Divine doctrines, and to
persist in them, and, if occasion be, willingly to die for
them."

Why Apocryphal Books are not Included with the Hebrew Scriptures.

The number of books which, in the foregoing extract, Josephus enumerates as being contained in the
Hebrew Scriptures is thirty-nine, exactly corresponding
with the number now in the Old Testament. But, it
may be asked, What about the fourteen Apocryphal
books which are in the Roman Catholic Bible? To
which it may be replied, that these were originally written in Greek and Latin, and never formed a part of
Hebrew literature. They were, therefore, never incorporated with the Hebrew Scriptures, or recognized by
the Jews as inspired or possessing any canonical authority, whatever value might attach to them as ordinary
histories of passing events. The writer of the preface
to the Commentary on the Apocrypha, published by the
Society for Promoting Christian Knowledge, under the
direction of the Tract Committee of the Church of England, makes the following remarks in reference to these
books :

"It is certain that the Apocrypha was written after
the age of Malachi, and that the greater part of it, if not
the whole, was composed before the coming of Christ,
and existed in the time of our blessed Lord; and it is
no less certain that it was not received by the Hebrew
Church as inspired, and that our blessed Lord communicated with the Hebrew Church, which called Malachi

the 'Seal of the Prophets,' and acknowledged that the succession of inspired writers had come to a close in his age, and that no books composed after it were to be regarded as inspired. Our Lord acknowledged her canon of the Old Testament as complete, and set His Divine seal upon it. The written Word, as received by the Hebrew Church, was accepted by the incarnate Word; it was received as the Word of God by the Son of God."

As a Theocracy the Jewish Nation Most Highly Valued the Inspired Writings.

The Jewish nation from the time of Moses, whether governed by judges or kings, was a theocracy, under the direct rule of Jehovah, and this they always recognized, no matter how grievously they sinned against Him and merited His chastisements. The children of Israel had been living under the first covenant made with Abraham, which was one of grace, down to the time when they voluntarily placed themselves under the second covenant made at Sinai, which was one of law. Through Moses God then spake to the children of Israel, saying, "Now, therefore, if ye will obey my voice indeed, and keep my covenant, then ye shall be a peculiar treasure unto me above all people; for all the earth is mine. And ye shall be unto me a kingdom of priests, and an holy nation"; and all the people answered together and said, "All that the Lord hath spoken we will do " (Ex. 19 : 5-8). From that time forward they were under a solemn covenant with Jehovah to obey all His commands, and He promised earthly blessings as the reward of their obedience, and threatened with earthly judgments as the consequence of disobedience. And now nearly forty years afterwards, when about to enter the promised land, Moses in that wonderful summary of God's dealings with them, and commandments to them, as given in the Book of Deuteronomy, reminded them thus of the covenant into which Jehovah had entered with

them : " For thou art an holy people unto the Lord thy
God; the Lord thy God hath chosen thee to be a special
people unto Himself above all people that are upon the
face of the earth. The Lord did not set His love upon
you, nor choose you because ye were more in number
than any people; for ye were the fewest of all people,"
etc. (Deut. 7 : 6, 7). And again He reminds them, " For
thou art an holy people unto the Lord thy God, and the
Lord hath chosen thee to be a peculiar people unto Himself above all the nations that are upon the earth" (Deut.
14 : 2).

It is little wonder that a nation so highly favoured by
God should lightly esteem the writings of uninspired
philosophers and works of fiction; and, therefore, we
find no place given to such literature among the collection of Hebrew books, which consisted only of inspired
writings, in which, through His prophets God had been
gradually unfolding His will to them, as we read, " The
Word of the Lord was unto them precept upon precept,
precept upon precept; line upon line, line upon line;
here a little and there a little," etc. (Isa. 28 : 13). And
all these writings by various persons in different ages,
predicting the coming of the Messiah, in whom, through
them, all nations should be blessed; or warning them
of coming judgments on account of their sins." Surely
the learned Professor must be willing to admit that such
a nation as this, with their inspired prophets, had no
need for either philosophy or fiction.

Scope of True Criticism and Qualifications for Its Exercise.

As has been already remarked, true criticism acknowledges the Divine inspiration and authenticity of
those Hebrew Scriptures comprising the Old Testament,
which have been handed down with such scrupulous care
through so many generations of God's chosen people,
and which have been used and commended as the Word
of God by the Son of God. But still there is a large field

for honest criticism in the detection and explanation of
interpolations by copyists and errors by translators,
which do not in any way affect either the inspiration or
authenticity of the Old Testament Scriptures. The only
persons, however, who are qualified to engage in this
work are those who are not only learned, but also
regenerate men, filled with the Holy Spirit, and thus
able to compare spiritual things with spiritual. It was
their high priests and their inspired prophets, who,
amongst the Jews, not only wrote, but had the custody
and criticism of the inspired writings down to the time
of Malachi, and from that time until the Lord Jesus
Christ entered upon His public ministry they were in
the custody of the priests, who were responsible for their
safe-keeping. But after the resurrection of Christ and
the descent of the Holy Spirit at Pentecost, a new dispensation was inaugurated. The Church of Christ was
formed by believers (Jew and Gentile) being baptized
by the Holy Spirit into One Body, of which Christ is
the head, and in that Church there was a new line of
prophets, inspired by God to reveal His will respecting
the new order of things that had been established. The
Messiah promised to the Jewish nation, the seed of Abraham, and " the seed of David according to the flesh, and
declared (or determined) to be the son of God with
power, according to the Spirit of holiness, by the resurrection from the dead" (Rom. 1 : 4) had come "unto His
own, but His own received Him not; but as many as received Him to them gave He power to become the sons
of God, even to them that believe on His name, which
were born, not of blood, nor of the flesh, nor of the will
of man, but of God" (John 1 : 11-13). He was rejected
by the Jewish nation, and by them crucified; and, as He
had promised to His disciples, He rose from the dead
on the third day. Before leaving them and ascending to
heaven from their very presence, He gave them the promise of the baptism with the Holy Spirit . . . and
said to them : " Ye shall receive *power* after that the
Holy Spirit is come upon you, and ye shall be witnesses

unto me, both in Jerusalem and in all Judea, and in Samaria, and unto the uttermost parts of the earth. And when He had spoken these things, while they beheld, he was taken up, and a cloud received Him out of their sight. And while they looked steadfastly toward heaven as He went up, behold two men stood by them in white apparel: which also said unto them, Ye men of Galilee, why stand ye gazing up into heaven ? This same Jesus which is taken up from you into heaven shall so come in like manner as ye have seen Him go into heaven" (Acts 1 : 5-11).

Descent of the Holy Spirit and New Revelations Completed.

With the descent of the Holy Spirit upon the whole Church various gifts were bestowed, among which was that of prophecy (1 Cor. 12 : 10). This gift was needful in the Church for revealing the will of God in the new dispensation before the New Testament was written. They, as well as the apostles, spoke as the Spirit gave them utterance, and, while the apostles exercised a general supervision of the spiritual work and revelations in the various assemblies of Christians, it is likely, from what we read in 1 Cor. 14 : 29-33, that in every assembly there were several of these inspired prophets. As, however, in the Mosaic dispensation there were false prophets, against whom the people were warned, and whose pretended revelations were rejected when subjected to inspired criticism, so in this new dispensation there was the danger of men professing to be prophets, through whom God was not speaking ; and, therefore, in the passage just referred to provision was made for the most careful criticism of all that was said, so that if the instructions given by the apostle were observed there was little danger of error being permitted amongst them. One of the special purposes for which the Holy Spirit came to dwell in the heart of each individual believer during this dispensation was that He might teach

them all things, and bring all things to their remembrance which the Lord Jesus Christ had said unto them
(John 14 : 26). Jesus, whom Professor Goldwin Smith,
like Nicodemus, calls the " Great Teacher," said to His
disciples again in John 16 : 13, " Howbeit when He, the
Spirit of truth, is come, He will guide you into all truth;
for He shall not speak *from* (R.V.) Himself, but whatsoever He shall hear that shall He speak; and He will
show you things to come." Even as their great Teacher
had been with them personally when present bodily on
earth, so now and henceforth they were to have dwelling
in their hearts continually another great Teacher, the
third person in the Godhead, by whose mighty power
the Lord Jesus Christ Himself had performed all His
wonderful works. And just as they yielded themselves
up to be taught and guided by this ever-present Teacher
would He guide them into all truth, and enable them
rightly to criticize and detect any errors that might be
advanced while as yet there was no written word. The
Church is being still " built upon the foundation of the
apostles and prophets, Jesus Christ Himself being the
chief corner-stone " (Eph. 2 : 20); but for the erection
of the superstructure it was needful that the record of
the life and works and teaching of Christ and His
apostles and the leading principles of Christian faith,
delivered at first orally or by letter through the inspired
apostles and prophets of this new dispensation, should
be embodied in more permanent form for the instruction of future generations. There were many histories
written of the life and sayings and doings of the Lord
Jesus Christ, but only four of these, the Gospels as we
now have them, passed the ordeal of criticism to which
they were subjected, and were received by the apostles
and prophets of the early Church as inspired writings,
and thus embodied in the New Testament Scriptures.
All the writings which make up this book were, it is
believed, published between A.D. 43 and A.D. 98. Before
this period the Church had received oral instruction
from Christ and His apostles and inspired prophets for

over twenty years. They recognized the fact that since
Pentecost the Holy Spirit was and ever would be their
teacher as they submitted to His guidance, but, as the
apostolic and prophetic gifts in the foundation were
passing away, the need was felt of preserving their inspired writings in permanent form for use in future ages,
and as authentic records of the life of Christ and the
teaching which had been received by the Spirit of Christ
through the gifts which He had bestowed.

Honest Criticism Required for Both Old and New Testaments.

For many centuries before the art of printing was
discovered the New Testament Scriptures were, like the
Old Testament Scriptures, copied with the pen on parchment; and as a matter of course there is just the same
reason in both cases why honest criticism should be
exercised for the detection of interpolations and other
errors by the copyists and of mistakes by translators into
various languages. For such criticism, however, mere
scholarship is not a sufficient qualification. The critic
should also, as already remarked, be a regenerated man,
and endued with power by the Holy Spirit, or he cannot
apprehend the true spiritual meaning of what he reads
so as to perform intelligently this necessary work.

Professor Smith Questions Authenticity of the Four Gospels and Acts.

Professor Goldwin Smith objects to the four Gospels,
because, as he says, "they were written by anonymous
writers and of uncertain dates"; and yet, with strange
inconsistency he accepts just so much of the life and
sayings of Jesus recorded in those Gospels as suits his
taste, and rejects all the rest. But his statement is not
correct if it implies that the writers were unknown. It
is doubtful if there are any writings of the same age in
existence the authorship of which is more clearly estab-

lished. That Matthew, the apostle, and formerly a publican, was the writer of the first Gospel was never questioned by any ancient authority, and that it was written
by him in Hebrew is the tradition of the ancient Church
from apostolic times, and Irenaeus says it was written
by Matthew when Peter and Paul were preaching at
Rome, about A.D. 63, or probably earlier.

Irenaeus says that Mark's Gospel was written about
A.D. 43 by John Mark, who acted as interpreter to
Peter, and also assisted both Barnabas and Paul. It
was written by him at Rome, and, as was supposed, under
the special influence and direction of Peter, from whom
he learned most of the facts.

Luke was not an eye-witness of the resurrection, but
was an honest compiler of the facts related by him and
doubtless received from many witnesses. It is not certainly known whether he was a Hellenistic Jew or a
convert from the Gentiles, but his companionship with
Paul during his missionary journeys and his imprison-
ment at Rome give assurance of the reliability of all his
statements. No doubt was ever felt in the Church as to
the authorship of this Gospel.

But the fourth Gospel is the one to which the Professor has the strongest objections, and yet, strange to
say, it is the one about which there is the strongest evidence, both as to authorship and date. It was published in Ephesus about A.D. 97 by the Apostle John
in his extreme old age, about the time of his banishment
to Patmos, at the urgent entreaty of the elders of the
Asiatic coast and of deputies sent from several churches
and many still surviving disciples of Christ, among whom
is said to have been the Apostle Andrew. It was said
to be his intention mainly to supplement the other three
Gospels already written, and this accounts for his omit-
ting most of the important things stated by them, and
only repeating three of the same events which they
have given besides the history of the Passion, Death
and Resurrection of Christ, viz., the feeding of the five
thousand, Jesus walking on the sea, and Mary anointing

Him; but he supplies a great deal that the other evangelists have not given, thus bearing out the theory that it was intended as a supplementary Gospel. He describes himself as "the disciple whom Jesus loved," and that "other disciple." A comparison of this Gospel with John's first Epistle should settle the question of authorship if there were any doubt about it. It does seem, however, that the special dislike of infidels generally to this Gospel must arise from the plain statements made in it as to the necessity of the new birth for salvation, and of the indwelling of the Holy Spirit for instruction in the truth, two things which, as a matter of course, neither they nor any other unregenerate man or woman can possibly understand.

Professor Goldwin Smith says that Luke was probably the author of the Acts, but that there is no positive evidence of the existence of this book till towards the close of the second century; and he thus insinuates a doubt in reference to its authorship for which there is no foundation whatever. The fact is that the Acts is just a continuation of the Gospel which Luke had written, both having been addressed to Theophilus, probably a Roman of high rank, to give him certain information about the things which he had been taught by Paul and himself. The fact of both books having been addressed to the same person makes it certain that no great length of time elapsed between the publication of the two.

In reference to the four Gospels Professor Goldwin Smith further says (page 175) : "A biography of Christ there cannot be. There are no genuine materials for it, as Strauss truly says. Four compilations of legend cannot be pieced together so as to make the history of a life. No ingenuity can produce a chronological sequence of scene such as a biographer requires."

Another objection that he makes (page 156) to the four Gospels is that "there are discrepancies in the narratives."

And a still further objection is (page 160) that "there is no trace of the death of Christ left in general history!"

And yet in the face of all these objections to the Gospels, which he calls a "compilation of legends," he makes the following remarks with apparent candour :

On page 137 he says : "The effect produced by the teaching of Jesus and His disciples is beyond question the most momentous fact in history!"

And on page 137 : "The conversion of Saul marks the greatness of the moral change!"

But on page 105 he had previously said : "A sudden and absolute change of nature is contrary to all our experience, which would lead us to believe that gradual progress is the law." If in this last statement he is speaking only on behalf of himself and the so-called "liberal theologians" the writer is not disposed to question its correctness; but every true Christian will declare that his or her experience accords with the statement of Scripture : "If any man be in Christ, he is a new creature; old things are passed away : behold, all things are become new" (2 Cor. 5 : 17).

The Gospels Not Intended as a Biography of Christ.

And now with regard to the three objections to the four Gospels which are quoted above. Let us consider briefly the circumstances of the case. According to the promises which Jesus had given to His disciples, the Holy Spirit had come down at Pentecost when "they were all with one accord in one place. And suddenly there came a sound from heaven, as of a rushing, mighty wind, and it filled all the house where they were sitting. And there appeared unto them cloven tongues, like as of fire, and it sat upon each of them; and they were all filled with the Holy Ghost, and began to speak with other tongues, as the Spirit gave them utterance" (Acts 2 : 1-4). It seems as if human language was inadequate to describe this wonderful transaction, the like of which had never before occurred in the history of the world; but there was an experience then entered upon by all present on that memorable occasion which could never afterwards be erased from their minds : " they were all filled with the Holy Ghost "; they had received the promised enduement of power from on high; a Divine Person had taken possession of each heart; and He, the Spirit of Christ, had strangely quickened their memories, and brought to their recollection the person of Jesus and His sayings and doings as vividly as if He was then speaking and acting in their midst. They no longer felt like comfortless orphans, who had been bereaved of their best and only friend. He was by His Spirit still with them as He had promised : "' Lo! I am with you alway, even unto the end of the age." They did not want a biography of One who was still present with them, and all whose words and actions were kept ever freshly before their minds, " written not with ink, but with the Spirit of the living God; not in tables of stone, but in fleshy tables of the heart " (2 Cor. 3 : 3).

Results of Enduement With Power.

The presence of Jehovah had been manifested in the Shekinah glory which had overshadowed them, and in the Shekinah fire which appeared as tongues of flame; and with the conscious indwelling of the Holy Spirit all timidity was gone. Peter and John and the other disciples preached the Word with all boldness in the power of the Spirit, and on the same day, the day of Pentecost, three thousand souls were converted, and we read: "And fear came upon every soul; and many wonders and signs were done by the apostles." This enduement of power by the Holy Spirit is the cause which produced the effect referred to by Professor Smith on page 137, where he makes the admission, " The effect produced by the teaching of Jesus and His disciples is beyond question the most momentous fact in history." After the healing of the lame man at the gate of the temple Peter and John were brought before the rulers and elders and scribes, where Annas, the high priest, presided, and they

were asked : " By what power or by what name have
ye done this ? Then Peter, filled with the Holy Ghost,
said unto them, Ye rulers of the people and elders of
Israel, if we this day be examined of the good deed done
to the impotent man, by what means he is made whole:
be it known unto you all, and to all the people of Israel,
that by the name of Jesus Christ of Nazareth, whom ye
crucified, whom God raised from the dead, even by Him
doth this man stand here before you whole. This is the
stone which was set at nought of you builders, which
is become the head of the corner. Neither is there salvation in any other; for there is none other name under
heaven given among men whereby we must be saved;
Now when they saw the boldness of Peter and John, and
perceived that they were unlearned and ignorant men,
they marvelled; and they took knowledge of them that
they had been with Jesus. And beholding the man that
was healed standing with them, they could say nothing
against it " (Acts 4 : 14). And twenty years afterwards,
when Paul at Thessalonica went into the synagogue and
reasoned with the Jews out of their Old Testament Scriptures, " opening and alleging that Christ must needs
have suffered and risen again from the dead; and that
this Jesus whom I preach unto you is Christ," a great
commotion was raised, and certain lewd fellows of the
baser sort cried : " These that have turned the world
upside down have come hither also " (Acts 17 : 6). And
after the death of the first martyr Stephen, the Church
at Jerusalem (except the Apostles) " were scattered
abroad throughout Judea and Samaria, and went everywhere preaching the Word " (Acts 8 : 1, 4). What
Word did they preach ? Only the Hebrew Scriptures,
which they read, and to the fulfilment of which in the
person of Christ they boldly testified. And the great
theme of their discourses always was, " Jesus and the
resurrection." They had no New Testament Scriptures,
and they needed none, for they spoke of the things which
they had themselves seen and heard, and which the Holy
Spirit, dwelling in them, was ever keeping freshly before

their minds and hearts, and for the truth of these things
they were willing to lay down their lives at any moment.
He whom they preached had told them that He was
going from them for a little while, but He was coming
again to receive them to Himself, that where He was
there they might be also (John 14 : 3). They fondly
treasured up the memory of His words and actions, and
looked forward with longing eyes to His expected return.
He had never, so far as we have heard, either written
anything Himself or commanded them to write anything
about Him or His works, or His teaching; and so long
as they lived, according to His promise to them, the
Holy Spirit brought all things to their remembrance
that He had said unto them (John 14 : 26). But as the
Second Coming of their Lord was delayed, and the living
witnesses to His life and death and resurrection passed
one by one from earth to heaven, the Holy Spirit put
it into the hearts of His disciples to commit to writing
those truths to which they had been witnessing during
their lives, and thus to provide the means whereby men
in future ages might be saved through believing their
testimony regarding Him.

God's Purpose in the Writing and Preservation of the Four Gospels.

To write all that He had said and done when here on
earth could not be expected, nor was it necessary. At
the close of the fourth Gospel, John, the beloved disciple, declared himself to be the writer of it in these
words, " This is the disciple which testifieth of these
things and wrote these things, and we know that his
testimony is true. And there are also many other things
which Jesus did, the which, if they should be written
every one, I suppose that even the world itself could
not contain the books that should be written." In this
oriental style of expressing himself the apostle shows
how impossible it would be to commit to writing within
reasonable bounds a full account of the sayings and

doings of the Lord Jesus Christ, and, as has been already remarked, his own Gospel was doubtless chiefly intended to be supplementary to the other three which had been already written. Each of the four Gospels appears to have been written from a different standpoint, and without any special care as to the chronological order in which the events were narrated. They were not intended as a history of the life of Christ, but rather to bring His person and work before the mind of the reader from the point of view at which the writer beheld Him. Matthew presents Him as the Messiah promised to Israel. Mark seems to regard Him specially as the servant of Jehovah. Luke as the Son of Man, and John as the Son of God. But the four books are written without any pre-arrangement between the authors, in different countries and at widely different dates, extending from A.D. 43 to A.D. 98. But there is agreement between them in all essential particulars which concern the salvation of men, presenting Him, notwithstanding all the bitter enmity aroused against Him as the only perfect man who ever walked this earth. Son of Man and Son of God, dying the shameful death of the cross for sins that were not His own, and rising again from the dead on the third day; the One who voluntarily laid aside the glory which He had with the Father from a past eternity, for whom a body had been prepared, in order that as a man He might identify Himself with this fallen race, revealing the infinite love of God to sinful men, to whom He is still speaking by His Holy Spirit.

Therefore, in reply to Professor Goldwin Smith's first objection to the four Gospels, it is a sufficient answer to say that they were never intended for the purpose of writing a history of His life in chronological order; and that it is absurd for anyone to try and represent as legends or fables the well-attested and thoroughly reliable records handed down to us in the Gospels regarding the life and ministry and the death and resurrection of the Lord Jesus Christ.

The Professor Objects to Discrepancies.

The next objection that he makes to the four Gospels is that there are " discrepancies between the narratives." Leaving aside for the time being the question of the inspiration of the writers, and regarding them simply as honest men, desirous of giving a truthful account of what they knew personally, or had learned from the most trustworthy sources, regarding this wonderful man; our faith in the truthfulness of their statements would be strengthened by the circumstance that there were discrepancies between them as to minor details, whilst there was substantial agreement as to all the main facts. Thus we find in the Gospels some things stated by one evangelist that are omitted by another, and where some events are related by all there are great differences in the manner of relating them. As the Professor has only made a general statement without giving any proof or particulars, it is, of course, impossible to guess at what discrepancies he may refer to; but if he will only consider the matter carefully he must admit that, as a general principle, some discrepancies between a number of independent witnesses are calculated to increase our confidence in the correctness of their statements about the main facts on which they are all agreed. At all events, this would be strong evidence that no combination had been entered into by the different narrators to impose upon the credulous.

Says there is no Trace of the Death of Christ in General History.

The other objection which he makes to the four Gospels is that " there is no trace of the death of Christ left in general history." To which it might be sufficient answer to say briefly if such is the fact : " So much the worse for general history !" But in another place the Professor himself refers to the death of Christ as a " judicial murder," and it cannot be supposed that he seriously questions the fact that Jesus died because general history did not mention it.

Says Writers of New Testament did not Claim to be Inspired.

Another remark which he makes regarding these New Testament Scriptures is that the writers themselves do not claim to be inspired. To which it may be replied, that their claiming to be inspired would not make them so. It is of much greater importance that their inspiration should be recognized, as it has been by other inspired writers, and by all other spiritual men in the Church of God, who are best qualified to judge upon such a subject. For those who are still unconverted it should be sufficient to know that they are reliable witnesses to the things which they have seen and heard, and that through believing their testimony regarding the Lord Jesus Christ they may have life through His name (John 20 : 31). But while the writers did not claim inspiration for themselves, or say what they thought about their own writings, there can be no doubt that they felt, whether speaking or writing, that they were under the guidance of the Holy Spirit, and that thus their ministry was a continuation of the ministry of Christ when He was upon earth.

After Resurrection of Christ the Church became the Custodian of the Scriptures.

The Old Testament Scriptures passed into the custody of the Christian Church; and with the Gospels, the Book of Acts, the Epistles, and the Book of Revelation, which formed the New Testament, have been carefully preserved by the early fathers, and many copies of them reproduced by monks secluded in cloisters throughout many ages since the time of the apostles; and these copies have been subjected to the most severe criticism by many competent and spiritual men, more especially since the multiplication of copies by the art of printing. That some few interpolations and errors by copyists in both Old and New Testaments may yet be discovered is quite possible. But it would be the height of folly for anyone to conclude because there are some things about the Bible which as yet he is unable to understand or explain, that, therefore, as infidel writers would fain have him think, the whole book is nothing but a compilation of fables, with which mankind has been gulled for some thousands of years. No other records in this world have ever been preserved with so much care through so many centuries, and none others have ever been subjected to such searching criticism by those who were best qualified to do this work.

Enmity of Ungodly Men against the Word of God.

For centuries past ungodly men have been doing their utmost to make it appear that the Word of God is neither authentic nor inspired, but thus far without success. It is true that infidelity is on the increase, but this arises, not from the soundness of arguments used against the Scriptures, but from the natural enmity of the human heart to the revelation which God has given therein of man's true condition by nature, and the necessity of the new birth, without which there can be no possible hope of salvation for impenitent sinners. With the increase of scientific knowledge, and the march of material improvement in many ways, in modern times, men are becoming more exalted in their own estimation, and more unwilling to see and confess their own utter depravity by nature as the Bible pourtrays it. Their pride will not allow them to take the place of lost sinners, and thus seek and find salvation through the atoning sacrifice of the Son of God upon the cross of Calvary. And so they try to persuade themselves that the Word of the living God is only a compilation of fables, by which mankind has been deluded through many generations. But, not content with thus destroying their own souls, they are generally bent on destroying the faith of others in the only revelation which God has given of the way of salvation, without giving them anything in exchange. While these writers may do much mischief to themselves and others, they can never shake the sure foundation of the Word of God. The One whom Professor Goldwin Smith recognizes as " the Great Teacher " said : " Heaven and earth shall pass away, but my Word shall not pass away" (Matt. 24 : 35); and we also read in 1 Peter 1 : 24, 25 : " For all flesh is as grass, and all the glory of man as the flower of grass. The grass withereth and the flower thereof fadeth away; but the Word of the Lord endureth for ever. And this is the Word which by the Gospel is preached unto you."

Professor Smith's Denial of the Fall, the Incarnation and Redemption.

Before closing this chapter two other statements (both on page 166) from Professor Goldwin Smith's book may be given to show the thorougrly infidel character of his publication.

In the first he disputes what he calls the Johanistic doctrine of the Trinity, and ridicules the idea of " a Being who fills eternity and infinity, becoming for the redemption of one speck of the universe an embryo in the womb of a Jewish maiden," and says that " for this stupendous doctrine our principal evidence is the anonymous work of a mystic writer." It is really extraordinary how one who is generally regarded as a learned and able writer can show such an utter disregard for facts when writing about the Word of God. It is quite true that the Apostle John clearly presents the doctrine of the Trinity in his Gospel (John 14 : 26), but it is not true, as has already been clearly shown in this chapter, that he was an anonymous writer, because in the closing verses of the Gospel he has declared himself to be the writer of it just as clearly as if he had signed his name

to it; and the immaculate conception of Christ is testified to by both Matthew and Luke in their Gospels.
Such a remark as that referred to shows how easy it is
for a man to deceive himself by thinking that he has an
exalted idea of the Divine Being when he is really limiting the attributes of Him who, as the Scriptures declare,
numbers the very hairs of our heads, and without whose
knowledge a sparrow does not fall to the ground. These
are the words of the Lord Jesus Christ Himself, whom
the Professor admits to be "the Great Teacher."

The other statement which he makes is this. He says:
"The Incarnation is the centre of this whole circle of
miracles, but, since his rejection of the authenticity and
authority of the Book of Genesis, the purpose and meaning of the incarnation have been withdrawn. If there
was no Fall of man there can be no need of redemption.
If there was no need of redemption, there can have been
no motive for the incarnation . . . . This is a vital
point." There is a perfectly logical sequence in these
conclusions, provided his first premise is correct, that
there was no Fall. But this is not true. In other Scriptures besides the Book of Genesis we have the clearest
statements as to man's natural condition as a sinner and
his need of redemption. Look, for instance, at what the
Lord Jesus Christ said to the two disciples whom He
overtook on the road to Emmaus after His resurrection.
"O fools, and slow of heart to believe all that the prophets have spoken! Ought not Christ to have suffered
these things, and to enter into His glory?" And, beginning at Moses and all the prophets, He expounded
unto them *in all the Scriptures* the things concerning Himself" (Luke 24 : 25-27). And these Scriptures which He
expounded to them were the Hebrew Scriptures then in
use by the Jewish people, which included the Book of
Genesis, from which He then doubtless explained to them
that the same Jesus who had died upon the cross and
risen again was the seed of the woman who was to bruise
the serpent's head, about whom God had spoken to Adam
in the Garden of Eden after the Fall. Who are we to

believe ?   Professor Goldwin Smith or the One whom
he professes to admire as the "Great Teacher," who
Himself claimed to be the Son of God, and who is twice
spoken of as God by the Apostle Paul, first in Rom.
9 : 5, thus : "Christ, who is over all, God blessed forever"; and again in Titus 2 : 13 : "Looking for the
blessed hope and appearing of the glory of our great
God and Saviour Jesus Christ."   Enough, however, has
been previously said to show that there is no reasonable
ground for objecting to the inspiration and authenticity
of the Book of Genesis, which the Lord Jesus Christ
recognized as one of the books of Moses.

It is a remarkable fact that in His three replies to
the temptations of Satan, the Lord Jesus Christ quoted
every time from the Book of Deuteronomy, whose authenticity and inspiration infidel writers have done their
utmost to dispute.

CHAPTER III.

GOD SPEAKING BY THE PROPHETS.

THERE were many true prophets since the Fall who have left no writings behind them, and some of their predictions were handed down either by reliable tradition or by documentary evidence, which was never incorporated in the canonical books of the Hebrew Scriptures. And some of these predictions are referred to and quoted by the inspired writers in the New Testament Scriptures. Take, for instance, that remarkable passage in Jude 14 : 15, "And Enoch also, the seventh from Adam, prophesied of these, saying, Behold, the Lord cometh with ten thousands of His saints to execute judgment upon all; and to convince all that are ungodly among them of all their ungodly deeds which they have ungodly committed, and of all their hard speeches which ungodly sinners have spoken against him." This prophecy by the man who walked with God for three hundred years before the Flood has not yet been fulfilled, but it has been confirmed by other prophecies in both Old and New Testament Scriptures. (See Zech. 14 : 5, and 2 Thess. 1 : 7-10). And, if we may judge by the rapid spread of infidelity, the time of its fulfillment is not far dstant.

Unfair Criticism by Professor Goldwin Smith.

Another instance of the same kind is in Matt. 2 : 23, which reads thus : "And he came and dwelt in a city called Nazareth, that it might be fulfilled which was spoken by the prophets, " He shall be called a Nazarene." Because this has been literally fulfilled in the person of Christ Professor Goldwin Smith tries to throw doubt upon it (page 167) by stating that there is nothing corresponding to it in the Old Testament. This is very unfair. The passage does not say that it was written in the Old Testament, but that it was "spoken by the prophets," so that the natural inference would be that, as in the case of Enoch's prophecy, the predictions of several prophets that He should be called a Nazarene had been handed down by tradition, and were well known when Matthew wrote his Gospel.

Many Divine Revelations Not Committed to Writing.

There can be no doubt that in the Old Testament Scriptures we have only a very small part of the teaching and predictions of the true prophets of Jehovah, through whom for so many ages He had been revealing His will to His chosen people. In the very nature of things it could not be otherwise. The Lord Jesus Christ during His public ministry was constantly speaking to the people day after day, and it is only a very small part of what He said that has been recorded. The Holy Spirit has, however, so guided that in each case there has been sufficient committed to writing and handed down to us in both Old and New Testaments to give a full revelation of His purposes which He desired us to know.

Divine Revelations Often Certified by Miracles.

God often accompanied the prophetic gift with miraculous powers when the circumstances called for such proofs that He was speaking through the prophets; and those to whom they were sent were thus compelled by the manifestation of supernatural powers to recognize them as ambassadors from a supernatural Being, who claimed their obedience. Thus Moses wrought many miracles before Pharaoh, which only had the effect of hardening his heart, until at length the judgment of God overtook him and his people, so that he was compelled to let the children of Israel go out of Egypt to worship Him. Thus when the people were hemmed in on every side, the Red Sea before them and Pharaoh's army

behind them, Moses at the command of God "stretched
out his hand over the sea: and the Lord caused the sea
to go back by a strong east wind all that night, and made
the sea dry land; and the waters were divided, and the
children of Israel went into the midst of the sea upon
the dry ground; and the waters were a wall unto them
on their right hand and on their left." After they had
got safely over the Egyptian army attempted to follow
them. But Moses stretched forth his hand again over
the sea, which came back and overwhelmed the host of
Pharaoh in the waters so that not one of them escaped.
And what was the effect of this miraculous deliverance ?
We read that "Israel saw that great work which the
Lord did upon the Egyptians : and the people feared
the Lord, and believed the Lord and His servant Moses"
(Ex. 14 : 31). After this the bitter water at Marah was
made sweet, and there God first covenanted to be their
Healer if they were obedient to His commands (Ex.
15 : 26). And then for their sustenance in their wilderness journeys the manna was provided, which they gathered fresh every morning for so many years. And again,
when in that arid, barren waste at Rephidim they cried
out for water to drink, the Lord commanded Moses to
smite with his rod the rock in Horeb and water would
come out of it; and Moses did so, and the thirst of the
people was assuaged. And by many other signs and
wonders did God, through the forthputting of His supernatural power, bear testimony to His people that Moses
was His prophet, and that He was speaking to them
through him.

After Joshua succeeded Moses as the prophet and
chosen leader of the host of Israel God caused Jericho
to be taken by the forthputting again of His own supernatural power; and thus, at the very outset of the work
he was commissioned to do, his own heart, and the hearts
of the people were encouraged by the manifest approval
of Jehovah. And after the land was conquered and
divided amongst the various tribes we read, "And the
people served the Lord all the days of Joshua, and all

the days of the elders that outlived Joshua, *who had seen all the great works of the Lord* that He did for Israel" (Judges 2 : 7).

God's Revelations often Certified by Judgments.

During the time of the Judges, who followed Joshua, God sometimes raised up strange instruments, as it appears to us, to execute His judgments, both on His own people and on the surrounding nations on account of their sins. The assassination of Eglon, King of Moab, who was oppressing the children of Israel, by Ehud, the left-handed son of Gera, a Benjamite (Judges 3 : 15). The death of Sisera, captain of the Canaanite host, which was warring against Israel, by the hands of Jael, the wife of Heber, the Kenite. The death of the cruel murderer, Abimelech by means of a millstone, which a woman cast upon his head. The terrible vengeance executed by the children of Israel upon the tribe of Benjamin for the murder and shameful outrage of the Levite's concubine, are all cases in point, and reveal to us the state of barbarism into which the nation had fallen for nearly three hundred years after the time of Joshua; and the sad picture is only relieved by the occasional history of some prophet, prophetess or judge whom the Lord raised up for their deliverance, under whose rule a temporary respite was enjoyed from the prevailing lawlessness. When the Law was given at Mount Sinai their forefathers had covenanted with Jehovah, "All that the Lord hath spoken we will do" (Ex. 19 : 8). But after Moses and Joshua, God's appointed prophets and rulers, and the elders who outlived Joshua had disappeared, and the people were left without any visible head, "they forsook the Lord God of their fathers which brought them out of the land of Egypt, and followed other gods . . . and provoked the Lord to anger; and they forsook the Lord and served Baal and Ashtaroth; and the anger of the Lord was hot against Israel, and He delivered them into the hands of spoilers that spoiled them, and He sold them into the hands of their enemies . . . Never-

theless the Lord raised up judges, which delivered them
out of the hand of those that spoiled them . . . And
when the Lord raised them up Judges, then the Lord was
with the Judge, and delivered them out of the hand of
their enemies all the days of the Judge. . . . And it
came to pass when the Judge was dead that they returned
and corrupted themselves more than their fathers in
following other gods to serve them, and to bow down
unto them; they ceased not from their own doings nor
from their stubborn way" (Judges 2 : 12-19). And the
general record of this highly favoured nation is summed
up thus : " In those days there was no king in Israel;
every man did that which was right in his own eyes "
(Judges 21 : 25). Before taking possession of the land
promised to Abraham and his seed they had failed to
cast out all the nations that were therein as God had
commanded; and God allowed them to remain, and the
reason is thus explained : "And they were to prove
Israel by them, to know whether they would hearken
unto the commandments of the Lord, which He commanded their fathers by the hand of Moses."

Under the Law given to them by Moses they had
failed and merited the judgments which came upon them
from the nations which they had not driven out; and,
on the other hand, God made use of them to punish
those who were afflicting them. Considering the conditions of society that existed in that age, those assassi-
nations would not probably seem more cruel to the
people where they took place than would executions
after a formal trial by court martial appear to those now
living in countries where the benign influence of Christianity has softened the asperities of war even amongst
those who do not themselves profess to be Christians.

The Professor Admits that if there is a Great Law-giver, He can Suspend the Operation of Law.

Professor Goldwin Smith candidly admits (page 143)
that the phrase, "Laws of nature," presupposes that there

must be a law-giver capable of suspending the operation of law. Believing this to be correct, is it unreasonable to suppose that if the great Law-giver and Ruler of the universe has given a revelation of His will through any human being He should suspend the operation of His laws for the purpose of testifying to the genuineness of the revelation given ? If this proposition is admitted there is no need for discussing the probability of any miracles having been wrought by Jehovah as an endorsement of any prophets who claimed to speak in His na.ne. We only require, therefore, to investigate the evidence that such miracles were really performed, just in the same manner that we would investigate any other historical facts.

Authentic Records of Miracles in Old Testament Scriptures.

There are many cases besides that of Moses in which God has thus set the stamp of His approval upon prophets who delivered His messages to His chosen people. and upon leaders raised up for their deliverance. When the angel of the Lord appeared to Gideon and commissioned him to save the children of Israel from the Midianites, he was overwhelmed with a sense of his own insufficiency. And the Lord gave him the assurance. "Surely I will be with thee." But he wanted a miracle performed to convince him that it was really the angel of God who was speaking to him; and the Lord graciously complied with his request (Judges 6 : 17-21). And again, when about to go forth to battle with the enemies of Israel, he twice asked God to work a miracle as a proof that he would obtain the victory, and again God complied with both his requests, and the assurance was given (vs. 36-40).

The feats of strength performed by Samson were all miracles, as we read in connection with each of them that "the Spirit of the Lord came mightily upon him" (Judges 14 : 6), or "the Spirit of the Lord came upon

him " (Judges 14 : 19). The slaying of Goliath by David
in the presence of all Israel was evidently a miracle
wrought by the power of God to show that He was with
him, although in this case it was not necessary to suspend the operation of natural law. The claim of Elijah,
the Tishbite, to be regarded as a true prophet of Jehovah,
was certified to by many miracles, including the provision of meal and oil made for the widow who had supplied his wants. and the healing of her son (1 Kings 17),
and the calling down of fire from heaven in the presence
of four hundred and fifty prophets of Baal which consumed the burnt sacrifice, that had been first drenched
with water. Elisha's position as a prophet was also
certified in a similar way by the miracles which he
wrought, including the dividing of the waters of the
Jordan, which he struck with the mantle of Elijah, saying, "Where is the Lord God of Elijah ?" the restoration to life of the Shunamite woman's dead child, and
the healing of Naaman of leprosy. The account of these
miracles appears in authentic history, and we have no
right to question its correctness without positive evidence
to the contrary.

Fulfillment of Predictions by Prophets.

The most general way, however, by which God certified His true prophets was by the fulfillment of their
predictions, and the spiritual power that accompanied
their words as judged by spiritual men. When Deborah,
the prophetess, judged Israel, she predicted the defeat
of the Canaanites, and told Barak, her captain, that the
Lord would deliver Sisera into the hand of a woman,
and it all literally came to pass as she said. When
Samuel told Eli of the judgment that was to come upon
his house on account of the wickedness of his sons, the
prediction was literally fulfilled. Nathan told David
that the child which Bathsheba bore to him should surely
die, and it died the seventh day afterwards. And the
predictions made by Elijah and Elisha were also literally
fulfilled. When King Hezekiah was sick the prophet

Isaiah was sent to him with a message from God to set his house in order, because he should die and not live. And when Hezekiah prayed to God and wept before Him, the prophet was sent to him again with another message that He would heal him, and that He had added fifteen years to his life, and this prediction was fulfilled. These are but a few familiar instances of the way in which God fulfilled the predictions of His prophets, and thus compelled His people to recognize the fact that through them His word was spoken.

But as we come down to the Psalms and the prophetic writings we find that there is a much fuller revelation of many things that in former ages had, as we suppose, been only dimly outlined, and looked forward to by types and shadows, such as the coming of the Messiah, His rejection and death, and His Second Coming and glorious reign over Israel, in whom all nations will be blessed.

Old Testament Saints and Prophets Knew More than is Recorded of them in Scripture.

In order, however, to a right understanding of the prophetic Scriptures it is necessary to bear in mind that all the revelations which God has given have not been handed down to us. We must take into account the effect produced upon the minds of those with whom God held personal converse if we would rightly estimate the fulness of the revelations they received, instead of supposing that they only knew so much of truth as has been committed to writing. Abel and Noah, and doubtless Adam, also knew the significance of the altar and its bleeding victim, and Enoch prophesied of the coming of the Lord with ten thousands of his saints; but this information must have been communicated to them by personal revelations from God, of which we have no record in the Old Testament Scriptures. Melchizedek, King of Salem (which means King of Peace), to whom Abraham paid tithes, would not have been officiating as priest of the Most High God (Gen. 13 : 18) without an intelligent apprehension of truth, which must have been made known to him by Noah and his descendants, or by direct revelation from Jehovah, of which we possess no record. Abraham, Isaac and Jacob showed by their altars and sacrifices their knowledge of the need of atonement for sin before entering into the presence of God. And Jacob's blessing on his sons showed that he looked forward to the coming of the Messiah, but we have nothing recorded in Scripture to inform us how or when they obtained the knowledge of these truths, which were afterwards so clearly revealed. The only distinct promise of redemption of which we read in the Book of Genesis was that given in the Garden of Eden that the seed of the woman should bruise the serpent's head, and that the serpent should bruise his heel. This is quite intelligible to us now in the light of subsequent revelations, but if we had not these we would not be likely, from the statement made to the serpent, to see any need of the sacrifice, or any prospect of the coming glory of Christ. It is quite evident that in the cases of all these saints of God in the patriarchal ages there was a preparation of mind and heart for the reception of that fuller revelation given through Moses in the ceremonial law, and the various sacrifices as types of the Lamb of God, who was to take away the sin of the world. And it is evident also from the prophesies to which we have referred that they had a like preparation of mind and heart for the fuller revelations to be given through other prophets prior to His coming. In like manner through the darkest periods of human history and national failure, there were doubtless many who cherished the knowledge of those glorious truths which they had received from their fathers, and looked forward to the fulfillment of the promises that had been given. Thus it was in the days of Elijah, when he thought that all the prophets of Jehovah had been slain and he alone was left; and the Lord Himself with the still, small voice assured the discouraged prophet that he had seven thousand men

left in Israel who had not bowed the knee to Baal
(1 Kings 19 : 10, 18). Therefore, in looking at various
texts in the Old Testament Scriptures, which may be
regarded as Messianic prophecies, we must not look at
them as isolated passages, from which alone the people
to whom they were addressed were to obtain their knowledge of the Person and the events to which they refer,
but rather as landmarks in a vast field of truth, in which
much more had already been revealed. In this way these
otherwise isolated passages assume a new significance,
and we get a more definite conception of the manner in
which the One Infinite Being has " at sundry times and
in divers manners spoken in time past unto the fathers
by the prophets." Through many channels, " precept
upon precept, line upon line, here a little and there a
little," as it is expressed in Isa. 28 : 13. God had thus
been revealing more and more information upon subjects
already in a great measure understood through revelations previously made to themselves and their fathers.
Bearing these facts in mind, let us now look at some
passages in the Old Testament which refer to the Coming
One, who is the sum and substance of all revelation from
God to man.

Professor Smith Denies that the First Advent of Jesus was Predicted in Scripture.

Professor Goldwin Smith says (page 76) that no
real and specific prediction of the advent of Jesus, or of
any event in His life, can be produced from the books
of the Old Testament. This, like many of his other
objections, is not a fair way of putting the matter. We
have no right to surmise that the Old Testament is not
the Word of God if we cannot find one isolated passage
giving full particulars of some future event, when there
may be much stronger evidence from many passages,
each of which gives different phases of the same event.

Let us look at the statements made by various prophets apart from those which have been already quoted,

and bearing in mind from what has been stated that the
predictions respecting the Coming Messiah require to
be looked at as a whole if we wish to get any adequate
idea of their application to, and fulfillment in, the person
of the Lord Jesus Christ.

Christ Predicted as Ruler of the Tribe of Judah.

In Gen. 49 : 10, where Jacob blesses his son, Judah,
we read : " The sceptre shall not depart from Judah,
nor a law-giver from between his feet until Shiloh come;
and unto him shall the gathering of the people be."
Another translation of this verse is as follows : " The
sceptre shall not depart from Judah, nor the leader's
staff from between his feet, until he comes to Shiloh, and
to him will be the obedience of the peoples." It matters
not which of these translations is adopted. It is plainly
shown by either of them that the future *Ruler* of Israel
was to be of the tribe of Judah.

Christ Predicted as Prophet and Mediator.

In Deut. 5 : 23-28 and Ex. 20 : 19 we find that the
Israelites could not bear to have Jehovah speak directly
to them, and they entreated Moses to act as their *Mediator*. And in Deut. 18 : 15-19 Moses said to the children
of Israel : " The Lord thy God will raise up unto thee
a *Prophet* from the midst of thee of thy brethren, like
unto me; unto him ye shall hearken, according to all
that thou desirest of the Lord thy God in Horeb in the
day of the assembly, saying, Let me not hear again the
voice of the Lord my God, neither let me see this great
fire any more, that I die not. And the Lord said unto
me, They have well spoken that which they have spoken.
I will raise them up a Prophet from among their brethren
like unto thee, and will put my words in his mouth; and
he shall speak unto them all that I shall command him."
This Prophet which was to be raised up from among His
brethren, like unto Moses, was to be, as he was, a
Mediator between them and God.

Christ Predicted as King of the Seed of Abraham and Jacob.

In Num. 24 : 15-19, when God compelled Balaam to bless Israel instead of cursing them, as Balak desired, we find him saying, " I shall see him, but not now. I shall behold him, but not nigh; there shall come a *Star* out of Jacob, and a sceptre shall rise out of Israel, and shall smite the corners of Moab, and destroy all the children of Seth. And Edom shall be a possession; Seir also shall be a possession for his enemies: and Israel shall do valiantly. Out of Jacob shall come he that shall have dominion, and shall destroy him that remaineth of the city." An evident prediction of the glorious reign of the Coming Messiah as *King* over all the earth. Taking this passage in connection with Ex. 15 : 18 in the Song of Moses, "The Lord shall reign for ever and ever"; or, as another translation renders it, " Jehovah shall be King for ever and ever," we see that God is to reign, and the seed of Jacob is to reign; or, in other words, God manifest in the flesh, the Messiah promised to Israel of the seed of Abraham, is to reign for ever and ever.

After the removal of the Benjamite King Saul, and the enthroning of David as the anointed king of the house of Judah over a theocratic kingdom, he evidently regarded himself as the vicegerent of Jehovah, having God's enemies as his enemies, and being, indeed, in many respects a type of the Coming King, who was to be of his seed. Peter, when filled with the Holy Spirit on the day of Pentecost, spoke of him as a Prophet (Acts 2 : 30); and there can be, therefore, no question about the propriety of applying to the Lord Jesus Christ those passages in the Psalms which were evidently fulfilled in Him, more especially when we remember that He Himself after His resurrection spoke to them about those things in the Psalms referring to Himself (Luke 24 : 44).

The Sufferings of Christ Predicted.

The sufferings of Christ, as prophetically described in Psalm 22, transcended anything in David's own actual experience, and, therefore, cannot, by any stretch of imagination, be made to apply to him. The first verse commences with the very words which the Lord Jesus Christ uttered on the cross, "My God! my God! Why hast Thou forsaken me?" (Matt. 27 : 4-6 and Mark 15 : 34). The eighteenth verse says, "They part my garments among them, and cast lots upon my vesture." And this prediction was literally fulfilled by the Roman soldiers at His crucifixion, as we read in Matt. 27 : 35; and also in John 19 : 23, 24. "Then the soldiers, when they had crucified Jesus, took his garments and made four parts, to every soldier a part; and also His coat. Now the coat was without seam, woven throughout. They said, therefore, among themselves, Let us not rend it, but cast lots for it, whose it shall be. . . . These things, therefore, the soldiers did." ' Surely this is the fulfilment of a specific prediction of an event in the life of Jesus which ought to be satisfactory to Professor Goldwin Smith. In this Psalm it is evident that the spirit of prophecy impelled David to write things of which he had no personal knowledge, and which could only be understood in the light of their New Testament fulfillment. This is also true of the first twenty-one verses of Psalm 69, which describe the sufferings of Christ, and end with the words, "They gave me also gall for my meat, and in my thirst they gave me vinegar to drink." The literal fulfillment of this prediction we find in Matt. 27 : 34. "They gave him vinegar to drink, mingled with gall; and when he had tasted thereof he would not drink." But the most remarkable prediction in either of these two Psalms is that in Psalm 22 : 16, "They pierced my hands and my feet," which literally described the manner of His death by crucifixion, which could not have been present to the mind of the Psalmist, as this mode of execution was afterwards introduced by the Romans.

The Genealogy of Jesus as the Son of David.

In 2 Sam. 7 : 12-18 God announced to David through the prophet, Nathan, " Thine house and thy kingdom shall be established for ever. The sins of David and his descendants afterwards could not frustrate the Divine purpose thus expressed. And so we find that the Lord Jesus Christ came of the seed of David. His genealogy, according to Jewish law, was reckoned not after the mother, but after the father. He was reckoned as the legitimate son of Joseph, who was of the house of David, because, although not begotten by him, He was born into his marriage relationship (Matt. 1 : 20, 21). In Matthew's Gospel the genealogy is shown from David through Solomon to Joseph, the son of Jacob; and in Luke's Gospel Joseph is spoken of as the son of Eli (Luke 3 : 23), and the genealogy is traced back from him through Nathan to David, so that there is a double line from David to Christ, one through Solomon and the other through Nathan; and this double line may possibly be accounted for in this way : that Mary may have been a daughter of Eli, and thus also of the house of David, and that Joseph, the son of Jacob, may have been brought up with her in the house of Eli, and married her, when their genealogical descents from David would thus be united but her name could not appear.

Predictions of Christ in Psalm CX.

In Psalm 110 there is a manifest reference to the Coming Messiah. The first verse, " The Lord said unto my Lord, Sit thou at my right hand until I make thine enemies thy footstool," is quoted by Peter on the day of Pentecost, after which he pressed home their guilt upon the Jewish nation, saying, " Therefore, let all the house of Israel know assuredly that God hath made that same Jesus, whom ye have crucified, both Lord and Christ" (Acts 2 : 34-36). And the fourth verse of this Psalm, " The Lord hath sworn and will not repent, Thou art

a *priest* for ever after the order of Melchizedek," com-
pletes the threefold picture of Christ as Prophet, Priest
and King, His priesthood not being after the order of
Aaron in the tribe of Levi, but "a priest for ever after
the order of Melchizedek," of whose pedigree nothing
is known (Heb. 5 : 6), but his name means, "My King
is righteous," which is very significant.

David's Confidence in Fulfillment of God's Covenant.

In 2 Sam. 23: 1-7 David presented a wonderful picture
of the Coming Messiah : "The Spirit of the Lord spake
by me, and His word was in my tongue. The God of
Israel said, the Rock of Israel spake to me. He that
ruleth over men must be just, ruling in the fear of God;
and he shall be as the light of the morning, when the
sun riseth, even a morning without clouds; as the tender
grass, springing out of the earth, by clear shining after
rain. Although my house be not so with God; yet he
hath made with me an everlasting covenant, ordered in
all things, and sure, for this is all my salvation and all
my desire, although he make it not to grow." In this
passage as well as in Psalm 110 and others, written after
his great sin in the matter of Uriah the Hittite, we
cannot help recognizing how strongly conscious he had
become of the difference between his life and the ideal of
the divinely anointed One who was to come after him;
and yet he clings with assured confidence to the "everlasting covenant ordered in all things, and sure," which
God had made with him, that the Messiah would be of
his seed. And there is no fact more fully recognized in
the public ministry of the Lord Jesus Christ than this,
that He belonged to the house of David, apart from the
genealogies that are recorded in Matthew and Luke
already referred to. In Matt. 9 : 27 the two blind men
followed him, saying, "Thou Son of David, have mercy
on us."

Christ Proclaimed and Recognized as Son of David.

In Matt. 15 : 22 the woman of Canaan cried unto him, "Have mercy on me, O Lord, thou son of David." In Matt. 20 : 30 two blind men cried out after Him, saying, "Have mercy on us, O Lord, thou Son of David." In Matt. 21 : 9 we read of the multitudes crying out to Him, "Hosanna to the son of David! Blessed is he that cometh in the name of the Lord. Hosanna in the highest!" and in the fifteenth verse we read that the children cried out. "Hosanna to the son of David!" and the chief priests and scribes who heard them, and were sore displeased. did not deny His right to be thus addressed. In Rom. 1 . 3 He is spoken of as being of the seed of David. In 2 Tim. 2 : 8 He is spoken of in the same way. In Rev. 3 : 7 He is spoken of as being the Key of David, and in Rev. 22 : 16 as "the root and offspring of David."

Prediction in Job of Christ as the Redeemer.

In the Book of Job, supposed to be the oldest in the Bible, and to have been written by Moses, in chap. 33 : 24, atonement for sin is referred to by Elihu speaking on behalf of God in these words : "Then he is gracious unto him and saith, Deliver him from going down to the pit; I have found a ransom," or, as the margin has it, "An atonement." This is doubtless an intimation of Christ as the *Redeemer*, who Himself said in Matt. 20 : 28, "Even as the Son of man came not to be ministered unto but to minister, and to give his life a ransom for many"; and of whom we read in 1 Tim. 2 : 5, 6, "For there is one God, and one Mediator between God and men, the man, Christ Jesus, who gave Himself a ransom for all, to be testified in due time."

Prediction of Christ as the Divine King.

In Psalm 45 is a song in praise of the Divine King. and, whatever may have been the occasion of writing it originally, it is evidently, according to the prophetic

word, to be understood as a song of praise to Messiah
as King, and having a distinct reference to the marriage
of the Lamb. The sixth verse of this Psalm is quoted
in Heb. 1 : 8 as addressed to the *Son of God.* "Thy
throne, O God, is for ever and ever; a sceptre of righteousness is the sceptre of thy kingdom."

Predictions of Christ in Joel.

In Joel we have some very distinct prophecies regarding the Lord's Second Coming to execute vengeance
and to establish His millennial kingdom, which, as a
matter of course, are not yet fulfilled, and in chap.
2 : 28, 29 that remarkable prophecy about the outpouring
of the Holy Spirit, which had a partial fulfilment at
Pentecost, which is still being fulfilled in these last days
in the cases of individual Christians, but which is to have
its complete fulfillment at the Second Coming of Christ.
"And it shall come to pass afterward that I will pour
out my Spirit upon all flesh; and your sons and your
daughters shall prophesy, your old men shall dream
dreams, your young men shall see visions. And also
upon the servants and upon the handmaids in those days
will I pour out my Spirit." Referring to this prediction
Peter quoted it at Pentecost, prefacing his quotation with
these words : "This is that which was spoken by the
prophet, Joel," and he thus declared that in the fulfilment of the promise made by the Lord Jesus Christ to
His disciples after His resurrection the prediction by
Joel was also fulfilled (Acts 2 : 16).

Predictions of Christ in Isaiah.

But the most definite Messianic prophecies are those
of Isaiah. Look, for instance, at chap. 7 : 14. "Therefore the Lord Himself shall give you a sign : Behold,
a virgin shall conceive and bear a son, and shall call his
name Immanuel." The literal fulfillment of this prophecy
we find recorded in Luke 1 : 26-36 and in Matt. 1 : 23,
with the additional information that His name, Immanuel or Emmanuel, means "God with us."

Again in Isa. 9 : 6, 7 we read, " For unto us a child
is born, unto us a son is given, and the government shall
be upon his shoulder; and his name shall be called
Wonderful, Counsellor, the Mighty God. the Everlasting
Father, the *Prince of Peace*. Of the increase of his government and peace there shall be no end upon the throne
of David, and upon his kingdom, to order it and to
establish it with judgment and justice from henceforth,
even forever. The zeal of the Lord of hosts will perform
this." There is no possibility of any unprejudiced
enquirer failing to comprehend who is meant by this
prediction. The Apostle Paul, in 1 Cor. 15 : 25, says
regarding Christ, " For He must reign till He hath put
all enemies under His feet." The Lord Jesus Christ was,
indeed, a wonderful personage. His enemies were
obliged to confess, " Never man spake like this man "
(John 7 : 46). And He was certainly the Prince of
Peace, for He made peace by the blood of His cross.
In His last address before leaving them, by His sufferings and death, to make atonement for sin, He said,
" Peace I leave with you, my peace I give unto you, not
as the world giveth give I unto you. Let not your heart
be troubled, neither let it be afraid " (John 14 : 27). And
after His resurrection from the dead, when He appeared
in their midst, the first words He uttered were, " Peace
be unto you " (John 20: 19, 26). He came and "preached
peace " to those that were afar off and to those that were
nigh (Eph. 2 : 17), and He Himself is now " our peace "
(Eph. 2 : 14).

In Isa. 10 : 1-5 we read, "And there shall come forth
a rod out of the stem of Jesse, and a *Branch* shall grow
out of his roots; and the Spirit of the Lord shall rest
upon him, the spirit of wisdom and understanding. the
spirit of counsel and might, the spirit of knowledge and
of the fear of the Lord; and shall make him *of quick
understanding* in the fear of the Lord; and he shall not
judge after the sight of his eyes, neither reprove after
the hearing of his ears; but with righteousness shall he
judge the poor, and reprove with equity for the meek

of the earth : and he shall smite the earth with the rod
of his mouth, and with the breath of his lips shall he
slay the wicked. And righteousness shall be the girdle
of his loins and faithfulness the girdle of his reins."
And in v. 10 of the same chapter we read, "And in that
day there shall be a *root of Jesse*, which shall stand for
an ensign of the people; to it shall the Gentiles seek;
and his rest shall be glorious." These verses also appear
clearly to point to the Lord Jesus Christ as descended
from Jesse, the father of David, more especially when we
couple them with Zech. 3 : 8 and 6 : 12, in both of which
passages He is referred to as the Branch. That He was
of quick understanding at twelve years of age was shown
by his discoursing with the doctors in the temple, when
" all that heard him were astonished at his understanding
and answers " (Luke 2 : 47), and at His baptism by John
the heavens opened, and the Spirit of God was seen
" descending like a dove, and lighting upon Him, and
lo, a voice from heaven saying, This is my beloved Son,
in whom I am well pleased" (Matt. 3 : 17). Part of the
predictions in Isa. 10 have already been literally fulfilled as we find by the passages just quoted. Others
await fulfillment in the future.

Prediction of Christ as the Son of God.

In Psalm 2 : 6, 7 the future Messiah is declared to be
the *Son of God:* "Yet have I set my King upon my holy
hill of Zion. I will declare the decree : the Lord hath
said unto me, Thou art my Son; this day have I begotten thee," and in v. 12, " Kiss the Son lest he be
angry and ye perish from the way, when his wrath is
kindled but a little. Blessed are all they that put their
trust in him." The Lord Jesus was accused of blasphemy, condemned to death, and crucified because He
declared Himself to be the Son of God. This prediction was, therefore, literally fulfilled in the person of
Christ.

Prediction of Christ as the Corner Stone.

In Isa. 28 : 16 there is another statement, which also evidently refers to the Coming Messiah, " Therefore thus saith the Lord God, Behold, I lay in Zion for a foundation, a stone, a tried stone, a precious *corner-stone*, a sure foundation; he that believeth shall not make haste." In Matt. 21 : 42 we read, " Jesus saith unto them, Did ye never read in the Scriptures, The stone which the builders rejected, the same is become the head of the corner; this is the Lord's doing, and it is mar- vellous in our eyes ?" referring to Psalm 118 : 22, which is again referred to in Acts 4 : 11 by Peter. And also in Rom. 9 : 33 and in Eph. 2 : 20 we read about the Church being " built upon the foundation of the apostles and prophets, Jesus Christ Himself being the chief corner- stone." There is, therefore, no doubt about the person referred to as the corner-stone and the sure foundation.

Predictions of Babylonish Captivity and Deliverance.

In Micah 4 : 10 there is a prediction of the Babylonish captivity and of the deliverance from it as follows : " Be in pain and labour to bring forth, O daughter of Zion, like a woman in travail : for now thou shalt go forth out of the city, and thou shalt dwell in the field, and thou shalt go to Babylon; there shalt thou be delivered; there the Lord shall redeem thee from the hand of thine enemies." This prediction of the captivity was literally fulfilled about one hundred years afterwards, and in due time the deliverance was also effected.

Micah's Prediction of Destruction of Jerusalem and Its Fulfillment.

In Micah 3 : 11, 12 there is a definite prediction of the destruction of Jerusalem in these words : " The heads thereof (the house of Israel) judge for reward, and the priests thereof teach for hire, and the prophets thereof divine for money; yet will they lean upon the

Lord and say. Is not the Lord among us ? None evil can come upon us. Therefore shall Zion for your sake be ploughed as a field, and Jerusalem shall become heaps, and the mountain of the house as the high places of the forest." This was fulfilled in the destruction of the city by the Romans under Titus about eight hundred years afterwards.

In Micah 4 : 1-5 there is a remarkable prediction of the coming glory of the Messiah's reign at Jerusalem during the Millennium, the fulfillment of which is, of course, yet future.

Predictions of the Birth of Christ in Bethlehem.

But in Micah 5 : 2 we have the most remarkable Messianic prediction by this prophet : " But thou, *Bethlehem*-Ephratah, though thou be little among the thousands of Judah, yet out of thee shall he come forth unto me that is to be ruler in Israel : whose goings forth have been from of old, from everlasting "; or, as the marginal reading has it (" from the days of eternity "). The literal fulfillment of this prediction is recorded in Matt. 2 : 1, and should be of itself a conclusive answer to Professor Goldwin Smith's objection, that " No real and specific predictions of the advent of Jesus or of any event in His life can be produced from the books of the Old Testament." This is the *Ruler* of the tribe of Judah to whom Jacob referred in Gen. 49 : 10 when blessing his sons. This is the One spoken of in John 1 : 1. " In the beginning was the Word, and the Word was with God, and the Word was God." and again referred to in Col. 1 : 15. " Who is the image of the invisible God, the first-born of every creature." Jerusalem was the royal city of David, where his sins had brought disgrace upon himself and dishonour upon the name of Israel's God; but Bethlehem, " Too small to be reckoned among the districts of Judah," as it is rendered in another translation, had been the birth-place of David and the home of his father, Jesse, before grace had found him and made him the anointed ruler of Israel. How

fitting it was, then, that the Second David, who was at
the same time David's Son and David's Lord, should
be born there, where, as another writer puts it, " The
Davidic royal house is reduced to its root and renews
its youth," and the predictions regarding "the Branch
(Isa. 11 : 1, 10) out of the root of Jesse" should be
fulfilled.

Isaiah's Prediction of the Captivity in Babylon and Its Fulfillment.

In Isa. 39 the captivity in Babylon is distinctly foretold. The King of Babylon had sent letters and a present
to Hezekiah, King of Judah, and Hezekiah was glad, and
showed the messenger all his treasures, and the Lord
sent this message to him by the prophet, " Behold, the
days come that all that is in thine house, and that which
thy fathers have laid up in store until this day shall be
carried to Babylon; nothing shall be left, saith the Lord.
And of thy sons which shall issue from thee, which thou
shalt beget, shall they take away, and they shall be
eunuchs in the palace of the King of Babylon." About
one hundred years afterwards this prediction was literally fulfilled (2 Kings 25 and 2 Chron. 36).

Prediction of Destruction of Nineveh and Its Fulfillment.

In Nahum 3 : 7 it is predicted that Nineveh was to
be laid waste, and this was literally fulfilled about one
hundred years afterwards.

In Jer. 23 : 5-8 we have a very distinct prediction of
the coming reign of the Messiah, " Behold, the days
come, saith the Lord, that I will raise unto David a
righteous Branch, and a King shall reign and prosper,
and shall execute judgment and justice in the earth. In
his day Judah shall be saved, and Israel shall dwell safely;
and this is his name whereby he shall be called, THE
LORD OUR RIGHTEOUSNESS. Therefore, behold the days
come, saith the Lord, that they shall no more say, The

Lord liveth, which brought up the children of Israel out
of the land of Egypt; but the Lord liveth, which brought
up and which led the seed of the house of Israel out
of the north country, and from all countries whither I
had driven them; and they shall dwell in their own
land." As a matter of course, this prediction will not be
completely fulfilled until after the Lord's Second Coming, which cannot now be far distant; but it is important
to mark the names here given to the Messiah as the
Branch out of the stem of Jesse, spoken of by Isaiah,
who is identical with the Ruler that was to be born at
Bethlehem, the home of Jesse, spoken of by Micah.
There is a similar prediction again in Jer. 30 : 15, 16.

Predictions of Christ as the Shepherd of His People.

In Ezek. 34 : 23-25, where the prophet is speaking of
the future glory of Messiah's kingdom, we read, "And
I will set up one *Shepherd* over them, and he shall feed
them, and he shall be their shepherd. And I, the Lord,
will be their God, and my servant, David, a prince
among them; I, the Lord, have spoken it. And I will
make with them a covenant of peace . . . and I will
make them and the places round about my hill a blessing;
and I will cause the showers to come down in his season;
there shall be showers of blessing." In John 10 : 14, 15
the Lord Jesus Christ says : " I am the good shepherd,
and know my sheep, and am known of mine. As the
Father knoweth me, even so know I the Father : and I
lay down my life for the sheep." And, as we have seen
before, He is also their Prince of the house of David.

In Ezek. 37 : 21-25 there is a promise to restore the
children of Israel to their own land. "And say unto
them, thus saith the Lord God, Behold, I will take the
children of Israel from among the heathen whither they
be gone, and will gather them on every side, and bring
them into their own land; and I will make them one
nation in the land upon the mountains of Israel, and one

King shall be king to them all; and they shall be no more two nations, neither shall they be divided into two kingdoms any more at all . . . and David, my servant, shall be king over them; and they shall have one shepherd . . . and David, my servant, shall be their prince forever." These predictions, so far as Israel is concerned, have yet to be fulfilled, but the mention of David as the future king and shepherd of Israel, taken in connection with other passages previously quoted, show that the Lord Jesus Christ is the person referred to in this prophecy.

Remarkable Predictions in Deutero-Isaiah, and Their Fulfillment.

There is considerable difference of opinion as to the authorship of the last twenty-seven chapters of Isaiah, often spoken of as Deutero-Isaiah, which are supposed to have been written during the captivity in Babylon, but there is no question as to their inspiration. From the beginning of chap. 40 there appears to be a decided widening of the scope of those blessings which were to come through the Messiah to the world. Look, for instance, at Isaiah 45 : 21-23, "Tell ye and bring them near; yea, let them take counsel together, who hath declared this from ancient time ? who hath told it from that time ? have not I the Lord ? and there is no God else beside me; a just God and a Saviour; there is none beside me. Look unto me and be ye saved, all the ends of the earth; for I am God, and there is none else." But especially is this true of chap 53, which presents such a wonderful picture of the Lord Jesus Christ as the Suffering Surety for sinners, and in which Israel is not once specially referred to. And to this world-wide significance of His death we seem to have an introduction in the last two verses of the preceding chapter: "As many were astonished at thee ; his visage was so marred more than any man, and his form more than the sons of men; so shall he sprinkle many nations; the kings

shall shut their mouths at him ; for that which had
not been told them shall they see, and that which
they had not heard shall they consider " (52 : 14, 15).
The whole of chap. 53 predicts His substitutionary sufferings and death so vividly that there can be no question
in the mind of any Christian as to its meaning, and it
is certain that the New Testament writers regarded it in
the same light. With respect to its literal fulfillment in
the person of Christ, consider some of these verses
singly :

PREDICTIONS IN ISAIAH 53.	FULFILLMENTS.
Verse 1. " Who hath believed our report? and to whom is the arm of the Lord revealed ? "	John 1 : 14. "He came unto His own, and His own received Him not." John 12 : 37. " But though He had done so many miracles before them, yet they believed not on Him."
Verse 3. " He is despised and re-jected of men ; a man of sorrows, and acquainted with grief; and we hid, as it were, our faces from Him ; he was despised, and we esteemed Him not."	Luke 23 : 18. "They cried out all at once, Away with this man, and release unto us Barrabas ! " Heb. 4 : 15. " For we have not an high priest which cannot be touched with a feeling of our infirmities, but was in all points tempted like as we are, yet without sin."
Verse 4. " Surely he hath borne our griefs (or sickness) and carried our sorrows (or pains), yet we did esteem him stricken, smitten of God and afflicted."	Matt. 26: 37, 38. "And he took with him Peter and the two sons of Zebedee, and began to be sorrow-ful and very heavy. Then saith he unto them, My soul is exceeding sorrowful even unto death."
Verse 5. " But he was wounded for our transgressions, he was bruis-ed for our iniquities ; the chastise-ment of our peace was upon him ; and with his stripes we are healed."	1 Peter 2: 24. "Who his own self bare our sins in his own body on the tree, that we, being dead to sins, should live unto righteousness : by whose stripes ye were healed."

PREDICTIONS IN ISAIAH 53.	FULFILLMENTS.
Verse 6. "All we like sheep have gone astray; we have turned every one to his own way; and the Lord hath laid on him the iniquity of us all."	Rom. 4 : 25. "Who was delivered for our offences, and raised again for our justification." 1 Peter 2 : 25. "For ye were as sheep going astray, but are now returned unto the Shepherd and Bishop of your souls." 1 Peter 3 : 18. "For Christ also hath once suffered for sins, the just for the unjust, that He might bring us to God, being put to death in the flesh, but quickened by the Spirit."
Verse 7. "He was oppressed, and he was afflicted; yet he opened not his mouth; he is brought as a lamb to the slaughter, and as a sheep before her shearers is dumb, so he openeth not his mouth."	Mark 15: 3-5. "And the chief priests accused him of many things; but he answered nothing. And Pilate asked him again, saying, Answerest thou nothing? Behold how many things they witness against thee. But Jesus yet answered nothing, so that Pilate marvelled."
Verse 9. "And he made his grave with the wicked and with the rich in his death, because he had done no violence, neither was any deceit in his mouth."	Matt. 27 : 57-60. "When the even was come, there came a rich man of Arimathaea, named Joseph, who also himself was Jesus' disciple. He went to Pilate and begged the body of Jesus. Then Pilate commanded the body to be delivered. And when Joseph had taken the body he wrapped it in a clean linen cloth, and laid it in his own new tomb, which he had hewn out in the rock; and he rolled a great stone to the door of the sepulchre and departed."

Prediction of Christ Riding on an Ass.

In Zech. 9 : 9 we read, " Rejoice greatly, O daughter of Zion; shout, O daughter of Jerusalem; behold, thy King cometh unto thee; he is just, and having salvation; lowly, and riding upon an ass, and *upon a colt, the foal of an ass.*" The literal fulfilment of this prediction we find in John 12 : 12-15, which reads : "On the next day much people that were come to the feast, when they heard that Jesus was coming to Jerusalem, took branches of palm trees, and went forth to meet him, and cried, Hosanna! Blessed is the King of Israel that cometh in the name of the Lord. And Jesus, when he had found a young ass, sat thereon; as it is written, Fear not, daughter of Zion; behold thy King cometh, sitting on an ass's colt."

Prediction of Christ's Betrayal for Thirty Pieces of Silver.

In Zech. 11 : 13 we read, "And the Lord said unto me, Cast it unto the potter : a goodly price that I was prized at of them. And I took the *thirty pieces of silver,* and cast them to the *potter* in the house of the Lord." The fulfillment of this prediction is given in Matt. 27 : 3-10, "Then Judas, which had betrayed him, when he saw that he was condemned, repented himself, and brought again the thirty pieces of silver to the chief priests and elders, saying, I have sinned in that I have betrayed the innocent blood. And they said. What is that to us? See thou to that. And he cast down the pieces of silver in the temple and departed, and went and hanged himself. And the chief priests took the silver pieces and said, It is not lawful for to put them into the treasury, because it is the price of blood, and they took counsel and bought with them the potter's field, to bury strangers in. Wherefore that field was called the field of blood unto this day." It is stated in Matt. 26 : 15 that the chief priests before the betrayal had covenanted to give him thirty pieces of silver.

Prediction of the Manner of His Death.

In Zech 12 : 9-11 we read, "And it shall come to pass in that day that I will seek to destroy all the nations that come against Jerusalem, and I will pour upon the house of David, and upon the inhabitants of Jerusalem, the spirit of grace and of supplications; and they shall look *on me whom they have pierced*, and they shall mourn for him as one mourneth for his only son, and shall be in bitterness for him, as one that is in bitterness for his firstborn.   In that day there shall be a great mourning in Jerusalem as the mourning of Hadadrimmon in the valley of Megiddon" (that is, like the mourning for Josiah, their best beloved king).   This prediction will be fulfilled at the Second Coming of Christ with all His saints to execute vengeance upon the nations that are gathered against Jerusalem to battle, spoken of in Zech 14, when His kingdom is to be established over all the earth.   But the remarkable thing in connection with it for our present purpose is that here, as well as in Psalm 22, the death of the Lord Jesus Christ by crucifixion is plainly referred to in the words, "They shall look upon me whom they have pierced," and thus in the manner of His death there was a fulfillment of the prophecy.

Predictions of Christ in Malachi.

In Mal. 3 : 1 there is definite prediction in connection with the first coming of Christ which has been fulfilled, " Behold, *I will send my messenger*, and he shall prepare the way before me, and the Lord, whom ye seek, shall suddenly come to his temple, even as the messengers of the covenant, whom ye delight in : behold, he shall come, saith the Lord of hosts." The fulfillment of this prediction in the person of John the Baptist as the forerunner of Christ is found in Luke 1 : 76 where Zechariah prophesies concerning him, "And thou, child, shalt be called the Prophet of the Highest; for thou shalt go before the face of the Lord to prepare his ways." And in Luke 7 : 27 the Lord Jesus Christ Himself says of John the Baptist, " This is he of whom it is written, Behold, I send my messenger before thy face, which shall prepare thy way before thee."

Predictions of Christ in Daniel.

The Book of Daniel does not claim to have been actually written by the Prophet Daniel, but the predictions are his, and are among the most remarkable in the whole canon of Old Testament Scripture. And there is no more question about the inspiration of this book than about the inspiration of Hebrews, which is only supposed to have been written by either Paul or Barnabas. As already remarked, however, on a previous page, the knowledge of an author's name does not determine the question of the inspiration of a book, which must be judged on its own merits by spiritual men otherwise properly qualified for such work. The most remarkable passage in this book is that referring to the death of the Messiah in Dan. 9 : 24-27 in these words : " Seventy weeks are determined upon thy people, and upon thy holy city to finish the transgression, and to make an end of sins, and to make reconciliation for iniquity, and to bring in everlasting righteousness, and to seal up the vision and the prophecy, and to anoint the Most Holy. Know, therefore, and understand that from the going forth of the commandment to restore and to build Jerusalem unto the Messiah, the Prince, shall be seven weeks and threescore and two weeks; the street shall be built again, and the wall even in troublous times And after threescore and two weeks *shall Messiah be cut off*, but not for himself; and the people of the prince that shall come shall destroy the city and the sanctuary; and the end thereof shall be with a flood; and unto the end of the war desolations are determined. And he shall confirm the convenant with many for one week; and in the midst of the week he shall cause the sacrifice and oblation to cease; and for the overspreading of abominations he shall make it desolate, even until the consummation; and that determined shall be poured upon the desolate." It would be outside the purpose of this book to attempt an exposition of this prophecy upon which volumes have been written. It is sufficient to say that in it the death

of the Messiah is clearly predicted, and in the death of
Christ this was fulfilled.

We have seen in the preceding pages some of the
things which Jesus as " the Great Teacher of humanity "
explained to His disciples out of Moses and the Psalms
and the prophets concerning Himself after His resurrection from the dead.   But, although they had been with
him so much, and had seen His mighty works and witnessed His death, and were now witnesses to His resurrection, they were slow to learn the lessons which He
taught them, and failed to comprehend their meaning
fully until after the Holy Spirit came down at Pentecost,
and guided them into all truth, and brought all things
to their remembrance which Jesus had said unto them.
It was out of the Old Testament Scriptures that He was
teaching them; and if, with all their advantages, as His
disciples, taught by Himself, they were so slow to learn
without the Spirit's teaching, how futile must be the
efforts now of the most highly cultured men to understand by their own unaided intellects the same Scriptures
out of which He instructed them.

Some of Professor Smith's Objections to the Prophecies.

Let us now look at some of the remarks and objections which Professor Goldwin Smith makes to the prophecies.

On page 167 of his book he asks, " Was there *miraculous* fulfilment of Hebrew prophecies ?" It is difficult
to understand what he means by such a question. The
passages which have been quoted prove the *literal* fulfilment of very many, more especially in connection with
the Lord Jesus Christ as the Messiah, to whom the Jewish
nation had been long looking forward, but the fulfilment
generally took place in the most natural manner possible. The miracle of the Messianic prophecies consisted in the predictions themselves, from so many persons, extending over so many ages, all centreing upon,

and finding their fulfillment in, the one Divine Person of the Lord Jesus Christ as the Jewish Messiah and the Redeemer of mankind. Some other examples of the literal fulfilment of prophecy have been given, including the death of David's son by Bathsheda, the healing of Hezekiah, the Captivity in Babylon, and the Release from it, the destruction of Nineveh, the destruction of Babylon, and the destruction of Jerusalem, to which might be added many others if necessary.

He says, on page 168, that the expression, "An ass, and a colt, the foal of an ass," spoken of in Matt. 21 : 5-7, does not mean two things, but two expressions for one thing. This is doubtless correct, as appears from John 12 : 12-15, where the expression used is simply, " Sitting on an ass's colt."

He says, on page 168, in regard to Psalm 22 : 18, " They part my garments among them, and cast lots upon my vesture," are taken as denoting two actions, when they are only a double expression for one, after the manner of Hebrew poetry." In this suggestion he is entirely wrong, as is plainly seen by the record of the fulfillment of that prediction, given in John 19: 23, 24, from which it is evident that the garments and the coat were different articles of apparel. " Then the soldiers, when they had crucified Jesus, took his garments, and made four parts, to every soldier a part; *and also his coat:* now the coat was without seam, woven throughout." There does not appear to be much need for calling in the aid of Hebrew poetry to make this remarkable prediction seem to mean something different from that which the plain language implies, and thus, if possible, weaken the Scripture testimony to the atonement of Christ.

He says, on page 169, that the words, " I called my son out of Egypt," in Hosea 11 : 1, can by no ingenuity be referred to anything but the Exodus, not to mention the strong suspicion of a story raised to correspond with the supposed prophecy! Here, again, the Professor is wrong, and it will not require much ingenuity to prove it. The whole verse reads: " When Israel was a child, then I loved him, and called my son out of Egypt." Now, in the first place, God never called Israel His Son; and, in the second place, the verse contains two distinct statements : one, that He loved Israel when he was a child; the other, that He called His Son out of Egypt. If the child, Jacob or Israel, whom He loved, and the Son whom He called out of Egypt were one and the same person, the verse would have read something like this, " When Israel was a child I loved him, and called him out of Egypt." The love of God to Jacob as a child by the election of grace is declared in Mal. 1 : 2, 3, " Was not Esau Jacob's brother, saith the Lord; yet I loved Jacob, and I hated Esau ".; and in Rom. 9 : 13, "As it is written, Jacob have I loved, but Esau have I hated." The insertion of the word *then* in the text also shows that it is the election by grace of Jacob as a child to which reference is made, and, as already remarked, God never called Jacob His Son. To say the least, this is a very slender pretext on which to raise a doubt about one of the predictions concerning the Messiah; and that it is only a pretext is evidenced by the fact that when attacking the authenticity of the Pentateuch (page 65) he seriously questions the probability of the Israelites ever having been in Egypt at all, because " nothing certainly Egyptian seems to be traceable in Hebrew beliefs or institutions!" This should settle his doubt about the passage in Hosea, for, if Israel never was in Egypt, it could not refer to him, and must apply to the Lord Jesus Christ as stated in Matt. 2 : 15.

On page 169 he makes this extraordinary statement, that the words, " Behold, a virgin shall conceive and bear a son," in Isaiah 7 : 14. is evidently a sign given by the prophet in relation to a crisis in contemporary history, which has plainly not the remotest connection with the immaculate conception of Jesus. The cool assurance with which this bold statement is made is amazing. There is not the slightest use in wasting time in argument on a point upon which the Scriptures speak so plainly. It must surely be sufficient to refer the reader to the passages in Matt. 1 : 23 and Luke 1 : 26-38, which speak so clearly on this subject, proving the literal fulfillment of this prediction, which was a miracle; but he cannot reject the testimony of Scripture on this ground, for a miracle is something contrary to the laws of nature, and on page 143 he admits that the phrase, "Laws of nature," presupposes that there must be a law-giver, capable of suspending the operation of law."

Mistaken Criticism Arising from Defective Knowledge of Scriptural Truth.

He says, on page 169, that the prediction, "'The sceptre shall not depart from Judah, nor the ruler's staff from between his feet until Shiloh come, and unto him shall the obedience of the peoples be,' not only were not fulfilled, but were contradicted by the history of Jesus, who was not a temporal- ruler or deliverer, and was, therefore, not recognized as the Messiah by the Jews." These remarks are a striking proof of the absolute inability of any one to undertake the criticism of Scripture who is not acquainted with the leading truths which it unfolds. All prophecies regarding the Coming of Christ or the Messiah represent Him in one or other of two aspects. Either, *first*, as the future King of the tribe of Judah and of the house of David, who was to reign gloriously at Jerusalem, and whose advent was to usher in a time of wonderful temporal and spiritual blessing to them as a nation, and through them to all other nations. It was in this sense that the Jewish people looked forward to His coming. Or, *second*, as the Lamb of God to take away the sin of the world by laying down His life to make atonement for sin. In this sense His coming was not understood except by those whose spiritual eyesight was enlightened by the Holy Spirit, as was the case with John the Baptist, the "messenger sent before His face," who proclaimed Him as the Lamb of God that taketh away the sin of the world; and as was also the case with the angels who appeared to the shepherds on the Plains of Bethlehem, saying, "Fear not : for, behold, I bring you good tidings of great joy, which shall be to all people. For unto you is born this day in the city of David a Saviour, which is Christ, the Lord. And this shall be a sign unto you : ye shall find the babe, wrapped in swaddling clothes, lying in a manger. And suddenly there was with the angel a multitude of the heavenly host, praising God, and saying, Glory to God in the highest, and on earth peace, good-will toward men" (Luke 2 : 10-14).

To this latter aspect of His coming the minds of the Jewish people as a nation were blinded; and, although He was duly heralded by the people on His way to Jerusalem with shouts of "Hosanna! Blessed is the King of Israel that cometh in the name of the Lord," yet He was rejected and despised by the rulers and the nation at large, who, instead of a crown, gave Him a cross; and thus, without knowing it, carried out the purpose of God in providing redemption for a fallen race by His atoning sacrifice for sin. And thus all the types of the ceremonial law, and all the prophecies as to His sufferings were at once and for ever fulfilled when Christ, our Passover, was sacrificed for us. For their "judicial murder," as the Professor calls it, of the Lord Jesus Christ, the judgment of God in fulfilment of prophecy descended upon the Jewish people, Jerusalem was destroyed and the people scattered throughout the earth, a hissing and a bye-word among all other nations; but the fulfillment of their hopes is only deferred for a time until the Church of God, composed of Jew and Gentile, is completed, and taken to be with Himself in the glory, after which the Messiah will come again and establish His kingdom with the Jewish people as His subjects, through whom all other nations of the earth will then be blessed, and all those prophecies that speak of Messiah as King and of the glories of His reign will be fulfilled as literally as were the predictions relating to His humiliation, and suffering, and death. If Professor Gold-

win Smith had understood these truths and borne them
in mind his remarks upon this passage in Gen.49 : 10
would not have been so hopelessly mixed. Christ has
come as the Messiah of the tribe of Judah as therein
predicted, and He has been proclaimed as King, but
rejected and crucified, so that His work of redemption
might be accomplished, after which He is coming again
to establish His kingdom and rule over His people and
this whole earth righteously during His millennial reign,
and "unto Him shall the obedience of the peoples be."
It is true there is some difference between critics as to
the proper translation of the part of that verse relating
to Shiloh, but that is only a small matter compared with
the important truth contained in it in reference to Christ
as the Lion of the tribe of Judah, and we can afford to
wait the result of sanctified criticism on the other part
of the passage, when its meaning will doubtless be made
perfectly clear.

Professor Smith's Gross Misrepresentation of Predictions in Isaiah LIII.

He says, in reference to Isa. 53. "None, in short, of
the so-called prophecies will be found to be more than
applications, and many of them, as applications, are far
fetched. This is true of even the most remarkable of the
number, the description of the oppressed and sorrowing
servant of Jehovah in Isa. 53 : 3. the author of which
cannot be said to have distinctly foretold anything in
the history of Jesus, even if we take Jesus to have been
so pre-eminently a man of sorrows. . . . In no single
case can Jesus or any event in His life be said to have
been present to the mental eye of the prophet." This is
about the most glaring attempt that could possibly be
imagined to destroy the effect of the predictions contained in that wonderful chapter regarding the atoning
sufferings of the Lord Jesus Christ. If it is a specimen
of the kind of criticism his friends. the "liberal theologians," indulge in, the world can afford to do without

them. We would ask the readers of this book to look back to pages 106 and 107, at the remarks made on this chapter, especially at the separate verses that are quoted, with the evidence of their fulfillment set opposite; and then to turn back to the above remark of Professor Goldwin Smith, and say what they think of such a misrepresentation of the plain statements of Scripture.

The Professor Takes the Churches to Task.

On page 79 he blames the churches for ascribing the authorship of the Pentateuch to Moses, of the Book of Daniel to the Prophet Daniel, and of both parts of the Book of Isaiah to the Prophet Isaiah, but he has failed to inform us to whom the writing of these books should be ascribed; and how the knowledge of the author's name affects the inspiration and authenticity of a book which he has written containing clear predictions of future events, which have been literally fulfilled in after ages, and the revelations in which, as regards the character and purposes of Jehovah, are in complete accord with other books which we have no doubt are inspired. It is unnecessary to say more on this subject here as it has been more fully dealt with in preceding pages. But in reference to Moses being the author of the Pentateuch, we would direct attention to Matt. 8 : 4, in which the Lord Jesus Christ referred to a command in Leviticus which He said was given by Moses; and also to Matt. 19 : 7, 8, in which He referred to another command in Deuteronomy, which He also said was given by Moses. This is certainly a higher authority for the authorship of those books than Professor Goldwin Smith or the "liberal theologians."

Professor Smith's Incredibilities.

On page 94 he speaks of certain things as *manifest incredibilities*, such as the stoppage of the sun, Baalam's speaking ass, Elisha's avenging bears, and the transformation of Nebuchadnezzar, but he cannot bring for-

ward one tittle of proof that those things did not occur,
while the Word of God assures us that they did; and
that Word also assures us that with God " all things are
possible."   But he is not the first man to have been
troubled with incredibilities about Divine things.   The
Apostle Paul, when speaking for himself before King
Agrippa, said : " Why should it be thought a thing
incredible with you that God should raise the dead ?"
(Acts 26 : 8). And if He has raised the dead, why should
we doubt anything else that His Word declares to be
true ? The great trouble, however, with Professor Goldwin Smith seems to be that he finds almost everything
incredible that God has revealed.

His Denial of the Miracles of Christ.

On page 173 he says with regard to the miracles of
Christ that " The Jews were further prepared for the
acceptance of fresh miracles by their traditional acceptance of those of the Old Testament.   So devoid were
they of any . conception of natural law, or of anything
except a direct action of the Deity, that with them a
miracle would hardly be miraculous."   How absurd, and
yet how plausible! The Professor admits that there is
a great Being who somehow or other rules the universe.
He admits there are natural laws.   But he goes further,
and says that the phrase, "Laws of nature," pre-supposes
that there must be a law-giver capable of suspending the
operation of law.   And it is presumed that he would
define a miracle to be something done contrary to the
laws of nature.   Let it be borne in mind that from the
very beginning of their existence as a people the Jews'
religion was a supernatural one.   They had a supernatural God to deal with, who had repeatedly manifested
His presence and His power in a supernatural way, and
the record of these supernatural manifestations had been
most carefully handed down to them through many generations; but they were an intelligent race, not likely
to be imposed upon by trickery.   If the Professor's

remark last quoted means anything, it means this, that
when the Lord Jesus Christ entered upon His public
ministry He found the Jews a credulous people, who
believed a lot of traditions that had come down to them
from former ages, and were, therefore, likely to be easily
imposed upon by pretended miracles, and, being unac-
quainted with the operation of natural laws, they ascribed to Divine power the mighty works that were done
by Him. And hence we may conclude that he disputes
all the miracles wrought by the Lord Jesus Christ, whom
he calls "the great Teacher of humanity," and would
apparently have us believe that He was an imposter, who
was deceiving the people by tricks of legerdemain
through the operation of natural laws, and at the same
time declaring that He was the Son of God, who had
come to seek and save those that were lost and to call
sinners to repentance. Or, perhaps, he would have us
believe that there were no miracles performed by Jesus,
and that the reports of them were only invented by His
disciples after His death, which would be contrary to
the testimony of reliable history from various sources.

Concluding Remarks.

In this and the two preceding chapters we have seen
that God has, indeed, spoken at sundry times and in
divers manners in time past unto the fathers by the prophets; that the earliest of the revelations thus given
were embodied in history and carefully preserved as
sacred writings by the Jewish nation, and thus handed
down to future generations; and we have also seen that
those sacred writings, known by us as the Old Testament Scriptures, were recognized and endorsed by the
Lord Jesus Christ as the Word of God.

In confirmation of historical facts referred to in the
Book of Genesis it may be remarked that in recent ex-
plorations of ruins of ancient Assyrian cities archaeolo-
gists have discovered stone tablets with inscriptions
telling of the conquests of Chedorlaomer, King of Elam,
and of other kings who are spoken of in connection

with the history of Abram in Genesis 14; and also telling of Melchizedek, who was King of Salem and priest of the most high God (Gen. 14 : 18).

It may also be mentioned that Sir J. W. Dawson, our most eminent Canadian geologist and scientist, says that the Book of Exodus is an Egyptian book, with numerous words and phrases descriptive of Egyptian manners, and coloured with Israelitish ideas of desert life; that the plagues spoken of in that book were natives of the climate and soil of Egypt, and that the golden calf was an imitation of the Egyptian deity, Apis.

There is, therefore, not the slightest excuse for supposing with Professor Goldwin Smith that the Pentateuch was written during the Babylonish captivity, about 1,000 years after the Exodus of the children of Israel out of Egypt; and that Moses was not the author of those five books when all Jewish history and the Lord Jesus Christ Himself have certified that he was.

CHAPTER IV.

GOD SPEAKING BY HIS SON.

IN Isaiah 5 : 7 we read, " For the vineyard of the Lord of hosts is the house of Israel, and the men of Judah his pleasant plant : and he looked for judgment, but, behold! oppression: for righteousness, but behold a cry." And in Mark 12 : 1-9 we are informed that the Lord Jesus Christ spake the following parable to the chief priests and scribes and elders who had come to Him : "A certain man planted a vineyard, and set an hedge about it, and digged a place for the winefat, and built a tower, and let it out to husbandmen, and went into a far country, and at the season he sent to the husbandmen a servant, that he might receive from the husbandmen of the fruit of the vineyard. And they caught him and beat him, and sent him away empty. And again he sent unto them another servant; and at him they cast stones, and wounded him in the head, and sent him away shamefully handled. And again he sent another, and him they killed, and many others, beating some and killing some. Having yet, therefore, one son, his well-beloved, he sent him also last unto them, saying, They will reverence my son. But these husbandmen said among themselves, This is the heir. Come, let us kill him, and the inheritance shall be ours. And they took him and killed him, and cast him out of the vineyard. What shall, therefore, the Lord of the vineyard do ? He will come and destroy the husbandmen, and will give the vineyard unto others. Have ye not read this Scripture, The stone which the builders rejected is become the head of the corner. This was the Lord's doing, and it was marvellous in our eyes." And then we read in the following verse, "And they (that is, the

chief priests, scribes and elders) sought to lay hold on
him, but feared the people; for they knew that he had
spoken the parable against them; and they left him, and
went their way." The Scripture the Lord quoted to
them was from Psalm 118 : 22, 23, referring to Himself
as the head stone of the corner.

Jesus Proclaimed in Jerusalem as the Promised Messiah.

The time when Jesus thus spoke to the chief priests,
and scribes, and elders was the day after His triumphal
entry into Jerusalem riding upon the ass's colt, which
trod upon the garments and branches the multitude
strawed in the way as they shouted, " Hosanna to the
Son of David! Blessed is he that cometh in the name
of the Lord! Hosanna in the highest!" After which,
as we read in Matthew's Gospel, " When he was come
into Jerusalem, all the city was moved, saying, Who
is this ? And the multitude said, This is Jesus, the
prophet of Nazareth of Galilee. And Jesus went into
the temple of God, and cast out all them that sold and
bought in the temple, and overthrew the tables of the
money changers, and the seats of them that sold doves:
and said unto them, It is written, My house shall be
called a house of prayer, but ye have made it a den of
thieves. And the blind and the lame came to him in the
temple, and he healed them. And when the chief priests
and scribes saw the wonderful things that he did, and the
children crying in the temple and saying, Hosanna to the
Son of David! they were sore displeased, and said unto
him, Hearest thou what these say? And Jesus said unto
them, Yea; have ye never read, Out of the mouths of
babes and sucklings thou hast perfected praise ?" (Matt.
21 : 9-16).

In order to understand the full force of the parable
which He had spoken to the chief priests, and scribes,
and elders, who were members of the Sanhedrim that
soon afterwards condemned Him to suffer death by

crucifixion, let us look at some passages in the Old
Testament Scriptures with which His hearers were
familiar. In 2 Kings 17 : 9-23, "And the children of
Israel did secretly those things that were not right
against the Lord their God. . . . For they served
idols, whereof the Lord their God had said unto them,
Ye shall not do this thing. Yet the Lord testified against
Israel and against Judah, by all the prophets, and by
all the seers, saying, Turn ye from your evil ways, and
keep my commandments and my statutes, according to
all the law which I commanded your fathers, and which
I sent unto you by my servants, the prophets. Notwithstanding they would not hear, but hardened their necks,
like to the neck of their fathers, that did not believe in
the Lord their God. . . . Therefore the Lord was
very angry with Israel, and removed them out of His
sight : there was none left but the tribe of Judah only.
. . . The Lord removed Israel out of His sight, as He
had said, by all His servants, the prophets. So was
Israel carried away out of their own land unto Assyria
unto this day."

In 2 Chron. 36 : 16 we read, " But they mocked the
messengers of God, and despised his words, and misused
his prophets, until the wrath of the Lord arose against
his people till there was no remedy."

In Neh. 9 : 26 we read, " Nevertheless they were disobedient and rebelled against thee, and cast thy law
behind their backs, and slew thy prophets, which testified against them to turn them to thee; and they wrought
great provocations."

In Jer. 25 : 4-12, "And the Lord hath sent unto you
all his servants the prophets, rising early and sending
them; but ye have not hearkened, nor inclined your ear
to hear. . . . Therefore, thus saith the Lord of hosts,
Because ye have not heard my words, behold, I will
send and take all the families of the north, saith the
Lord, and Nebuchadnezzar, the King of Babylon, my
servant, and will bring them against this land, and
against the inhabitants thereof, and against all these

nations round about ; and this whole land shall be a desolation and an astonishment; and these nations shall serve the King of Babylon seventy years. And it shall come to pass when seventy years are accomplished that I will punish the King of Babylon, and that nation, saith the Lord, for their iniquity, and the land of the Chaldeans, and will make it perpetual desolations." Both of which predictions were literally fulfilled.

Chief Priests, Scribes and Pharisees alarmed and Determined to put Jesus to Death.

From these and similar passages in the Hebrew Scriptures those whom the Lord Jesus Christ addressed knew well that they and their predecessors were the husbandmen referred to. They felt it keenly. This Nazarene, in an obscure station of life, had for over three years been attracting much attention by His teaching many things contrary to all 'their traditions, and by many wonderful miracles that He wrought. His fame was spread throughout the whole country, and multitudes followed Him wherever He went. The day before they had seen Him riding into Jerusalem as Zechariah had predicted upon an ass's colt, and they had heard the crowds shouting, " Hosanna to the Son of David!" thus proclaiming Him as their Coming Messiah; and this son of a poor village carpenter had actually gone into the temple in their very presence, and upset the tables of the money changers, and charged them with making the house of God a den of thieves. Such audacity they had never witnessed before, and they were determined to put a stop to his career. After the severe rebukes He had given them in the parable about the vineyard they sought to lay hands on Him, but they feared the multitude, who regarded Him as a prophet. In the following chapter we find them repeatedly trying to entrap Him in His speech in order to find some ground of accusation against Him, but without success; and we read in Matt. 22 : 46, "And no man was able to answer·

Him a word. Neither durst any man from that day forth ask Him any more questions." And in chap. 23 we have His final terrible denunciation of the Scribes and Pharisees who had rejected Him as their Messiah, and were now seeking His life. Eight times over He says, " Woe unto you, Scribes and Pharisees, hypocrites," as He brings various charges against them. Twice He says to them, " Ye fools and blind." Twice He calls them " blind guides," and He thus concludes His address to them, " Ye serpents, ye generation of vipers! How shall ye escape the damnation of hell ? Wherefore, behold, I send unto you prophets, and wise men and Scribes : and some of them ye shall kill and crucify; and some of them shall ye scourge in your synagogues, and persecute them from city to city; that upon you may come all the righteous blood shed upon the earth, from the blood of righteous Abel unto the blood of Zacharias, son of Barachias, whom ye slew between the temple and the altar. Verily, I say unto you, all these things shall come upon this generation. Oh, Jerusalem, Jerusalem, thou that killest the prophets, and stonest them that are sent unto thee, how often would I have gathered thy children together, even as a hen gathereth her chickens under her wings, and ye would not! Behold, your house is left unto you desolate. For I say unto you, Ye shall not see me henceforth till ye say, Blessed is he that cometh in the name of the Lord." This was His valedictory address to the chief priests, Scribes and Pharisees, who were thenceforth bent on securing His death at the earliest possible moment. They had missed their opportunity. Had they received and acknowledged Him as their Messiah when He had come just as Zechariah had predicted, riding on the ass's colt, and proclaimed by the multitude, who cried. Hosanna! " Blessed is the King of Israel, who cometh in the name of the Lord" (John 12 : 13), His glorious reign might have been commenced. and all the temporal blessings promised to them as a nation might have been ushered in; but they had deliberately and blindly rejected Him

(as He knew they would), who, as the Son of God, had
come to His Father'svineyard and spoken to them; even
as their fathers had rejected, persecuted, and slain the
prophets who had been sent to them and spoken to them,
in the name of the Lord. He had often told His.dis-
ciples about His death, which was now near at hand, and
said to them that He would rise again from the dead on
the third day, but they never seemed to fully comprehend what He meant by such a strange statement until
after His resurrection had actually taken place, and the
evidence of their natural senses convinced them that it
was a reality.

The Earlier Public Ministry of Jesus.

We have seen from the Scriptures just quoted how
He spoke to the chief priests and scribes and elders about
the way in which their fathers had treated the prophets
whom God had sent unto them, and about the way in
which they themselves would treat His Son after all the
proofs that He had given to them that He was the promised Messiah. Let us now look back at the earlier
part of His public ministry and consider how the Son
of God has spoken, not simply to the Jews, as in the
Scriptures to which we have referred, but to us, Gentiles
as well as Jews; and in doing so we must take into
account not only the matter and manner of His speech,
but also the miracles which He performed, and which
attested His Divine character and mission.

After His baptism by John the Baptist in the Jordan
the heavens were opened, and the Spirit of God was seen
descending upon Him like a dove, and lighting upon
Him, and a voice from heaven was heard saying, " This
is my beloved Son, in whom I am well pleased." Afterwards, when filled with the Holy Spirit, He was tempted
of Satan in the wilderness for forty days, after which He
commenced His public ministry in Galilee, and, as we
read in Matt. 4 : 23, 24, "Went about all Galilee teaching
in their synagogues, and preaching the Gospel of the
Kingdom, and healing all manner of sickness, and all

manner of disease among the people. And his fame went throughout all Syria; and they brought unto him all sick people that were taken with divers diseases and torments, and those which were possessed with devils, and those which were lunatic, and those that had the palsy; and he healed them." This is the way in which God first spoke to us by His Son—by teaching, preaching, and healing the physical diseases of the people. Then it was that He preached that wonderful sermon upon the mountain to the multitudes who followed Him, in which He announced the inauguration of a new era of grace in the dealings of men one with another, and the need of a righteousness and a purity which are not merely confined to external acts, but which must also pervade the secret thoughts and intents of the heart. The beatitudes in the beginning of this discourse are a beautiful expression of spiritual truths contained in the Gospel; and yet immediately following them He declares, " Think not that I am come to destroy the law or the prophets. I am not come to destroy, but to fulfil. For verily, I say unto you, Till heaven and earth pass, one jot or one tittle shall in no wise pass from the law till all be fulfilled." This corresponds with the statement made in John 1 : 17, " For the law was given by Moses, but grace and truth came by Jesus Christ."

In Luke 4 : 16-22 we read what may have been His first public announcement of His Divine mission. "And he came to Nazareth, where he had been brought up; and, as his custom was, he went into the synagogue on the Sabbath day, and stood up for to read; and there was delivered unto him the book of the Prophet Esaias. And when he had opened the book, he found the place where it was written, " The Spirit of the Lord is upon me, because he hath anointed me to preach the Gospel to the poor; he hath sent me to heal the broken-hearted, to preach deliverance to the captives, and recovering of sight to the blind, to set at liberty them that are bruised, to proclaim the acceptable year of the Lord. And he closed the book, and gave it again to the minister, and sat down; and the eyes of all them that were in the synagogue were fastened on him. And he began to say unto them this day is this Scripture fulfilled in you ears, and all bare witness and wondered at the gracious words which proceeded out of his mouth." The passage that the Lord Jesus Christ here read was in Isa. 61 : 1, 2, and the remarkable thing in connection with His quotation was that He stopped reading in the middle of the second verse, the whole of which is as follows : "To proclaim the acceptable year of the Lord, and the day of vengeance of our God; to comfort all that mourn," and sat down without reading, "and the day of vengeance of our God"; after which He said, "This day is this Scripture fulfilled in your ears," thus intimating to His hearers that a new dispensation of grace had been entered upon, and that the day of vengeance had been postponed.

Professor Smith Denies that Isaiah Wrote what Jesus quoted from His Writings.

It will, perhaps, be a surprise to Professor Goldwin Smith to find that the passage in the book of the Prophet Isaiah, from which the Lord Jesus Christ read at this time, was in that part of the book which He, without producing any proof for his statement, asserts was not written by the Prophet Isaiah. The gracious words which Jesus spoke at Nazareth were followed by some plain truths that pricked the consciences of His fellow-townsmen, and they were filled with wrath, and would have killed Him if they could; but He, passing through their midst, went His way.

The Miracles and Teaching of Jesus in His Earlier Public Ministry.

He next went to Capernaum and taught them on the Sabbath day. "And they were astonished at his doctrine: for His word was with power" (Luke 4 : 33). There He cast an unclean demon out of a man in the synagogue, and we read in v. 36, "And they were all amazed, and spake among themselves, saying, What a word is this! for with authority and power He commandeth the unclean spirits, and they come out." There the Roman centurion came and asked Him to heal his servant, and Jesus said to him, " Go thy way; and as thou hast believed, so be it done unto thee," and his servant was healed the self-same hour. It was there that He entered into Peter's house and found "his wife's mother sick of a fever, and He touched her hand, and the fever left her; and she arose and ministered unto them." After which we read in Matt. 8 : 16, " When the even was come, they brought unto him many that were possessed with demons, and He cast out the spirits with His word, and healed all that were sick." After that He entered into a ship with His disciples to go to the other side of the Sea of Galilee; and there arose a great storm, but He was fast asleep. And they awoke Him, saying, " Lord, save us; we perish. And He said unto them, Why are ye fearful ? Oh, ye of little faith! Then He arose and rebukèd the winds and the sea; and there was a great calm. But the men marvelled, saying, What manner of man is this, that even the winds and the sea obey Him!" After crossing to the other side of the lake He cast the demons out of two men who " dwelt in the tombs, exceeding fierce, so that no man might pass that way; and they cried out, saying, What have we to do with thee, Jesus, thou Son of God ? Art thou come hither to torment us before the time." They asked Him if He cast them out of the two men to allow them to enter a herd of swine that was near. He did·so. The men were healed, but the swine ran down a steep place into the sea and perished. And in consequence of this serious loss of property the whole city came out and besought Jesus to depart out of their coasts. It was also as we find in Luke 7 : 12-15 during this part of His ministry while at Capernaum that He raised to life the widow's son who was being carried to his burial. " Now when they came nigh to the gate of the city, behold, there was a dead man carried out, the only son of his mother, and she was a widow; and much people of the city was with her. And when the Lord saw her He had compassion on her, and touched the bier, and they that bare him stood still. And He said, Young man, I say unto thee, Arise. And he that was dead sat up and began to speak. And he delivered him to his mother." And after that we read in v. 16 the effect produced by this miracle, "And there came a fear on all; and they glorified God, saying, That a great prophet is risen up among us; and that God hath visited his people."

Now, up to this time it appears that God was speaking by His Son, almost exclusively, by the miracles of mercy that He was constantly performing, and the result was that God was glorified; and the people were obliged to confess that Jesus was a prophet, thereby fulfilling the prediction of Moses, "A Prophet shall the Lord your God raise up unto you of your brethren like unto me; him shall ye hear in 'all things whatsoever he shall say unto you."

Bitter Enmity of the Scribes and Pharisees.

After recrossing the Sea of Galilee to Capernaum we find that the Scribes and Pharisees have begun to watch Him, and find fault with Him at every opportunity. In Luke 5 : 17-26 we read, "And it came to pass on a certain day, as he was teaching, that there were Pharisees and doctors of the law sitting by which were come out of every town of Galilee, and Judea, and Jerusalem; and the power of the Lord was present to heal them. And behold, men brought in a bed a man which was taken with a palsy; and they sought means to bring him in and lay him before Him; and when they could not find by what way they might bring him in because of the multitude, they went upon the house top, and let him down through the tiling with his couch into the midst before Jesus. And when he saw their faith he said unto him, Man, thy sins are forgiven thee, and the Scribes and Pharisees began to reason, saying, Who is this which

speaketh blasphemies ? Who can forgive sin but God
alone ? But when Jesus perceived their thoughts he,
answering, said unto them, What reason ye in your
hearts ? Whether is easier to say, Thy sins be forgiven
thee, or to say, Rise up and walk ? But that ye may
know that the Son of Man hath power on earth to forgive sins (he said unto the sick of the palsy), I say unto
thee, Arise, and take up thy couch, and go into thine
house. And immediately he rose up before them, and
took up that whereon he lay, and departed to his own
house glorifying God. And they were all amazed, and
they glorified God, and were filled with fear, saying. We
have seen strange things to-day." From this time forward we find that while "the common people heard Him
gladly," as stated in Mark 12 : 37. He was a marked
man by the Scribes and Pharisees, who constantly sought
to entrap Him in His words, and find some occasion
against Him.

In Matt. 9 we have the account of His restoring to
life the ruler's daughter; of the healing of the woman
that had the issue of blood; of His giving sight to two
blind men, and of His casting a dumb devil out of a man,
so that he afterwards spake. The Pharisees could not
dispute the miracles that they witnessed, but they said.
" He casteth out devils through the prince of the devils "
(Matt. 9 : 34), after which we read that " Jesus went
about all the cities and villages, teaching in their synagogues and preaching the Gospel of the kingdom, and
healing every sickness and every disease among the
people."

Commission to the Twelve Apostles.

At length He sent out the twelve apostles whom He
had chosen, and commissioned them to preach the Gospel
of the kingdom which He had been preaching, and commanded them, saying, " Go not into the way of the Gentiles, and into any city of the Samaritans enter ye not;
but go rather to the lost sheep of the house of Israel.
And as ye go preach, saying, The kingdom of heaven is

at hand, heal the sick, cleanse the lepers, raise the dead, cast out devils; freely ye have received, freely give" (Matt. 10 : 5-8). Thus they were empowered to work miracles as He did, and to preach the Gospel of the kingdom which He preached, and to proclaim that the Messiah had come of the seed of David to establish His kingdom. After this He sent out other seventy disciples, two and two, with power to heal the sick and to preach the same Gospel of the kingdom. The twelve had obeyed His word, and gone through the towns preaching the Gospel and healing everywhere. They came back and told Him what they had done, and He took them aside privately into a desert place to rest awhile with Himself. But the multitudes followed, and He who never turned a deaf ear to the poor and needy, healed all that had need of healing. And then, as if to encourage His disciples' hearts, He gave them that wonderful proof of the inexhaustible fulness that was in Him by feeding the five thousand men with the five loaves and two fishes, and after they had all eaten, twelve baskets of fragments remained. He then prevailed on His disciples to get into a ship and go before Him to the other side of the sea whilst He sent the multitudes away, and when this was done, " He went up into a mountain to pray, and when the evening was come He was there alone; and in the fourth watch of the night He went to His disciples walking on the sea. And when the disciples saw Him walking on the sea they were troubled, saying, It is a spirit; and they cried out for fear. But straightway Jesus spake unto them, saying, Be of good cheer; it is I; be not afraid. And Peter answered him, and said, Lord, if it be thou, bid me come unto thee on the water. And He said, Come. And when Peter was come down out of the ship he walked on the water to go to Jesus. But when he saw the wind boisterous he was afraid; and, beginning to sink, he cried, saying, Lord, save me! And immediately Jesus stretched forth his hand, and caught him and said unto him, Oh, thou of little faith; wherefore didst thou doubt ? And when they were come

into the ship the wind ceased. Then they that were in
the ship came and worshipped him, saying, Of a truth
thou art the Son of God. And when they had gone over
they came into the land of Gennesaret. And when the
men of that place had knowledge of him, they sent out
into all that country round about, and brought unto him
all that were diseased; and besought him that they might
only touch the hem of his garment; and as many as
touched were made perfectly whole. Then came to Jesus
Scribes and Pharisees which were of Jerusalem, saying,
Why do thy disciples transgress the tradition of the
elders ? for they wash not their hands when they eat
bread" (Matt. 14 : 24-36 and 15 : 1, 2). After answering
their question He rebuked them sharply in these words,
"Ye hypocrites! Well did Esaias prophesy of you saying, This people draweth nigh unto me with their mouth,
and honoureth me with their lips; but their heart is far
from me. But in vain do they worship me, teaching for
doctrines the commandments of men" (Matt. 15 : 7-9).

Commission to the Seventy Disciples.

The seventy disciples whom He had sent out also
" returned to Him again with joy, saying, Lord, even the
devils are subject to us through thy name. And he said
unto them, I beheld Satan as lightning fall from heaven.
Behold, I give you power to tread on serpents and
scorpions, and over all the power of the enemy; and
nothing shall by any means hurt you. Notwithstanding
in this rejoice not, that the spirits are subject unto you;
but rather rejoice, because your names are written in
heaven. In that hour Jesus rejoiced in spirit, and said,
I thank thee, O Father, Lord of heaven and earth, that
thou hast hid these things from the wise and prudent
and hast revealed them unto babes; even so, Father, for
so it seemed good in thy sight. All things are delivered
to me of my Father; and no man knoweth who the Son
is but the Father, and who the Father is but the Son, and
he to whom the Son will reveal him. And he turned
him unto his disciples and said privately, Blessed are the

eyes which see the things which ye see; for I tell you, that many prophets and kings have desired to see those things which ye see, and have not seen them, and to hear those things which ye hear, and have not heard them" (Luke 10 : 17-34).

How richly were both the twelve apostles and the seventy disciples rewarded for the service which they had done for the Master! The twelve had witnessed the miraculous feeding of the five thousand, and had seen Him walking on the water, and were forced to exclaim, "Of a truth thou art the Son of God." And the seventy were assured that their names were written in heaven, that nothing should by any means hurt them, and that He was, indeed, the promised Messiah, to whom many prophets and kings had been looking forward.

Only a few of the miracles performed by the Lord Jesus Christ, and they chiefly in the early part of His public ministry, have been specially mentioned in this chapter. They are enough, however, to show that He was constantly exercising supernatural power; and this fact was not questioned by His bitterest enemies, the chief priests and Scribes and Pharisees, who admitted the miracles, but declared that they had been performed by the power of Satan. As we have already seen in a previous chapter, there can be no reasonable doubt about the authenticity of the four Gospels, which contain the records of those miracles, and have been carefully preserved and handed down to us. But the resources of infidel skepticism are apparently as inexhaustible as they are futile, which we shall see farther on.

Professor Smith's Ingenious Device to Rule Out Evidence of the Miracles of Christ.

Professor Goldwin Smith has adopted a most ingenious rule for limiting the evidence that he thinks should be allowed in proof that a miracle has been performed, and that is, only to receive the testimony of an actual eye-witness to the occurrence in question. But

in event of this rule failing to set aside the testimony
in favour of miracles, he has another in reserve which
is still more sweeping, and that is, to throw doubt upon
the authenticity of the four Gospels, without even
attempting to produce any reasonable evidence that they
are not authentic. Thus, respecting the miraculous feeding of the five thousand men, besides women and children, and respecting Jesus walking on the water, all the
apostles having been present, including Matthew and
John, the writers of the two Gospels which bear their
names, the first rule would not apply. He can, therefore, conveniently fall back upon the second, and say
that it is not known who were the writers of those
Gospels. The absurdity of setting up and applying such
rules to the investigation of historical facts is self-evident,
but may, perhaps, be made more plain by applying the
same principle to the criticism of profane history. Supposing, for instance, that some ultra skeptic were to deny
that Julius Caesar had been murdered, would we refuse
to receive any evidence of that fact except that of some
person or persons who had witnessed the commission
of the crime ? And if we had placed in our hands two
well-known histories by independent writers, who both
claimed to have been present when the assassination
took place, and if these records differed somewhat in
the details, but agreed in regard to the main facts; and
if, moreover, the testimonies thus given were confirmed
by the writings of two other co-temporary authors, who
only compiled the accounts they had received from a
great many different persons who were eye-witnesses of
the tragedy, would any sane man declare that it was very
doubtful if such an event had ever taken place, although
for over two thousand years it had never been questioned, simply because he chooses to doubt the authenticity of the four independent histories in our possession without giving some substantial reason for his
doubts ? And yet this is the kind of arguments with
which modern skeptics are trying to throw dust in the
eyes of the rising generation, and thus prevent them

from searching the Scriptures for themselves with unbiased minds, and finding therein what wonderful things
God has spoken to us in these last days by His Son.

Says that Paul Does Not Testify to Any Miracle Except the Vision.

On page 149 Professor Goldwin Smith says that Paul
does not testify to any miracle other than the vision!
This statement is made in pursuance of his ironclad
rule only to receive the testimony of an eye-witness
himself. But we have the testimony of Luke as author
of the Acts, who travelled with Paul as to the blinding
of Elymas, the sorcerer (Acts 13 : 8-12); the healing of
the cripple at Lystra (Acts 14: 8-10); Paul's own miraculous healing after having been stoned (Acts 14 : 19, 20);
his casting the spirit of divination out of the damsel at
Philippi (Acts 16 : 16-18); his deliverance from prison,
and the conversion of the Philippian jailer and his family
(Acts 16 : 23-35); the "special miracles which God
wrought by the hands of Paul; so that from his body
were brought to the sick handkerchiefs or aprons, and
the diseases departed from them, and the evil spirits went
out of them" (Acts 19 : 11, 12); and the healing of
Publius and others on the Island of Melita (Acts 28 :
8, 9). Surely the evidence of Luke, the companion of
Paul in his travels, ought to be sufficient to satisfy any
reasonable man as to these facts, which were well known,
and never controverted in the early Church when the
narrative was written.

Denies that Peter Testified to the Resurrection of Christ.

On page 150 he says that in the first Epistle of Peter
there is no allusion to the resurrection of Christ. This
is not correct; there is a very distinct reference to it in
chap. 3, v. 21. But it would seem from his remark that,
having denied the authenticity of the four Gospels, he

would in this way try to get rid of Peter's testimony as an eye-witness to the resurrection; after which he would set aside all the testimony given in Paul's writings because he was not an eye-witness to that miracle, and would probably contend that his vision on the way to Damascus was only an optical illusion, although attended with very substantial results!

Also Questions the Authenticity of Second Peter.

On the same page he says that in Second Peter there is an allusion to the Transfiguration and the voice from heaven. See 2 Peter 1 : 16-18. " For we have not followed cunningly devised fables when we made known unto you the power and coming of our Lord Jesus Christ, but were eye-witnesses of his majesty. For he received from God the Father honour and glory, when there came such a voice to him from the excellent glory, This is my beloved Son, in whom I am well pleased. And this voice, which came from heaven, we heard when we were with him in the holy mount." This is certainly a strong testimony to a most extraordinary miracle, given in plain words which cannot be mistaken. But the Professor in his book, instead of quoting the passage, only refers to it as " an allusion to the Transfiguration," And he adds that " the authenticity of Second Peter is *strongly* impugned and *feebly* defended!" But he does not say by whom or on what grounds it is impugned so strongly, or by whom it is defended so feebly. Very likely it is strongly impugned by his friends, " the liberal theologians " and " higher critics," who are doubtless referred to in the beginning of chap. 2 as " false teachers," but in order to get the connection read from the verses quoted above in chap. 1 : 19-21, " We have a more sure word of prophecy : whereunto ye do well that ye take heed, as unto a light that shineth in a dark place, until the day dawn and the day star arise in your hearts; knowing this first that no prophecy of the Scripture is of any private interpretation. For the prophecy came not in old time by the will of man; but holy men of God spake as they were moved by the Holy Ghost," and then follows the solemn warning in chap. 2 : 1-3, " But there were false prophets also among the people, even as there shall be false teachers among you, who privily shall bring in damnable heresies, even denying the Lord that bought them, and bring upon themselves swift destruction. And many shall follow their pernicious ways; by reason of whom the way of truth shall be evil spoken of. And through covetousness shall they with feigned words make merchandise of you: whose judgment now of a long time lingereth not, and their damnation slumbereth not."

Desparate Attempts to Create Doubt Respecting Miracles.

On page 155 he says that to some of the miraculous parts of the Gospels there would be no eye-witnesses, such as the annunciation and the immaculate conception, of which the only possible witness tells us nothing. In reply to this it may be said that we have no knowledge of Mary having ever written anything, but she was a constant companion of Jesus and the apostles, and her home was with John after the crucifixion; so that all the particulars were doubtless obtained by the writers from her own lips. In the same way he also speaks of the temptation, the agony in the garden, and the descent of the angel, to which it should be a sufficient answer to say that the Lord Jesus Christ conversed much with His disciples after His resurrection, and He afterwards sent down the Holy Spirit to dwell in their hearts, and to bring to their remembrance all that He had said unto them, of which but little is recorded.

On page 161 he says: " The demoniac miracles are clearly stamped with the mark of Jewish superstition, and they are all absent from the fourth Gospel, because the first three Gospels were written for Jewish readers, while the fourth was written for an intelligent circle, to which they were not congenial, perhaps, at a later day"; all of which statements are mere assertion on his part, without a tittle of evidence to support them. Professor Goldwin Smith is continually shifting his ground so as to create doubt, if possible, about everything that God has revealed. Is it not remarkable that he and the "liberal theologians" should have the greatest aversion to the fourth Gospel, which, he says, was written for the "intelligent circle." But it has already been shown in a previous chapter that John wrote that Gospel as supplementary to the other three, and, therefore, he repeated but little of what they had stated, and stated things which they had omitted. As to demoniacal possession, it was not necessary for John to repeat what had already been stated in the first three Gospels.

Says the Four Gospels are Anonymous.

On page 150 he says: "The four Gospels are anonymous; and two of them, the second and third, are not even ascribed to eye-witnesses. The first Gospel (Matthew), if he were its author, would be the work of an eye-witness; and the preface to the third implies that it is not the work of an eye-witness, but a compiler; and to the fourth Gospel there is an attestation, but it is anonymous and misleading"; all of which statements are most insidious and misleading, and made for the purpose of destroying faith in the testimony which these Gospels give as to the miracles wrought by the Lord Jesus Christ, including His own resurrection from the dead. That these statements are all incorrect has already been shown in a previous chapter, and it is, therefore, unnecessary to say more on this subject at present. But it would, perhaps, not be out of place here to ask the learned Professor to mention, if he can, a single instance of an authentic history which has ever been written by any man who was himself eye-witness to all the facts which he recorded. Are not all true historians compilers of facts which they have learned from others, who may or may not have been eye-witnesses ?

On page 150 he also says : " The above is the sum total of the ocular evidence producible for the miraculous part of Christianity, and, besides this, there is nothing but traditions of unknown origin, recorded by unknown writers, at a date uncertain, and, for aught we know, many years after the events." These assertions and insinuations, so insidiously made, have already been refuted, and it is only necessary to say that the " ocular evidence " is that referred to under the first of his two rules for setting aside all evidence in regard to the performance of miracles. (See page 134.)

And on page 173 he adds: " If we must resign the miracles, the Messianic prophecies, and their supposed fulfillment in Christ, and the Trinitarian creed, what remains to us of the Gospel ? There remains to us the character, the sayings and the parables, which made and have sustained moral, though not ritualistic, dogmatic, or persecuting Christendom. There remain the supremacy of conscience over law, and the recognition of motive as that which determines the quality of action." And it is worthy of notice that the only place where he can get these things is in the Scriptures, whose authenticity he denies.

But as we go on to consider the sayings of Jesus, and learn how God has spoken to us by His Son, we shall find Professor Smith and the " liberal theologians " are just as much opposed to His teaching as to His miracles.

The Teaching of Jesus Distasteful to the Ruling Classes.

Whilst Jesus preached the Gospel of the kingdom, and performed so many miracles that both friends and foes were obliged to recognize His mighty works, there were things He spoke which were very distasteful to many of the listeners, and especially to the chief priests, the Scribes and Pharisees and elders of the people, most of whom probably looked forward to the reign of their expected Messiah as a time of earthly glory and worldly prosperity, when all their ambitions would be gratified. Riches and honour they doubtless expected as a matter of course. But this extraordinary man, who had only kind words for the poor and needy, and healing for those who were suffering from bodily sickness and infirmities, and even life for the dead, reproved their sins, rebuked their pride, and exposed their hypocrisy; and told them of a kingdom of God that was within them, when the Pharisees asked Him when the kingdom of God should come (Luke 17 : 21). He spoke to them of a spiritual kingdom, to enter which they must become as little children (Mark 10 : 15). When the Scribes and Pharisees murmured because He ate and drank with publicans and sinners, He said that He came not to call the righteous but sinners to repentance (Luke 5 : 30-32). And He had come to seek and to save that which was lost (Luke 19 : 10). He had spoken against them the parables of the Pharisee and the publican (Luke 18 : 9-16). He had set Himself up as Lord of the Sabbath, and allowed His disciples to do things that were unlawful on the Sabbath day (Matt. 12 : 1, 8). He had declared that whosoever should say to his brother, " Thou fool," would be in danger of hell fire (Matt. 5 : 22); that whosoever looked on a woman to lust after her had committed adultery with her already in his heart (Matt. 5 : 28); and that they were to love their enemies, bless them that cursed them, do good to them that hated them, and pray for those who despitefully used them and persecuted them (Matt. 5 : 44). He had told them that they should forgive a brother who had offended them seventy times seven (Matt. 18 : 22); and He had told them that it was the evil thoughts and lusts allowed in the heart that defile a man, and not the neglect of the washing of cups and pots and hands, as required by their traditions (Mark 7). He had told one of their rulers, a Pharisee named Nicodemus, and probably many others, that except a man be born again he could not even see the kingdom of God, much less enter therein; and in ex-

planation of this He had told them that, as Moses lifted
up the serpent in the wilderness, even so must He Himself be lifted up; that whosoever believed in Him should
not perish, but have eternal life, for God so loved the
world that He had given His only begotten Son, that
whosoever believeth in Him should not perish, but have
everlasting life; and that those who did not believe on
Him were condemned already (John 3 : 1-18). He said
He had living water to give, of which, if a man drank,
he would never thirst again. And, nothwithstanding that
Jerusalem was the place where God had chosen to put
His name, He had actually declared that the hour was
coming when the Father would be worshipped, neither
in that mountain nor in Jerusalem, but the hour cometh,
said He, and now is, when the true worshippers shall·
worship the Father in spirit and in truth, for the Father
seeketh such to worship Him; and that God is a spirit,
and they that worship Him must worship in spirit and
in truth (John 4 : 14-24). And again and again He had
repeated the declaration that those who believed in Him
should not perish, but had everlasting life, and they
should not come into condemnation (John 5 : 24). He
had invited all that laboured and were heavy laden to
come unto Him and He would give them rest (Matt.
11 : 28). On the last great day of the feast, when the
Pharisees and chief priests sent officers to take Him He
cried out, " If any man thirst, let him come unto me and
drink. He that believeth on me, as the Scripture hath
said, Out of his belly shall flow rivers of living water ";
and when the officers returned to the chief priests and
Pharisees and were asked why they had not brought Him.
they answered, " Never man spake like this man " (John
7 : 27-46). He had told them that " if any man came to
Him He would in no wise cast him out." He had told
the Jews who were opposing Him that they were of their
father, the devil, and that if they did not believe in Him
they would die in their sins. He had declared that He
was the good Shepherd, who was to lay down His life
for the sheep, and that He would give them eternal life;

and they should never perish; neither should any man pluck them out of His hand (John 10 : 15, 28). And He had also declared that He was the resurrection and the life; that he that believed in Him, though He were dead, yet should he live; and that whosoever liveth and believeth in Him should never die (John 11 : 25, 26).

God spoke these things by His Son to the Jews, who listened to His words as they came from His own lips. He speaks them to us now by His Son through the Word which the Holy Spirit inspired His disciples to write, bringing, as Jesus had promised, all things to their remembrance which He had said unto them.

God's Speaking by His Son excited the Deadly Enmity of the Chief Priests, Scribes and Pharisees.

The effects produced through God thus speaking by His Son to the Jews are described in John 7 : 12, "And there was much murmuring among the people concerning him; for some said He is a good man; others said, Nay, but he deceiveth the people." Also in John 7 : 40-43, "Many of the people, therefore, when they heard this saying, said, Of a truth, this is the Prophet." Others said, This is the Christ. But some said, Shall Christ come out of Galilee? Hath not the Scripture said that Christ cometh of the seed of David, and out of the town of Bethlehem where David was? So there was a division among the people because of him." And again we read in John 9 : 16, "Therefore, said some of the Pharisees, This man is not of God, because he keepeth not the Sababth day. Others said, How can a man that is a sinner do such miracles? And there was a division among them."

The chief priests, and scribes, and elders, from the things that He had publicly spoken against them, believed that they would receive no favour from Him if He was raised to the throne of Israel, and they had no sympathy with the doctrines He was teaching, which were

so much at variance with all that they had formerly
learned and taught; and their enmity against Him was
intensified by the miracle which He wrought in raising
Lazarus from the dead. This was followed by importan;
results. Some of the Jews who had seen Lazarus raised
went to the Pharisees and told them what Jesus had
done, after which we read, "Then gathered the chief
priests and the Pharisees a council, and said, What do
we ? for this man doeth many miracles. If we let him
thus alone, all men will believe on him, and the Romans
will come and take away our place and nation. And
one of them named Caiaphas, being the high priest that
year, said unto them, Ye know nothing at all, nor consider that it is expedient for us, that one man should
die for the people, and that the whole nation perish not.
And this spake he not of himself; but, being high priest
that year, he prophesied that Jesus shou!d die for that
nation; and not for that nation only, but that also he
should gather together in one the children of God that
were scattered abroad. Then from that day forth they
took counsel to put him to death " (John 11 : 46-53).

His triumphal entry into Jerusalem soon afterwards
amid the plaudits of the multitude confirmed them in this
determination, and their hatred was increased by the
stinging rebukes that He administered to them in public
soon afterwards. That they would seize Him and put
Him to death at the Passover feast was a foregone conclusion, and they must act swiftly and surely, as many
thousands who had heard Him speak and witnessed His
miracles would also be there; and, if they were not
expeditious in their movements, His friends might effect
a rescue; and, as they had already proclaimed Him
King, they might place Him on the throne. They must
not lose an hour between His condemnation and execution. They expected to justify themselves before the
people, because He was guilty of blasphemy in calling
Himself the Son of God, and before the Roman governor,
because He declared that He was the King of the Jews.

Last Address of Jesus to His Disciples Before His Crucifixion.

Jesus gathered His disciples in an upper room to partake with them of the Passover feast for the last time before Himself going to the cross to suffer as the Lamb of God that beareth away the sin of the world (John 1 : 29). He had done with speaking to the Jews as a nation. They had despised and rejected Him. But now, as they all sat together at that feast, His heart went out in tender love and pity to those whom He was about to leave so soon, and whose hopes He knew would be blighted for a season by His death. After they had partaken of the Passover Supper He instituted another feast, to be partaken then and afterwards till He should come again, as a memorial of His dying love. And then with tenderest love and sympathy He comforted their sorrowing hearts, saying: " Let not your heart be troubled ; ye believe in God, believe also in me. In my Father's house are many mansions; if it were not so I would have told you. I go to prepare a place for you. And, if I go and prepare a place for you, I will come again, and receive you to myself; that where I am, there ye may be also. And whither I go ye know, and the way ye know. Thomas saith unto him, Lord, we know not whither thou goest, and how can we know the way ? Jesus saith unto him, I am the way, the truth, and the life; no man cometh unto the Father but by me " (John 14 : 1-6). And then He went on to tell them that those who believed on Him were to do greater works than He had done, because He was going to the Father, and whatsoever they asked in His name He would do it. And He spoke to them repeatedly of that wonderful Person whom He was to send to dwell in their hearts as another Comforter, and said that He would not leave them comfortless. And He told them that this Comforter, who is the Holy Spirit, would teach them all things, and bring all things to their remembrance that He had said unto them; and He would guide them into all truth, and testify of Him; and He repeated the words of comfort, saying, "Peace I leave with you, my peace I give unto you; not as the world giveth, give I unto you; let not your heart be troubled, neither let it be afraid; ye have heard how I said unto you. I go away, and come again unto you" (John 14 : 26, 27). And then He exhorted them to abide in Him, and obey His commands, and love one another as He had loved them. He told them that the hour was come when they would be scattered, every man to his own home, and leave Him alone, and concluded with these words, "These things have I spoken unto you that in me ye might have peace. In the world ye shall have tribulation ; but be of good cheer: I have overcome the world" (John 16 : 33).

The Lord's Prayer for His Disciples.

And then followed that wonderful prayer to the Father on behalf of those whom He was about to leave so soon, who had been given to Him by the Father out of the world, and yet left in it to witness for Him in separation from it, that they might be kept and sanctified through the truth, and that they all might be one, that the world might believe that the Father had sent Him; and finally, that they might hereafter be with Him and behold His glory.

Although then, as it were, under the very shadow of the cross to which, as He knew, He would be nailed on the following day, the Lord Jesus Christ seemed to forget all about His own sufferings in His desire to comfort the humble followers whom He was about to leave, and through whom, in the power of the Holy Spirit, He was to continue to speak to His Church and to the world.

Shameful Treatment and Agonizing Death of the Son of God.

After singing a hymn they went out to the Mount of Olives and into the garden of Gethsemane, where for a short time alone, in communion with the Father, He looked forward, in deepest agony, to that fearful ordeal through which He was so soon to pass as the Sin-bearer, suffering instead of sinners the judgment due to them. Soon Judas came with the officers of the chief priests and betrayed Him to them with a kiss. He was arrested and taken before the high priests for trial, and condemned for blasphemy in saying that He was the Christ, the Son of God, after which they spat in His face and smote Him, and told Him to prophesy who smote Him. Then He was taken before Pilate, the Roman governor, charged with claiming to be the King of the Jews. Pilate examined Him, and said that he could find no fault in Him, and wished to release Him, but he finally yielded to the clamour of the Jews, who shouted, "Away with him! Crucify him!" And when he asked them, "Shall I crucify your king?" the chief priests answered, "We have no king but Caesar." And they also said, "His blood be on us and on our children," and the soldiers stripped Him, and put on Him a scarlet robe and a crown of thorns, and said, "Hail! King of the Jews," and they again spat on Him and mocked Him. He was then delivered to them and crucified between two malefactors, and Pilate wrote this title and put it on the cross : JESUS OF NAZARETH, THE KING OF THE JEWS. While hanging on the cross, and slowly dying that shameful, agonizing death, He spoke some words that told at the same time the depth of His anguish, the strength of His love to the perishing, and His thoughtful care for the mother whom He was leaving behind. Forsaken by all His disciples, oppressed by the burden of sin He was bearing, and suffering intense torture from His wounds, He looked upon His murderers and prayed for them, saying, "Father, forgive them, for they know not what they do." To the conscience-stricken thief at His side He gave the assurance that his sins were forgiven. To his mother and His beloved disciple, John, He spoke, providing a home for her with him. And after three hours, when darkness overspread the earth, and He realized that God, the Father, had hid

His face from Him, and that without any help from God or man He was bearing alone the judgment due to sin, the cry came from His lips with which the twenty-second Psalm opens, " My God! my God! why hast Thou forsaken me ?"   And at length, after saying, " It is finished," He bowed His head and died, and the Roman centurion and those that were with him said, " Truly, this was the Son of God!"

Resurrection of Christ and Subsequent Interviews With His Disciples.

He rose from the dead on the third day as He had promised, and appeared to Mary Magdalene, and " the same day at evening on the first day of the week, the doors being shut, He appeared in the midst of the disciples, saying unto them, Peace be unto you. And when He had so said, He showed them His hands and His side.   Then were the disciples glad when they saw the Lord.   Then said Jesus to them again, Peace be unto you; as my Father hath sent me, even so send I you. And when he had said this, he breathed on them and said, Receive ye the Holy Ghost," etc. (John 20 : 19-22). But Thomas was not with the other disciples on that occasion.   And he would not believe what they had told him.   So we read again in v. 26, "And after eight days again His disciples were within, and Thomas with them; then came Jesus, the doors being shut, and stood in the midst, and said, Peace be unto you.   Then said He to Thomas, Reach hither thy finger, and behold my hands, and reach hither thy hand, and thrust it into my side; and be not faithless but believing.   And Thomas answered and said unto him, My Lord and my God. Jesus said unto him, Thomas, because thou hast seen me thou hast believed; blessed are they that have not seen and yet have believed" (John 20 : 26-29). Again He appeared to seven of His disciples at the Sea of Tiberias, (Peter being one of the number), who had been fishing all night and caught nothing.   Then He told them to cast their

net on the right side of the ship, and they would find.
They did so, and were not able to draw it in for the
multitude of fishes. They had not known Him at first,
but now John said to Peter, "It is the Lord," and Peter,
with his usual impetuosity, at once cast himself into the
sea and went to Him. The rest soon followed, and they
found a fire of coals, with fish and bread laid thereon;
and He invited them to dine with Him, and also took
bread Himself. This was the third time He had appeared
to them, and after they had dined He asked Peter three
times in succession if he loved Him, and on being
assured that he did, He told him to feed His lambs, and
to feed His sheep. Paul states, in 1 Cor. 15 : 6, 7, that
he was seen of above five hundred brethren at once, of
whom the greater part were then alive, but some had
died; and that after that He was seen of James, and then
again of all the apostles; and last of all by Himself
also as of one born out of due time. And against all
this positive evidence for the resurrection of the Lord
Jesus Christ there is only, as has been already remarked,
the evidence of the Roman guards at His tomb, who
were bribed to say that His disciples had come and
stolen Him away while they slept. In Matthew's Gospel
we are informed that He said to His disciples, "All
power is given unto me in heaven and in earth. Go ye,
therefore, into all nations, baptizing them in the name
of the Father, and of the Son, and of the Holy Ghost;
teaching them to observe all things whatsoever I have
commanded you; and lo! I am with you alway, even
unto the end of the world " (Matt. 28 : 18-20). In Mark's
Gospel we are told that " He appeared to the eleven as
they sat at meat, and upbraided them with their unbelief
and hardness of heart because they believed not them
which had seen Him after He was risen. And He said
unto them, Go ye into all the world, and preach the
Gospel to every creature. He that believeth and is baptized shall be saved; but he that believeth not shall be
damned." etc. (Mark 16 : 14-16). In Luke's Gospel we
are told that in conversing with the two disciples on

the way to Emmaus He said, "O fools, and slow of heart
to believe all that the prophets have spoken! Ought
not Christ to have suffered these things and to enter into
His glory? And beginning at Moses and all the prophets, He expounded unto them in all the Scriptures
the things concerning Himself" (Luke 24 : 25-27). And
also to the eleven apostles at Jerusalem He said, "These
are the words that I spake unto you while I was yet with
you, that all things must be fulfilled which were written
in the law of Moses, and in the prophets, and in the
Psalms concerning me. Then opened he their understanding that they might understand the Scriptures, and
said unto them, Thus it is written, and thus it behoved
Christ to suffer, and to rise from the dead the third day,
and that repentance and remission of sins should be
preached in His name among all nations, beginning at
Jerusalem. And ye are witnesses of these things. And,
behold, I send the promise of my Father upon you; but
tarry ye in the city of Jerusalem until ye be endued with
power from on high. And he led them out as far as to
Bethany, and he lifted up his hands and blessed them.
And it came to pass while he blessed them he was parted
from them and carried up into heaven. And they worshipped Him, and returned to Jerusalem with great joy;
and were continually in the temple, praising and blessing
God" (Luke 24 : 44-53). And in John's Gospel we read
of Him after His resurrection, "And many other signs
truly did Jesus in the presence of His disciples which
are not written in this book; but these are written that
ye might believe that Jesus is the Christ, the Son of God;
and that, believing, ye might have life through His
name" (John 20 : 30, 31).

Insidious Question by Professor Smith.

On page 176 Professor Goldwin Smith asks, " Did
Jesus give Himself out, or allow His followers to designate Him as the Messiah? It is impossible to tell. All
that we can say is that His disciples . . . desired to
identify Him with the hope of Israel, and applied, or

wrested, passages of the Old Testament to that intent."
This question reminds one forcibly of the question
which the serpent asked Eve in the garden, " Yea, hath
God said, Ye shall not eat of every tree of the garden ?"
And it is evident that the intention in putting both questions was the same: just to raise a doubt as to what God
had really said, when the questioner knew perfectly well
what the answer should be. It is impossible to suppose
that any man of Professor Goldwin Smith's intelligence
does not know what has already been fully shown by
the Scriptures quoted in this chapter, that throughout
His whole ministry the Lord Jesus Christ claimed to be
the Messiah, of the seed of David, and Son of God as
well as Son of man, and that His disciples thus regarded
Him. At His baptism in the Jordan and on the Mount
of Transfiguration the voice from heaven had said, "This
is my beloved Son." When on the ass's colt He entered
Jerusalem with the multitude shouting, " Hosanna to
the Son of David!" and " Blessed be the King of Israel,
that cometh in the name of the Lord," thus proclaiming
Him as the Messiah, did He not recognize that in doing
so they were simply fulfilling the prophetic word concerning Him ? He was condemned to death by the
chief priests because He said He was the Son of God;
and Pilate allowed Him to be crucified because He was
the King of the Jews; and He would not deny either
of these charges to save His life. The statement about
wresting Old Testament Scriptures to identify Him with
the hope of Israel has already been fully met in a previous chapter and is not worthy of further notice.

On page 139 he quotes approvingly from the author
of " Supernatural Religion " as follows : " The system
of Jesus might not be new, but it was in a high sense
the perfect development of natural morality, and it confined itself to two fundamental principles, love to God
and love to man." The writer of that book had perhaps not read the discourse of the Lord Jesus Christ
with Nicodemus, in the third chapter of John's Gospel,
in the course of which He told that honest enquirer that

he must be born again or never enter heaven. It is really a wonder how the author of "Supernatural Religion" (whoever he may be) could write such unmitigated nonsense in the face of the plainest statements of Scripture. There is really no such thing as natural morality, but natural immorality has often presented a respectable, and even refined, exterior, through the restraints of law and society, but especially of Christian civilization. Where these are wanting the natural immorality develops rapidly.

Incorrect Statement by Professor Smith.

On page 116 he says that, "Apart from the miraculous resurrection of Christ, and Christ's miraculous raisings from the dead, no one has been heard from after death." This is not correct. The Lord Jesus Christ Himself, who knew all things, told, in Luke 16 : 19-31, about a certain rich man and a beggar named Lazarus, who both died. The beggar was carried by the angels to Abraham's bosom, and the rich man was buried (and doubtless had a grand funeral), but in Hades he lifted up his eyes, being in torments, and saw Abraham afar off, and Lazarus in his bosom; and he cried out to have Lazarus sent to dip the tip of his finger in water, and cool his tongue, for he was tormented in that flame. This request was refused, and he then wanted some one sent back from the dead to warn his five brethren lest they also should come into that place of torment. But Abraham said to him, "If they hear not Moses and the prophets, neither will they be persuaded though one rose from the dead." It is perfectly safe to predict that if any one rose from the dead, and were to go through the world describing from his own experience the terrible doom of lost souls, who had died without being born again, he would be denounced as a lunatic or an imposter by Professor Goldwin Smith and all the "liberal theologians" and "higher critics."

The Professor wants Christianity without Christ Crucified.

After having done his best to destroy all faith in the miracles wrought by the Lord Jesus Christ, and denied that He was the Son of God or the promised Messiah, as He claimed to be, on page 187 Professor Goldwin Smith thus closes his essay on the "Miraculous Element in Christianity" with the following remarks upon the person of Jesus : " In His character there is no doubt a large element of sorrow, without which He would not have touched humanity. Yet we think too much of Jerusalem, and of the closing scene, with its agonies, its horrors, and the circle of dark, and even dreadful, dogma, which has been formed around it. We think too little of the preaching of the Word of Life, and of the land in which the Word of Life was preached. Let us sometimes draw a veil over the cross, banish from our imaginations Jerusalem and its temple, reeking with bloody sacrifices, its fanatical Judaism, its hypocritical Phariseeism, its throng of bigots yelling for a judicial murder. Let us learn to see the great Teacher of humanity in the happy days of His mission, while He gathers round Him the circle of loving disciples and of simple hearts, thirsting for the waters of life, in the village synagogue, on the summer hillside or lake shore, amidst the vines and oleanders and lilies of Galilee." Now that is a very beautiful and poetic peroration, but it reminds one too much of the kiss with which Judas betrayed his Master. The Word of God declares that " the preaching of the cross is to them that perish foolishness," and that the preaching of " Christ crucified was unto the Jews a stumbling-block, and unto the Greeks foolishness "; and it is so still. And Paul said that he was determined not to know anything amongst the Corinthians save Jesus Christ and Him crucified, and that he was with them in weakness and fear and much trembling, and his speech and his preaching were not with enticing words of man's wisdom, but in demonstration

of the Spirit and of power that their faith should not
stand in the wisdom of men, but in the power of God
(1 Cor. 2 : 2-5).

Untrue Statement Respecting Orthodox Theologians.

But the following extract from Professor Goldwin
Smith's book will, perhaps, give a better idea of its
insidious and dangerous character than anything else
that has been quoted notwithstanding his poetic references to Jesus as a mere man, and his professed recognition of a great Supreme Being, who somehow or other
rules this universe. On page 181 he says : " We have
done, too, forever with the mixture of Rabbinism and
Alexandrian theosophy with which Paul has been accused of overlaying the Christian faith. We may bid
farewell to his doctrine of Atonement. That doctrine is
bound up with the belief in the Fall of Adam, and the
Fall of Adam is now abandoned as a fact even by orthodox theologians, though they would fain substitute for
it some lapse of the human race from a more perfect
state without any proof either of the more perfect state
or of the lapse." As the learned Professor has not informed us what he thinks the original Christian faith
really was, and who it was that accused Paul of overlaying it with something that has obscured its lustre, we
are entirely in the dark as to the meaning of the first
sentence in this extract; but it may be remarked that all
true Christians are generally under the impression that
Paul, through the special revelations made to him by
the Lord Jesus Christ, was the instrument used in unfolding the Gospel of the grace of God more fully than
any other. If he wants to learn Paul's opinion of Jewish
Rabbinism in connection with Christianity, he should
read carefully the Epistle to the Galatians; and if he
wants to know what amount of sympathy there was
between him and the cultured intellectual theosophists
of Athens he should read Acts 17 : 18-34. " Then certain

philosophers of the Epicureans, and of the Stoics encountered him. And some said, What will this babbler say? other some, He seemeth to be a setter forth of strange gods; because he preached unto them Jesus and the resurrection. And they took him and brought him unto Areopagus, saying, May we know what this new doctrine whereof thou speakest is? for thou bringest strange things to our ears; we would know, therefore, what these things mean. . . . Then Paul stood in the midst of Mar's Hill, and said, Ye men of Athens, I perceive that in all things ye are too superstitious. For as I passed by and beheld your devotions, I found an altar with this inscription, To THE UNKNOWN GOD. Whom, therefore, ye ignorantly worship, him declare I unto you. . . . And the times of this ignorance God winked at; but now commandeth all men everywhere to repent; because he hath appointed a day, in the which he will judge the world in righteousness by that man whom he hath ordained; whereof he hath given assurance to all men, in that he raised him from the dead. And when they heard of the resurrection of the dead, some mocked; and others said, We will hear thee again of this matter. So Paul departed from among them. Howbeit certain men clave to him and believed; among the which was Dionysius, the Areopagite, and a woman named Damaris, anc others with them." So we see that Paul's preaching to the philosophers of either Greece or Alexandria was not likely to be acceptable to those proud men, who were so filled with self-conceit and self-sufficiency with their own intellectual attainments that they would not take the place of little children, without which "the great Teacher of humanity" had said that they could not enter into the kingdom of God. In his Epistle to the Colossians the same apostle warned them against philosophers thus: "Beware lest any man spoil you through philosophy and vain deceit, after the tradition of men, after the rudiments of the world, and not after Christ. For in Him dwelleth all the fulness of the Godhead bodily." As to the learned Professor bidding farewell

to the doctrine of the Atonement, that is of very little
consequence, as a mere intellectual belief of sound doctrine will not save any one.   There must be a personal
taking of shelter under the precious blood of Atonement
which Jesus shed upon Calvary before any lost sinner
(no matter how sound his creed may be) can possibly
escape the doom of the rich man in Hades, and have any
assurance of a blessed eternity with the Lord Jesus
Christ in glory.   As to the doctrine of the Atonement
being bound up with the Fall of Adam, he is quite correct, but he says what is untrue in stating that the Fall
of Adam is now abandoned as a fact by orthodox theologians, for no man could be orthodox who rejects the
testimony of the Word of God, which has been so plainly
given upon that point.   But he says that these orthodox
theologians, who are probably the same persons as the
" liberal theologians," would fain substitute some lapse
of the human race from a more perfect state, without any
proof either of the more perfect state, or of the lapse.
This is really a very extraordinary method of reasoning,
which makes confusion more confounded.   Is it to be
understood that Professor Drummond and other evolu-
tionist theological professors are among the persons to
whom he refers as " orthodox theologians," who would
fain substitute "some lapse of the human race from a
more perfect state" for the Fall of Adam, as it is recorded
in Scripture.   Surely they could not suppose that man
was in a more perfect state when in the condition of the
missing link, to which he had been evoluted from the
lower animals, than he is in now, since he attained such
a development of intellectual superiority and " natural
morality!"

The Son of God still Speaking to Men by the Written Word.

We have seen in this chapter that God spoke by His
Son to the chief priests, scribes, and rulers who composed the Sanhedrim, or highest representative body in

the Jewish nation, charging home to them and their
fathers their guilt in rejecting the testimony of His servants the prophets, whom He had sent to them. We
have seen how He spoke to the multitudes in Galilee
and in Judea by the miracles of mercy which He wrought
in their presence, and by His tender sympathy and
gracious words to all who were suffering and sorrowing,
weary and heavy laden. He has spoken in His triumphal entry into Jerusalem as the promised Messiah
amid the hosannas of the people; and in His rejection by
the chief priests, scribes, and rulers, as He had predicted
in the parable about the vineyard, which He addressed
to them. He has spoken in that loving address to
His disciples at the Passover feast, and in that earnest
prayer to the Father on their behalf. He has spoken
silently by His agony in Gethsemane, by His meek
and lowly bearing in the presence of His persecutors
and judges; when falsely accused, clothed with robes of
mock royalty, crowned with thorns, spit upon and
buffeted, with back lacerated by the cruel scourges of
his enemies; by His dreadful sufferings on the cross,
His prayer for His murderers, and His care for His
mother in those awful hours when darkness overspread
the earth and that cry came from His lips, " My God!
my God! why hast thou forsaken me ?" He has spoken
by those words, " It is finished," when He bowed His
head and died for sins that were not His own, and
thus made full Atonement by offering Himself up as the
great Sacrifice for sin, of which all previous sacrifices
had been only types and shadows; 'for it was not possible for the blood of bulls and goats to take-away sins
(Heb. 10 : 4). He has spoken, after His resurrection, by the wounds in His hands and His side which
He showed to His disciples, by His instructions to them
from the writings of Moses, from the Psalms and from
the prophets as to the things therein concerning Himself, by His commission to preach the Gospel to every
creature, and by the assurance that all power is given unto
Him, and that He will be with us alway, even unto the

end of the world. And He has also spoken by His ascension into heaven, and by the assurance then given to those who witnessed it, from the two men in white apparel, " This same Jesus, which is taken up from you into heaven, shall so come in like manner as ye have seen him go into heaven " (Acts 1 : 11).

The promise given by the Lord Jesus Christ to His disciples the night on which He was betrayed was fulfilled when the Holy Spirit descended at Pentecost and filled the waiting disciples, and brought to their remembrance all things that He had said unto them, and guided them into all truth. Through the same blessed Teacher and Comforter other truths were also revealed to them concerning that wonderful redemption through which, out of Jew and Gentile, His Church was to be formed; and the mystery was thus revealed which had been kept secret since the world began (Rom. 16 : 25). The things thus brought to their remembrance, and revealed to the apostles and prophets in the early Church, have been embodied, as we have before seen, in the writings of the New Testament Scriptures, and through them God is still speaking to us by His Son, and is by the Holy Spirit guiding us into all truth, testifying to us of Christ, and showing us things to come.

In future chapters we shall consider some of those truths which God reveals to us by the Holy Spirit through His Word.

CHAPTER V.

GOD'S PURPOSE IN CREATION.

THE solution of the " Riddle of Existence " has been revealed in the Word of God, and cannot be otherwise or elsewhere discovered. In Rev. 4 and 5 is presented a wonderful vision, seen by the Apostle John in the Isle of Patmos, of things that must be hereafter. A door was opened in heaven, and a voice called to him, " Come up hither, and I will show thee things which must be hereafter." The first thing he saw was a throne set in heaven, and one sat on the throne, and he that sat was to look upon like a jasper and a sardine stone, and there was a rainbow round about the throne like unto an emerald, and round about the throne were four and twenty seats; and upon the seats were four and twenty elders sitting, clothed in white raiment; and they had on their heads crowns of gold. And out of the throne proceeded lightnings, and thunderings and voices; and there were seven lamps of fire burning before the throne, which are the seven Spirits of God; and before the throne there was a glassy sea (R.V.) like unto crystal, and in the midst of the throne, and round about the throne, were four living creatures (R.V.) full of eyes before and behind. And the first living creature was like a lion, and the second living creature like a calf, and the third living creature had a face as a man, and the fourth living creature was like a flying eagle. And the four living creatures had each of them six wings about him, and they were full of eyes within; and they rest not day and night, saying, " Holy, holy, holy, Lord God Almighty, which was, and is, and is to come." And when those living creatures give glory and honour and thanks to him that sat on the throne, who liveth forever and ever, the four and twenty elders fall down before him that sat on the throne, and

worship him that liveth forever and ever, and cast their
crowns before the throne, saying, "Thou art worthy, O
Lord, to receive glory and honour and power, for THOU
HAST CREATED ALL THINGS, AND FOR THY PLEASURE THEY
ARE AND WERE CREATED."

All Things Created for the Pleasure of the Creator.

This book is the last in the Bible; it is the revelation of Jesus Christ, which He gave to His servant,
John, and in this fourth chapter we have the beginning
of the revelation of those things that are to be hereafter.
It is a wonderful picture that is here presented to us. As
a matter of course the language used is symbolical, for
earthly speech would fail to describe celestial glories,
more especially the uncreated and inexpressible majesty
of the Great Being who rules the universe, and who is
described as being enthroned, and the object of the
adoring worship of all who are round about Him.
But who are those represented by the four and twenty
elders, sitting round about His throne with crowns of
gold upon their heads ? This is explained in the next
chapter where we read, "And I saw in the right hand of
Him that sat on the throne a book written within, and
on the back side, sealed with seven seals, and I saw a
strong angel proclaiming with a loud voice, Who is
worthy to open the book, and to loose the seals thereof ?
And no man in heaven nor in earth, neither under the
earth, was able to open the book, neither to look thereon.
And I wept much because no man was found worthy to
open and to read the book, neither to look thereon. And
one of the elders saith unto me, Weep not; behold, the
Lion of the tribe of Judah hath prevailed to open the
book, and to loose the seven seals thereof. And I beheld,
and lo! in the midst of the throne, and of the four living
creatures, and in the midst of the elders, stood a Lamb
as it had been slain, having seven horns and seven eyes,
which are the seven Spirits of God sent forth into all
the earth. And he came and took the book out of the

right hand of him that sat upon the throne. And when he had taken the book, the four living creatures and the four and twenty elders fell down before the Lamb, having every one of them harps, and golden vials full of odours, which are the prayers of saints. And they sung a new song, saying, Thou art worthy to take the book, and to open the seals thereof; for thou wast slain, and hast redeemed us to God by thy blood, out of every kindred and tongue, and people and nation, and hast made us unto our God kings and priests, and we shall reign on the earth " (Rev. 5 : 1-10).

There is no doubt, therefore, that the four and twenty elders " redeemed to God by the blood of the Lamb out of every kindred and tongue, and people and nation," represent the risen saints of all ages, twelve patriarchs of the old dispensation, and twelve apostles of the new, all raised to a place of glory such as no angel had ever enjoyed, seated and crowned in the very presence of God, while the four living creatures rest not day and night in their worship and service, saying, " Holy, holy, holy, Lord God Almighty, which was, and is, and is to come." The example of the four living creatures is followed by the four and twenty elders representing all the redeemed from earth, who fall down before Him that sat on the throne, and worship Him that liveth for ever and ever, and cast their crowns before the throne, saying, " Thou art worthy, O Lord, to receive glory, and honour, and power, for thou hast created all things, and *for thy pleasure* they are and were created." This is the purpose for which God created all things, animate and inanimate: for His own pleasure; and thus "The Riddle of Existence " is solved by the revelation of Jesus Christ from heaven speaking by His redeemed and glorified saints through His servant, John.

Man Created for God's Glory.

But whilst it is true, as we have seen, that all things in this vast universe were created by God for His own pleasure, there is an infinitely higher purpose which He

had in view in the creation of man in His own image
(Gen. 1 : 27). In Isa. 43 : 1-7 we read, " But now thus
saith the Lord that created thee, O Jacob, and he that
formed thee, O Israel, Fear not; for I have redeemed
thee, I have called thee by thy name; thou art mine.
. . . I will say to the north, Give up; and to the
south, Keep not back; bring my sons from far, and my
daughters from the ends of the earth, even every one
that is called by my name; for I HAVE CREATED HIM FOR
MY GLORY. I have formed him; yea, I have made him."

From both the Scriptures that have been quoted we
learn, that while all things were created by God for His
own *pleasure*, man was created for His *glory*. While it
is true, therefore, as we read in Psalm 19 : 1 that the
heavens declare the glory of God, and the firmament
showeth His handiwork "; there is a very special sense
in which man, created in the image of God, has been
formed for His glory, as we read in Heb. 2 : 6-8, " But
one in a certain place testified, saying, What is man
that thou are mindful of him ? or the son of man, that
thou visitest him ? Thou madest him for a little while
(marginal reading) lower than the angels ; thou
crownedst him with glory and honour, and didst set him
over the works of thy hands; thou hast put all things
in subjection under his feet." And this corresponds
with the original purpose of God as expressed in Gen.
1: 26, 27, "And God said, Let us make man in our image,
after our likeness; and let them have dominion over the
fish of the sea, and over the fowl of the air, and over
the cattle, and over all the earth, and over every creeping thing that creepeth upon the earth. So God created
man in his own image: in the image of God created he
him; male and female created he them."

Earth as the Chosen Scene of Incarnation and Redemption.

We know not how many ages elapsed between the
beginning, spoken of in Gen. 1 : 1, when God created
the heaven and the earth, and the time referred to in

Gen. 1 : 2, when the earth was without form and void, and the present condition of things on its surface was called into being; or what change, at this latter epoch, it may have sustained in its relation to other parts of the universe. Nor does it concern us much to know how it is that such a comparatively small planet as this earth, should occupy such a large place in the purposes of the great Creator and Upholder of all those heavenly bodies, rolling through illimitable space, of whose number and magnitude we can only get but a faint conception by the naked eye, and even with the most powerful telescope. It is sufficient for us to be informed by His Word that it has pleased Him to make this little planet of ours the scene of transactions "which the angels desire to look into" (1 Peter 1 : 12). There is an affectation of humility in the way that some modern skeptics speak about the improbability of the Great Being who rules the universe taking so much interest in this earth as the Word of God declares that He does; and they make this a pretext for doubting the authenticity of Divine revelation. Dr. Chalmers very truly said, "There is an imposing splendour in the science of astronomy; and it is not to be wondered at if the light it throws, or appears to throw, over other tracks of speculation than those which are properly its own should at times dazzle and mislead an enquirer. On this account we think it were a service to what we deem a true and righteous cause could we succeed in dissipating this illusion, and in stripping infidelity of those pretensions to enlargement, and to a certain air of philosophical greatness by which it has often become so destructively alluring to the young, and the ardent, and the ambitious."

There is no reason whatever why God should not make this planet, as well as any other, the theatre on which He should choose to display not only His creative power, but also the wonders of His grace, as revealed in the atoning sacrifice of the Lord Jesus Christ. Nor have infidel writers any right to assume that only this planet reaps any benefit from His work of redemption when we are informed that " every creature which is in heaven, and on the earth, and under the earth, and such as are in the sea, and all that are in them were heard saying, Blessing, and honour, and glory, and power be unto him that sitteth upon the throne, and unto the Lamb for ever and ever " (Rev. 5 : 13).

Cool Proposition of Professor Smith.

On page 103 Professor Goldwin Smith says : " We must clear our minds of geocentricism (which, in plain English, means having reference to the earth as a centre), and of Mosaic beginning and Apocaliptic end of things; float out into the universe we see in a star-lit night, in which we see ourselves as but living and conscious atoms. To fathom the mystery of the universe; that is, the mystery of existence, we cannot hope." Now, the great mistake that the learned Professor makes is in proposing to clear his mind of the Mosaic beginning and the Apocaliptic end of the Bible ; for without the one we could have no authentic records of the Creation, and of the early history of the human race; and without the other we would not have that wonderful revelation of Jesus Christ telling us of the future glory of the redeemed, and of those terrible judgments which are to come upon all Christ rejectors after the Church is taken away. And as to floating out into the universe on a star-lit night, and trying to fathom the mystery there, it will be utterly useless without the aid of that Divine revelation which he esteems so lightly. In Job 11 : 7 we read, " Canst thou by searching find out God ? Canst thou find out the Almighty to perfection ?" And in Job 36 : 26, " Behold, God is great. We know Him not, neither can the number of his years be searched out." And again, " Hast thou heard the secret of God ? and dost thou restrain wisdom to thyself ?" (Job 15 : 8). And in Deut. 29 : 29 we read, " The secret things belong unto the Lord our God ; but those things that are revealed belong unto us and to our children for ever, that we may do all the words of this law." The fact is that whilst infidel writers profess to be so lost in contemplating the wonders of the universe and the greatness of the Deity as to regard themselves as only "living and conscious atoms," they are unwilling to take the place of little children, and learn in God's school by the teaching of the Holy Spirit, through His Word, what are His purposes in Creation, which can never be discovered by either intellectual power or scientific research. On this point the following Scriptures should be carefully studied :

Touching the Almighty we cannot find Him out; He is excellent in power, and in judgment, and in plenty of justice (Job 37 : 23).

Thy way is in the sea, and thy path in the great waters, and thy footsteps are not known (Psalm 77 : 19).

Great is the Lord, and greatly to be praised; and his greatness is unsearchable (Psalm 145 : 3).

For my thoughts are not your thoughts, neither are your ways my ways, saith the Lord. For as the heavens are higher than the earth, so are my ways than your ways, and my thoughts than your thoughts (Isa. 55 : 8, 9).

Verily I say unto you, Except ye be converted and become as little children, ye shall not enter into the kingdom of heaven (Matt. 18 : 3).

Oh, the depth of the riches both of the wisdom and knowledge of God! How unsearchable are his judgments, and his ways past finding out! For who hath known the mind of the Lord ? and who hath been his counsellor ? (Rom. 11 : 33, 34).

Let no man deceive himself. If any man among you seemeth to be wise in this world let him become a fool that he may be wise (1 Cor. 3 : 18).

For if a man thinketh himself to be something, when he is nothing, he deceiveth himself (Gal. 6 : 3).

Beware lest any man spoil you through philosophy and vain deceit, after the tradition of men, after the rudiments of the world, and not after Christ (Col. 2 : 8).

O Timothy, keep that which is committed to thy trust, avoiding profane and vain babblings, and oppositions of science, falsely so called (1 Tim. 6 : 20).

While we cannot help admiring the wonders of the universe, so far as they have been revealed to us by astronomical science, we must bear in mind that God has also revealed to us in His Word, that there are more worlds than this earth which we inhabit. We read in Heb. 1 : 1, 2, "God who, at sundry times, and in divers manners, spake in times past unto the fathers by the prophets, hath in these last days spoken unto us by His Son, whom He hath appointed heir of all things, by whom also He made the worlds"; and again in Heb. 11 : 3, "Through faith we understand that the worlds were framed by the Word of God." But it does not seem to be the part of true wisdom to be so much occupied with other planets, and their possible inhabitants, as to shut our eyes to those wonderful things which God has revealed to us in the Scriptures regarding Himself and His purposes concerning the human race, upon the right apprehension of which our eternal destiny depends for either happiness or misery.

As Creator, God is Absolute.

As we have already seen, God's purpose in creating all things was for His own pleasure; and as Creator He became the absolute master of all that He created. The creature never had any rights whatever as against the will of the Creator; and this is plainly taught in the Word of God as we read in Isa. 29 : 15, 16, "Woe unto them that seek deep to hide their counsel from the Lord, and their works in the dark, and they say, Who seeth us ? and who knoweth us ? Surely your turning of things upside down shall be esteemed as the potter's clay; for shall the work say of Him that made it, He made me not ? or shall the thing formed say of Him that formed it, He hath no understanding ?" And again, in Isa. 45 : 9, "Woe unto him that striveth with his Maker! Let the potsherd strive with the potsherds of the earth. Shall the clay say to Him that fashioneth it, What makest thou ? or thy work, He hath no hands ?" And also in Rom. 9 : 17-21, "Therefore hath He mercy on whom He will, and whom He will He hardeneth. Thou wilt say then to me, Why doth He yet find fault, for who hath resisted His will ? Nay, but O man, who art thou that repliest against God ? Shall the thing formed say of Him that formed it. Why hast thou made me thus ? Hath not the potter power over the clay, of the same lump to make one vessel unto honour, and another unto dishonour ?"

Man has Failed to Glorify God.

But in the creation of man we have also seen that God had a still higher purpose. In the creation of other living creatures He spoke them into existence, and then commanded them to be fruitful and multiply in the earth, and God saw that all was good, and He had pleasure in His works. In the case of man, made in His own image, after His own likeness, we have a repetition, in greater detail, of his creation in Gen. 2, in which it is stated, "And the Lord God formed man of the dust of the ground; and breathed into his nostrils the breath of life; and man became a living soul" (Gen. 2 : 7). Thus, by the very breath of God, there was communicated to him a life that was infinitely higher than that of other earthly creatures. They had existence, and in their existence God had pleasure. But man had received life from God, in whose image he was formed, and, as viceroy of God over this fair earth, he had dominion over all other creatures; and God "brought them unto Adam to see what he would call them; and whatsoever Adam called every living creature, that was the name thereof" (Gen. 2 : 19). We have seen from Isa. 43 : 1-7 that man was created for God's glory, and from a being so highly favoured and endowed, and possessed of a holy nature and a free will, God had a right to expect implicit faith and perfect obedience. But sin came in through Satan in the form of a serpent tempting Eve, and through her

tempting Adam. And they came under the sentence of
death, which had been pronounced as the penalty of their
disobedience. While still continuing to exist as animate
and rational creatures, they lost the life that had been
breathed into them by God, and became dead in sin;
and, as those thereafter possessed of evil natures, they
communicated evil natures to all their posterity. And
so we read in 1 Cor. 15 : 22, " For as in Adam all die,"
etc., and again in Rom. 5 : 14, " Nevertheless, death
reigned from Adam to Moses," etc.

Man's Fallen Nature Utterly Corrupt.

This is a very unpalatable truth to unconverted men,
who have never seen the utter corruption of their own
fallen natures, and, therefore, rebel against the thought
that they are wholly unable to earn the favour of God
by any merit of their own. They try to persuade themselves that there is some germ of goodness about them,
which only needs to be cultivated and developed in order
to make them pleasing in His sight, before whom, conscience tells them, they must some time give an account
of the deeds done in the body. But, rather than take the
place now of guilty, ruined sinners before Him, many
prefer to try and persuade themselves that the record
which tells them of their true condition is only a myth,
and that the Bible, which contains it, is not a Divine
revelation from God to man.

If a man makes a complicated machine, he will take
pleasure in it just in proportion as it fulfills the end for
which it was made, and if it does not do this he has a
perfect right to destroy it. But if he could impart life
to it, with conscience, reason, and a free will, he would
expect more from it; and he would naturally feel very
indignant if, instead of obeying his word, it were to
thwart his plans, dishonour his name, and insult him to
his face. No man would submit to such treatment. He
would either destroy what he had made or inflict upon
it the severest punishment. And yet men seem to think
that God is an easy, good-natured Being, who is all love,

without any sense of justice, and who made them to live for their own pleasure and not for His, and will, therefore, allow them to disobey Him with impunity. For this reason they do not like the God of the Bible, who therein reveals Himself as a Being of spotless purity, who will judge His creatures righteously and punish them for their sins. As a just and holy God, in dealing with the nations of this world, He has frequently made them the means of chastising each other for their sins against Him, as we find by the records of Scripture; and these men profess to stand aghast at the deeds of cruelty which were thus committed; and point to passages in which God's terrible judgments have been visited upon various peoples in the course of His governmental dealings with them, and ask if we expect them to believe that God desired such things to come to pass, although His Word has plainly declared it; and He alone, who knew all the circumstances, was best able to judge what punishment was needed.

Professor Smith Objects to God's Manner of Punishing Sin.

On page 66 Professor Goldwin Smith says that we are in no way bound to believe that God so identified Himself with one family as to license it to invade other tribes and slaughter them: or that He rebuked His chosen people for saving alive the women and children of the Midianites.

On page 68 he objects in like manner to the slaughter of the Canaanites, the killing of Sisera, the assassination of Eglon, the hewing of Agag to pieces by Samuel, the prophet of the Lord. Elijah's massacre of the prophets of Baal, who were leading Israel away from the worship of Jehovah, and the hanging of Haman upon the gallows which he had erected for Mordecai.

He seems to have overlooked the fact that in these and many other cases there is an entire absence of personal malice on the part of those who were carrying out

what they believed to be the will of God upon His enemies. It is quite true that God could have rained down
fire from heaven upon them as He did upon Sodom and
Gomorrah if He had chosen that method of punishing
the parties referred to for their sins. But He chose other
means, and it would be very presumptuous in us to
question the wisdom and the justice of His actions
whether we understand them or not.

On page 68 he admires David, and accepts him as
the author of the Psalms, some of which, he remarks
on page 77, are spiritual as well as lyrical, and others
shocking. Now, in order to understand the language
used in some of the Psalms it is needful to bear in mind
that Israel was a theocratic kingdom, over which David
was reigning as the representative of Jehovah, and that
in the Psalms which appear to show a vindictive spirit
towards His enemies there is not a particle of personal
malice on his part; but as the mouthpiece of Jehovah
he speaks of God's enemies as if they were his own, and
thus cries for judgment on the wicked who are opposing
His holy will.

His Attempt to Disparage the Character of Christ Because of David's Sin.

On page 68 he also refers to David's great sin in the
matter of Uriah, the Hittite, but fails to point out how
speedily the judgment of God came upon him on account
of that sin, as recorded in 2 Samuel, "And Nathan said
to David, Thou art the man. Thus saith the Lord God
of Israel, I anointed thee king over Israel, and I delivered thee out of the hand of Saul. . . Wherefore
hast thou despised the commandment of the Lord to do
evil in His sight ? Thou hast killed Uriah, the Hittite,
with the sword, and hast taken his wife to be thy wife,
and hast slain him with the sword of the children of
Ammon. Now, therefore, the sword shall never depart
from thine house; because thou hast despised me, and
hast taken the wife of Uriah, the Hittite, to be thy wife."

When his sin was thus brought home to him David was humbled before God, his life was spared, and the sin put away, but the evil consequences remained. The child born to him by Bathsheba had to die, the sword did not depart from his house as long as he lived ; and the enemies of God have ever since made a handle of David's terrible sin to blaspheme the name of David's God, notwithstanding His speedy judgment upon the sin. In the face of these facts, and without mentioning them, the following remarks on page 68 by Professor Goldwin Smith on this subject are, to say the least, in extremely bad taste; although, as usual, the language used is not offensive. He says that David " was guilty of murder and adultery in the first degree; put to death with tortures the people of a captured city; on his deathbed bequeathed to his son a murderous legacy of vengeance, and shuts up his ten concubines for life," and then he adds " that it is not possible that the issues of spiritual life are so shut up that from this man's loins salvation should spring." The real attack made here so insidiously is upon David's Son, the Lord Jesus Christ, who is yet to sit upon David's throne, and through whom alone, as the sinner's substitute, in the work of Atonement salvation is to be found. The angel who announced His conception to Mary said, "That holy thing that shall be born of thee shall be called the Son of God"; and we read in Heb. 7 : 26 that He was " holy, harmless, undefiled, separate from sinners, and made higher than the heavens." The manner in which the learned Professor groups together David's real sin, which God severely condemned and punished; and for which David, after confession, obtained forgiveness; along with acts which he commanded to be done, in pursuance of his rightful authority as Jehovah's representative in executing judgment upon the sins of others, shows a deliberate intention not only to blacken the whole character of David himself, but also to make it appear that the Lord Jesus Christ, having come from such a polluted source, it is not likely that salvation should be alone through Him;

and, therefore, the allusion to David is only a pretext for a most insidious attack upon the person of the Lord Jesus Christ.

God Never Excuses Sin.

God never excuses sin, even in the cases of His most honoured servants. Sin must either be punished or atoned for, and without atonement forgiveness cannot be obtained. God has said that He " will by no means clear the guilty," and that " the soul that sinneth shall die." He cannot lie, and the sentence of judgment must be executed, either now or hereafter. Because of his sin Moses, the servant of God, with whom " God talked face to face as a man with his friend," could not enter the promised land; and David, because of his sin, was obliged to have war in his house all his days, and could not build the temple to Jehovah; and so with all, or nearly all, of God's chosen servants, we find sin and failure everywhere except in the case of the Lord Jesus Christ Himself, to whose charge no sin has ever been laid. In this respect the Bible is different from any other book. There is no attempt in it to cover over sin of any kind, no matter who may be implicated.

Only One Perfect Sinless Man.

God created man for His own glory, but there has been only one man who, looking back on the past, and about to leave this world, could lift up his eyes to the Father in heaven, and say, " I have glorified thee on the earth " (John 17 : 4): " I have finished the work which thou gavest me to do," and that was the Lord Jesus Christ. Paul was able to give a satisfactory testimony when he said, " I am now ready to be offered, and the time of my departure is at hand. I have fought a good fight. I have finished my course. I have kept the faith; henceforth there is laid up for me a crown of righteousness, which the Lord, the righteous judge, shall give me at that day; and not to me only, but unto all them that love his appearing" (2 Tim. 4 : 6-8); but he could not say of his whole life : " I have glorified God "; and wherein he failed at any time in this purpose of his existence he had sinned; but he could rejoice that the sin was put away by the atoning sacrifice of Christ, in whom he believed.

In Matt. 22 : 36-40 we read of a lawyer asking the Lord Jesus Christ : " Master, which is the great commandment in the law ? Jesus said unto him, Thou shalt love the Lord thy God with all thy heart, and with all thy soul, and with all thy mind. This is the first and great commandment. And the second is like unto it : Thou shalt love thy neighbour as thy self. On these two commandments hang all the law and the prophets." These are the words of the "Great Teacher of humanity," regarding whom, on page 184, Professor Goldwin Smith makes the following remarks: "Among the teachings of Jesus recorded in the Gospels, learning, literature, and science have no place. To the mind of Jesus, had they presented themselves, they would probably have seemed entirely alien. The simplicity of the child and the spiritual insight of poverty were, in His eyes, superior to the wisdom of the wise. In this respect His thorough-going disciples have generally reflected the image of their Master." Some readers may be inclined to suspect that there is a vein of sarcasm in these remarks, but truer words were never written, and it is refreshing to find something in the learned Professor's book which can be endorsed where there is so much that has to be disputed. In His answer to the lawyer's question the Lord Jesus Christ summed up, in the very simplest manner, what God has a right to expect from men whom He created for His own glory : that they should love Him " with all the heart, and soul, and mind."

Professor Smith's Opinion About the Soul of Man.

The Professor says, on page 102, regarding the soul : " Science (Darwinian and general) has put an end to the traditional belief in the soul as being separate from the body, breathed into it by a distinct act of the Creator." Science may have had this effect with him, and perhaps also with some of the so-called "liberal theologians," but certainly not with true Christians, as his remark would seem to imply. They have a much higher source of information in the unerring Word of God. It is true that the word "soul" is sometimes used as an interchangeable term for "life," and is often used to designate the whole person, as, for instance, in Acts 27 : 37, "And we were, in all, in the ship, two hundred threescore and sixteen souls." But there are many other passages in which the soul is mentioned as distinct from the body, the mind, the heart, or the life. Look, for example, at the following :

My soul is weary of my life (Job 10 : 1).

But his flesh upon him shall have pain, and his soul within him shall mourn (Job 14 : 22).

Why art thou cast down, O my soul ? and why art thou disquieted within me ? (Psa. 42 : 11).

So shall they be life unto thy soul (Prov. 3 : 22).

Behold, all souls are mine: as the soul of the father, so also the soul of the son is mine; the soul that sinneth it shall die (Ezek. 18 : 4).

Incline your ear and come unto me; hear, and your soul shall live (Isa. 55 : 3).

And fear not them which kill the body, but are not able to kill the soul, but rather fear him who is able to destroy both soul and body in hell (Matt. 10 : 28).

For what is a man profited if he shall gain the whole world, and lose his own soul (or life) ? or what shall a man give in exchange for his own soul (or life)? (Matt. 16 : 26).

But God shall say to him, Thou fool! this night thy soul (or life) shall be required of thee (Luke 12 : 20).

Now is my soul troubled; and what shall I say ? (John 12 : 27).

Because thou wilt not leave my soul in Hades, neither wilt thou suffer thine Holy One to see corruption (Acts 2 : 27).

He (David) seeing this before, spake of the resurrection of Christ, that his soul was not left in Hades, neither his flesh did see corruption (Acts 2 : 31).

And the very God of peace sanctify you wholly; and I pray God your whole spirit, and soul, and body be preserved blameless unto the coming of our Lord Jesus Christ (1 Thess. 5 : 23).

But we are not of them who draw back unto perdition, but of them that believe to the saving of the soul (Heb. 10 : 39).

Beloved, I wish above all things that thou mayest prosper and be in health even as they soul prospereth (3 John 2).

And I saw the souls of them that were beheaded for the witness of Jesus, and for the Word of God . . . and they lived and reigned with Christ a thousand years (Rev. 20 : 4).

The information contained in the above texts about the soul of man is much more reliable than anything that Mr. Darwin could furnish.

God, in His Word, Invariably Requires that Man Should Glorify Him.

As we have already seen, the Lord Jesus Christ declared that the first and great commandment is, "Thou shalt love the Lord thy God with all thy heart, and with all thy soul, and with all thy mind." Nothing less than this will satisfy the Creator, who has formed man for His own glory. And any failure to come up to this standard is sin, which can only be forgiven on the ground of atonement made. The supreme conceit which leads men who have not glorified God to talk as if He were under some obligations to them, to consult their wishes or promote their happiness, is really extraordinary: and the presumption with which they sit in judgment upon His character and governmental dealings with the human race is still more amazing, and can only be accounted for by their total blindness to what His Word declares

He requires. Look, for instance, at a few passages of Scripture in this connection :

This is it that the Lord spake, saying, I will be sanctified in them that come nigh me, and before all the people I will be glorified (Lev. 10 : 3).

O Lord, thou hast increased the nation, thou art glorified (Isa. 26 : 15).

Thus saith the Lord God . . . I will be glorified in the midst of thee (Ezek. 28 : 22).

Yea, all the people of the land shall bury them, and it shall be to them a renown, the day that I shall be glorified, saith the Lord God (Ezek. 39 : 13).

Thus saith the Lord of hosts, Consider your ways. Go up to the mountain, and bring wood and build the house (*i.e.*, the temple); and I will take pleasure in it, and I will be glorified, saith the Lord (Haggai 1 : 7, 8).

And said unto me, Thou art my servant, O Israel, in whom I will be glorified (Isaiah 49 : 3).

Thy people also shall be all righteous: they shall inherit the land forever, the branch of my planting, the work of my hands, that I may be glorified (Isa. 60 : 21).

Ye that fear the Lord, praise him; all ye, the seed of Jacob glorify him (Psa. 22 : 23).

I will deliver thee, and thou shalt glorify me (Psa. 50 : 15).

Whoso offereth praise glorifieth me (Psa. 50 : 23).

All nations whom thou hast made shall come and worship before thee, O Lord ; and shall glorify thy name (Psa. 86 : 9).

I will praise thee, O Lord my God, with all my heart; and I will glorify thy name for evermore (Psa. 86 : 12).

Therefore shall the strong people glorify thee (Isa. 25 : 3) . . . for the Holy One of Israel, for He hath glorified thee (Isa. 55 : 5) . . . and to the Holy One of Israel, because He hath glorified thee (Isa. 60 : 9).

And in the New Testament Scriptures the glorifying of God occupies as prominent a place as in the Old, as we see by the following passages :

Let your light so shine before men, that they may see your good works, and glorify your Father which is in heaven (Matt. 5 : 16). .

And they glorified the God of Israel (Matt. 15 : 31).

They were all amazed, and glorified God (Mark 2: 12).

And the shepherds returned, glorifying and praising God (Luke 2 : 20).

And He taught in their synagogues, being glorified of all (Luke 4 : 15).

And they were all amazed, and they glorified God (Luke 5 : 26).

And they glorified God, saying that a great prophet is risen up (Luke 7 : 16).

And immediately she was made straight, and glorified God (Luke 13 : 13).

And one of them, when he saw that he was healed, turned back and with a loud voice glorified God (Luke 17 : 15).

And Jesus said unto him, Receive thy sight; thy faith hath saved thee; and immediately he received his sight, and followed him, glorifying God; and all the people when they saw it gave praise unto God (Luke 18 : 42, 43).

Father, glorify thy name. Then came a voice from heaven, saying, I have both glorified it, and will glorify it again (John 12 : 28).

Jesus said, Now is the Son of man glorified, and God is glorified in him (John 13 : 31).

And whatsoever ye shall ask in my name, that will I do, that the Father may be glorified in the Son (John 14 : 13).

Herein is my Father glorified, that ye bear much fruit (John 15 : 8).

And all mine are thine; and thine are mine; and I am glorified in them (John 17 : 10).

This spake he, signifying by what death he should glorify God (John 21 : 19).

The God of Abraham . . . hath glorified his Son Jesus (Acts 3 : 13).

For all men glorified God for that which was done. For the man was above forty years old on whom this miracle of healing was shewed (Acts 4 : 21).

When they heard these things they held their peace and glorified God, saying, Then hath God also to the Gentiles granted repentance unto life (Acts 11 : 18).

And when they heard it they glorified the Lord (Acts 21 : 20).

Because that, when they knew God, they glorified him not as God, neither were thankful, but became vain in their imaginations, and their foolish heart was darkened; professing themselves to be wise, they became fools (Rom. 1 : 21, 22).

That ye may, with one mind and one mouth, glorify God, even the Father of our Lord Jesus Christ. Wherefore receive ye one another as Christ also received us to the glory of God (Rom. 15 : 6, 7).

That the Gentiles may glorify God for his mercy (Rom. 15 : 10).

For ye are bought with a price; therefore glorify God in your body (1 Cor. 6 : 20).

They glorify God for your professed subjection to the Gospel of Christ (2 Cor. 9 : 13).

And they glorified God in me (Gal. 1 : 24).

So also Christ glorified not Himself (Heb. 5 : 5).

They may by your good works, which they shall behold, glorify God in the day of visitation (1 Peter 2 : 12).

That God in all things may be glorified through Jesus Christ, to whom be praise and dominion for ever and ever (1 Peter 4 : 11).

On their part he is evil spoken of, but on your part he is glorified (1 Peter 4 : 14).

Yet if any man suffer as a Christian, let him not be ashamed; but let him glorify God on this behalf (1 Peter 4 : 16).

And they sing the song of Moses, the servant of God, and the song of the Lamb, saying, Great and marvellous are thy works, Lord God Almighty; just and true are thy ways, thou King of saints. Who shall not fear thee, O Lord, and glorify thy name ? for thou only art holy (Rev. 15 : 3, 4).

It is instructive to read over these Scriptures, and mark in what a variety of ways men may glorify God. This is the purpose for which they were created; for this they are allowed to exist on this earth and have been endowed with faculties, which, if rightly used, will enable them to glorify their Creator in their lives, here and now. But if, through pride and self-will, they refuse to obey Him, or believe His Word, they are condemned already. and He will be glorified in the execution of the righteous sentence of His broken laws. " The soul that sinneth, it shall die." Not the mere natural death of the body; but the second death in the lake of fire, into which are to be cast all whose names are not written in the Book of Life, including the fearful, and *unbelieving*, the abominable, and murderers, and whore mongers and sorcerers, and all liars (Rev. 21 : 8).

Only one man, as has been already remarked, could ever look back upon His whole life here and truthfully say, " I have glorified Thee on the earth." But all the redeemed, both in the Old and New Testament dispensations, have in some measure glorified God, if it was in nothing else than believing His Word, and accepting the full salvation purchased for them by the atoning sacrifice of the Lord Jesus Christ, and pressed upon their acceptance as a free gift. Only such have life in the proper sense of the word. All others only exist, and that they will continue to exist in a state of hopeless misery after the death of the body is plainly taught in the Word of God.

General Ignorance About the Nature of Sin.

In the light of God's requirements from man as the Creator it is astonishing what ignorance generally prevails as to the nature of sin, in the sight of a just and holy God, who knows the secret motives that prompt to every action. For the preservation of order in society it is necessary that severe penalties should follow the commission of certain crimes; but we have no right to assume that the sins which are most severely punished by men are more heinous in the sight of God than those which are not punished by men at all. The fearful, and unbelieving, and all liars, are to be cast into the same lake of fire with murderers, whoremongers, sorcerers, and idolators (Rev. 21 : 8). As a matter of fact, the greatest sins of which any human being can be guilty are those which most directly affect the character and person of God Himself. And thus it is a most heinous sin to make Him a liar by doubting His Word, and rejecting His Son and that salvation which He has purchased by the shedding of His precious blood. It is quite possible for a man to be a respectable member of society, intellectual, refined, genial, and benevolent, and at the same time to be a bitter enemy of God, as He has revealed Himself in the written Word and in the person of His incarnate Son; and to be guilty of idolatry, in making a god for himself after the imagination of his own heart, which he professes to worship. It will be apparent to any one who carefully searches the Scriptures that unbelief of His Word, rebellion, and idolatry are the sins which God has always most strongly condemned and most severely punished. Men are not going to be dealt with hereafter so much according to the way in which they have treated their fellow-creatures as according to the way in which they have acted towards their Creator, to whose long suffering they are indebted for continued existence. They may point with a sneer to the sins of David, which God severely punished and David bitterly repented of; but they omit to notice how loyal he was to God throughout his whole life, how he reverenced the Word of God, and wrote those inspired Psalms which have been used since his days in spiritual worship; and, above all things, how he looked forward in simple faith to the coming of the promised Messiah, and was, therefore, a man after God's heart, notwithstanding the sins into which he had fallen, and for which he had been punished.

The Lord Jesus Christ declared that the first and great commandment is, "Thou shalt love the Lord thy God with all thy heart, and with all thy soul, and with all thy mind." If this has not been done always, those who fail are law-breakers. Future obedience can never atone for past transgression. The law of God is inexorable. It is not a question of how much has a man sinned, but has he sinned at all. As we read in Rom. 3 : 19, "Now we know that what things soever the law saith, it saith to them who are under the law; that every mouth may be stopped, and all the world may become guilty before God." And again in Rom. 3 : 22, 23 "For there is no difference: for all have sinned and come short of the glory of God"; and we read also in the same chapter, "There is none righteous, no, not one; there is none that understandeth, there is none that seeketh after God. They are all gone out of the way; they are together become unprofitable; there is none that doeth good, no, not one." To come short of the glory of God is as much sin before Him as to commit murder, and unless all sin is put away it is impossible for any one upon whom it rests to ever enter heaven.

Insidious Questions and Remarks About the Son of God.

The insidious character of Professor Goldwin Smith's remarks is nowhere more plainly seen than in the following extract from page 180: "Did Jesus regard Himself or allow Himself to be regarded as God? Unitarians quote strong texts to the contrary. The Trinitarians get their texts chiefly from the fourth Gospel, which is manifestly imbued with the peculiar views of its writer and his circle. In fact, it may be said to be one note of the comparatively late composition of that Gospel that time must have elapsed sufficient for the Teacher of Galilee to become, first Divine, and then the

Second person of the Trinity, and the Alexandrian Logos. It seems unlikely that, even in those days of theosophic reverie, the author of the sayings and the parables should ever have been led by spiritual exaltation to form and promulgate such a conception of Himself."

A sufficient answer has already been given in Chapter IV. to a similar question asking if Jesus regarded Himself or allowed His followers to designate Him, as the Messiah. It is unnecessary to repeat what has been already said in answer to that question any further than to say that the learned Professor is perfectly well aware that Jesus did constantly declare Himself to be the Son of God, and that the question is only put for the purpose of raising doubt in the minds of others. But not only was He regarded as the Son of God, but He is spoken of as God by the Apostle Paul in the following passages: "Whose are the fathers, and of whom, as concerning the flesh, Christ came, who is over all, God blessed for ever" (Rom. 9 : 5). "Looking for that blessed hope and the glorious appearing of the great God and our Saviour, Jesus Christ" (Titus 2 : 13). The Jewish nation rejected the prophets of Jehovah, but their crowning sin was the rejection of the Son of God, who, by His life and teaching, and by the miracles of mercy which He wrought, gave ample proof that He was what He claimed to be, their promised Messiah, the Son of God, come down from heaven. For their rejection of Him they have been scattered throughout all other nations, and their land has been a desolation for many centuries. There is less excuse for Gentile heathens now, in so-called Christian countries, who have the Bible in their hands and see the results of Christian character and teachings. A terrible responsibility rests upon those, with so much light and privilege, who deliberately reject the Son of God, and treat His offers of mercy with contempt. This is a thousandfold worse than David's sin, and God will not hold him guiltless who spurns His offered grace.

Professor Smith's Ideas of Spiritual Life.

On page 5 Professor Goldwin Smith says: "What we call Spiritual Life seems, in fact, to be the cultivation of character, carried on under religious influence by a sort of inner self." This is certainly a strange definition of spiritual life to be given by one who says in another place: "Science (Darwinian and general) has put an end to the traditional belief in the soul as being separate from the body." What, then is the sort of inner self to which he refers? There is nothing more perplexing to unconverted men than the idea of receiving an entirely new life, direct from God, which is just as real as that with which they came into the world at their natural birth. And yet this is the truth taught in the Word, and enjoyed in the experience of every true Christian. Three times over Jesus impressed upon Nicodemus the necessity of the new birth as follows: "Verily, verily, I say unto thee, Except a man be born again he cannot see the kingdom of God. Nicodemus said unto Him, How can a man be born when he is old? Can he enter the second time into his mother's womb and be born? Jesus answered, Verily, verily I say unto thee, Except a man be born of water and of the Spirit he cannot enter into the kingdom of God. That which is born of the flesh is flesh, and that which is born of the Spirit is spirit. Marvel not that I said unto thee, Ye must be born again" (John 3 : 3-7). That the water here referred to has no reference to baptism is evident from the following Scriptures :

Eph. 5 : 25, 26. Husbands, love your wives even as Christ also loved the Church, and gave Himself for it; that He might sanctify and cleanse it with the washing of water by the Word.

James 1 : 17, 18. Every good gift and every perfect gift is from above, and cometh down from the Father of lights, with whom is no variableness neither shadow of turning. Of his own will begat He us with the Word of truth, that we should be a kind of first fruits of His creatures.

1 Peter 1 : 23. Being born again, not of corruptible seed, but of incorruptible, by the Word of God, which liveth and abideth for ever.

By these passages the necessity of the Word of God for the reception of spiritual life is plainly seen. The Word of God, applied by the Spirit of God to the hearts of men dead in trespasses and sins, is the only means whereby spiritual life can be received. A terrible responsibility rests, therefore, upon any man who attempts to shake the faith of others in that Word, without which he cannot receive spiritual life. It is bad enough for a man to lose his own soul, but it is far worse to be the means of dragging others down with him to a lost eternity. Cultivation of character will do no good where a new nature is required; and before any man receives that he must see his own lost and helpless condition, and then come to God in His own way as directed in His Word. The idea that unconverted men generally have about there being some germ of goodness about themselves, or some "natural morality," that only needs to be developed is a sham and a delusion, wholly opposed to the teaching of the Word of God and the experience of all Christians before regeneration. "Cultivation under religious influences" will never make a man a Christian; for the Lord Jesus Christ said, "That which is born of the flesh is flesh, and that which is born of the Spirit is spirit. Marvel not that I said unto thee, Ye must be born again."

In the first chapter of Romans we read, "For the wrath of God is revealed from heaven against all ungodliness and unrighteousness of men . . . Because that, when they knew God, they glorified him not as God, neither were thankful; but became vain in their imaginations, and their foolish heart was darkened; professing themselves to be wise they became fools, and changed the glory of the uncorruptible God into an image made like to corruptible man . . . and even as they did not like to retain God in their knowledge God gave them over to a reprobate mind," etc. This is man's natural condition and without a new nature, it is impossible for him to glorify God, and thus fulfil the purpose of his creation.

Vain Speculations About the Origin of Evil.

There has been much useless speculation about the origin of evil in the universe of God, and men are no wiser now than when they first began to speculate about it. This is one of the " secret things belonging to the Lord," which we have no right to pry into, as it is only " the things which are revealed which belong to us." All we know is that it does exist, and that the human race is subject to its power. We have reason to believe that man in a state of innocence as he came from the hand of God was the noblest creature that God had ever formed, because he was made in the very image and likeness of God Himself, and all other earthly creatures were subject to his will. If sin had not come in we know not how soon that wonderful intellect with which he was endowed might have mastered the knowledge of all the sciences and arts that are known at the present day. But this was not the purpose of his creation, and it might have served rather to glorify the creature than the Creator. What God required for His own glory were implicit faith and perfect obedince. Now look at the nature of the temptation presented by Satan in the form of the serpent, which led to the fall of Adam and Eve. He first suggested a doubt, then he boldly denied that what God said was true, and then he promised that they would be as gods, knowing good and evil. The great temptation after doubt and unbelief had taken root in the heart was to know more than God had chosen to reveal; and so, while the woman saw that the tree was good for food and pleasant to the eye, she concluded it was to be *desired* to make one wise, and with this desire for forbidden wisdom they disobeyed God and fell from their high estate. Hitherto they had only known that which was good; henceforth they knew both good and evil. Their increase of knowledge had cost them dearly. The life received from God was forfeited, although they continued to exist. Their posterity inherited their fallen nature; and God tried fallen man under the new conditions of his being, with the sad consequences of Adam's unbelief and disobedience before them, and the promise of redemption by the seed of the woman, who was to bruise the serpent's head, but very few walked with God as Enoch did for three hundred years, and who then ascended to heaven without dying when Noah's father was 113 years of age. Under these conditions man proved a failure, for by the time that Noah was five hundred years old he was the only man upon earth that walked with God, and all the rest had corrupted themselves; although many of them were mighty men which were of old, men of renown. All mankind except Noah and his family having been swept away by the flood, men were left to themselves again, with the warning of the Deluge and the knowledge of the altar of sacrifice and its meaning, but they soon departed from the way of righteousness again, and, instead of repenting of their sins, only sought to escape their consequences in case of a second Deluge. Again, under these new conditions, man with his free will proved a failure as before. Then God selected one man and his descendants, and entered into a covenant of grace with him. "Abraham believed God, and his faith was counted unto him for righteousness," and he knew the meaning of the altar and its sacrifice, and God treated him as a friend and gave him repeated promises of blessing, that was to come through his seed, upon all nations. Four hundred and thirty years after the covenant of grace made with Abraham, the Israelites, his descendants, were delivered from bondage in Egypt, and the law was given by God through Moses, which the whole nation promised to obey; and ceremonial worship was established, with sacrifices, all of which were typical of the One great sacrifice, which was to take away the sin of the world. Established as a theocratic nation, most highly favoured, with God Himself dwelling in their midst, in the most holy place, first in the tabernacle, and afterwards in the temple at Jerusalem, they were continually sinning and rebelling against Him, and receiving His judgments on account of their sins. Under these conditions again, with all the privileges that they enjoyed, the Jewish nation proved a failure, just as the human race had been a failure under all circumstances since the Fall of Adam. In no way that he had been tried had man glorified God, and thus fulfilled the purpose of his creation. His utter incapacity to do that which is right, whether without law or under law, had been plainly made manifest. Essentially corrupt by nature, and beyond all hope of improvement, nothing remained for him but the execution of God's righteous judgment against him as a sinner. " There is none righteous; no, not one "; " There is none that doeth good; no, not one." " That every mouth may be stopped, and all the world become guilty before God "; " for there is no difference: for all have sinned, and come short of the glory of God." This is the verdict of the Word of God, and doubtless also of all created unfallen beings, who are aware of the various conditions under which this wonderful creature (man) has been tried, who was originally made in the very image of God, and destined for His glory.

Riddle of Existence Solved by the Word of God.

This is the solution of the Riddle of Existence so far as man is concerned. The same temptations that led Adam and Eve astray are still all-powerful in preventing men from being reconciled to God. The lust of the flesh, and the lust of the eyes and the pride of life are always alluring; but—above all things in this age of intellectual progress and scientific research, the desire to be wise, or to be thought wise, are hindering proud men from taking the place of little children before God, without which they cannot possibly enter His kingdom. So

long as men are without Christ they are without life.
They only exist, and there is no bright future before
them, the reflection of which so often lights up the most
squalid scenes of poverty and the pallid features of the
dying saint; no hope beyond the grave; only an empty
void, to which they are looking forward, and insanely
trying to drag others with them, as if they thought there
would be some comfort in having companionship on
such a dark and dreary road.

Why should men *guess* at the Riddle of Existence
when God has so clearly revealed its solution ? Why
waste time in considering what a few frail mortals like
ourselves think about evolution when God's Word
plainly declares to us how the first progenitors of the
human race were created, and when the truth of the
Word of God has been confirmed by the Son of God,
who has died, and risen, and ascended into heaven, and
is soon coming again. Let men stop guessing and
believe the solution that Divine revelation has given.
Only thus can they obtain correct information and satisfactory results regarding the great problems of creation
and human existence.

CHAPTER VI.

GOD'S PURPOSE IN REDEMPTION.

"GOD so loved the world that He gave His only begotten Son, that whosoever believeth in Him should not perish, but have everlasting life" (John 3 : 16). These are the words of Jesus Himself, whom Professor Goldwin Smith calls "the great Teacher of humanity," as He explained to the Jewish ruler, Nicodemus, how the new birth was to be obtained. They proclaim a salvation provided for the whole world, to be received in the way which God has appointed.

Man's Utter Ruin by the Fall.

In the previous chapter we have seen how incurably corrupt man is by nature, and how faithless and disobedient he has always been, under all circumstances, in which he, as a highly endowed creature, with a free will, has been tried. There was only failure as the result of every trial, "Because that, when they knew God, they glorified him not as God, neither were thankful; but became vain in their imagination, and their foolish heart was darkened: professing themselves to be wise, they became fools . . . who changed the truth of God into a lie, and worshipped and served the creature more than the Creator, who is blessed for ever" (Rom. 1 : 21-25). "All had sinned and come short of His glory." "Angels which kept not their first estate . . . are kept in everlasting chains, under darkness, unto the judgment of the great day." Man is not by any means the first creature that has fallen from the condition of holiness in which he was created. But so far as we are informed, nothing but the righteous judgment of an infinitely holy

God awaited any who sinned against Him until the Fall
of man gave the opportunity for such a display of love
and grace as the universe had never before witnessed.
For four thousand years God had patiently borne with
men's selfish ingratitude and open rebellion. Only a
few out of the great mass of humanity looked by faith,
through the types, to the great Antitype, who was to
bear away sin by the sacrifice of Himself.

Advent and Rejection of the Messiah and His Victory Over Satan.

The Jewish nation had been looking for the advent
of their long-promised Messiah of the seed of Abraham
of the tribe of Judah, and of the house of David, to raise
them as a people to the pinnacle of earthly greatness,
and to reign gloriously at Jerusalem, as had been predicted by the prophets. If He had come as they expected,
they would doubtless have gladly hailed Him as their
deliverer from the Roman yoke, and been willing to lay
down their lives in His service. But they did not understand the purpose of God, who foresaw all their rebellion and rejection of His Son, and who purposed that
through His bearing away the sin of the world salvation
should be provided which was co-extensive with the
race; and that not only the Jewish people, but all other
nations throughout the earth, should thus share in the
benefits of His atoning sacrifice. So "when the fulness
of time was came, God sent forth His Son, made of a
woman, made under the law, to redeem them that
were under the law, that we might receive the adoption of sons" (Gal. 4 : 4, 5). Men through sin had
come under bondage to Satan, and the Lord Jesus Christ
came into the world to conquer and destroy this enemy
of God and of all righteousness. He defeated him in
the temptation in the wilderness, using no other weapon
than the Sword of the Spirit, which is the Word of God,
to repel all his attacks; but His crowning victory over
this great adversary was by His death and resurrection,

when as a man who was "tempted in all points like as we are, yet without sin" (Heb. 4 : 15), He went to the cross and died for sins that were not His own, and rose triumphantly from the dead on the third day thus show-ing that His sacrifice had been accepted, and that the justice of God was satisfied by that one Sacrifice of infinite value. Thus was the power of Satan broken, and the fatal wound given that will yet end in his complete overthrow, and confinement in the lake of fire, prepared for the devil and his angels (Matt. 25 : 41). In Heb. 2 : 14, 15 we read, "Forasmuch then as the children are partakers of flesh and blood he also himself likewise took part of the same; that through death he might destroy him that had the power of death, that is, the devil; and deliver them who through fear of death were all their lifetime subject to bondage."

Deliverance by His Death From the Curse of the Law.

The Israelites as a nation had voluntarily placed themselves under the law given by God through His servant, Moses, when they said, "All that the Lord hath spoken we will do," and, having broken the law, they came under the curses pronounced against law-breakers, as we read in Gal. 3 : 10-13, "For as many as are of the works of the law, are under the curse: for it is written, Cursed is every one that continueth not in all things which are written in the book of the law to do them. But that no man is justified by the law in the sight of God, it is evident; for the just shall live by faith. . . . Christ hath redeemed us from the curse of the law, being made a curse for us: for it is written, Cursed is every one that hangeth on a tree" (Gal. 3 : 10-13). The substitutionary character of the death of Christ is here very clearly expressed. The law of God, which is holy and just and good, can never save any one, because it requires a perfect obedience, and in default of this the curse is entailed upon the sinner, which can only be removed by payment of the full penalty. By full payment of this penalty when He was made a curse for us the Lord Jesus Christ purchased by His death upon the cross redemption for all who will receive it through faith in Him, and thus obtain deliverance from the curse which was resting upon them.

Deliverance From the Power of Sin.

Another sense in which redemption is spoken of in the Word of God is that referred to in Titus 2 : 13, 14, " Looking for that blessed hope, and the glorious appearing of the great God, and our Saviour Jesus Christ; who gave Himself for us that He might redeem us from all iniquity, and purify unto Himself a peculiar people, zealous of good works." This corresponds with the statement made by the angel to Joseph when announcing the conception of Jesus by the power of the Holy Spirit: " Joseph, thou son of David, fear not to take unto thee Mary, thy wife; for that which is conceived in her is of the Holy Ghost. And she shall bring forth a son, and thou shalt call his name JESUS, for he shall save his people from their sins."

The Cost of Redemption.

The price paid for the redemption of fallen men is very clearly stated in Scripture, as will be seen from the following passages: " In whom we have redemption through His blood, the forgiveness of sins, according to the riches of His grace " (Eph. 1 : 7), " Who hath delivered us from the power of darkness, and hath translated us into the kingdom of His dear- Son; in whom we have redemption through His blood, even the forgiveness of sins; who is the image of the invisible God, the firstborn of every creature: for by Him were all things created that are in heaven and that are in earth, visible and invisible, whether they be thrones, or dominions, or principalities, or powers; all things were created by him and for him; and he is before all things, and by him all things consist " (Col. 1 : 13-17). And

again, " Forasmuch as ye know that ye were not redeemed with corruptible things, as silver and gold, from
your vain conversation, received by tradition from your
fathers; but with the precious blood of Christ, as of a
lamb without blemish, and without spot . . . being
born again, not of corruptible seed, but of incorruptible,
by the Word of God, which liveth and abideth forever "
(1 Peter 1 : 18-22).   And again in Rev. 5 : 9, 10 there is
that wonderful picture of the redeemed after they have
been caught up to heaven, surrounding the " Lamb, as
it had been slain," who is also spoken of as the " Lion
of the tribe of Judah," and " the Root of David."   "And
they sing a new song, saying, Thou art worthy to take
the book, and to open the seals thereof; for thou wast
slain, and hast redeemed us to God by thy blood, out of
every kindred and tongue and people and nation, and
hast made us unto our God kings and priests; and we
shall reign on the earth."

It is thus evident from the teaching of the Word of
God that the redemption by Christ delivers from bondage to the devil, from the curse of a broken law, and
from the dominion of sin; and also that the price paid
in redemption was the precious blood of Christ, or, in
other words, the life of Christ, laid down on behalf of
sinners who were condemned to die, not only the natural
death of the body, which is common to all, but the
second death in the lake of fire, with the devil and his
angels (Matt. 25 : 41, 46).   That the blood refers to the
life is clear from the teaching in Lev. 17 : 11-14, " For
the life of the flesh is in the blood: and I have given it
to you upon the altar, to make an atonement for your
souls; for it is the blood that maketh an atonement for
your souls . . . for it is the life of all flesh; the blood
of it is for the life thereof."

Effect of Redemption not a Mere Restoration of Adamic Perfection.

The marvellous thing in connection with the work of
redemption by the Lord Jesus Christ is this, that it does

not merely restore man to a position of Adamic righteousness and innocence, such as our first parents had
before the Fall. That would be a great deal, but there
would still be the liability to fall again. But redemption provides something infinitely higher and better, for
under its provisions the sinner who receives Jesus as his
Saviour is reckoned by God as having died on the cross
in the person of Christ as his substitute, and as having
become a member of the new creation, of which the
Lord Jesus Christ is now the head: being made
partaker of His resurrection life, and having a new
nature, with new desires and new impulses, which leads
him to hate the things he formerly loved, and to love
the things he formerly hated. And even as, in the natural
body, the head directs all the members when in a healthy
condition, so in this new creation, of which the Lord
Jesus Christ, as the second Adam, is the head, all the
members, if in a right condition, will be subject to Him
in all things. God reckons them all as having not only
died, in the person of their Substitute, upon the cross;
but also as having been quickened together with Him,
and raised together with Him, when He rose from the
dead, and made to sit together with Him even now in
heavenly places (Eph. 2 : 5, 6); and they are kept by
the power of God through faith unto salvation, ready to
be revealed in the last time (1 Peter 1 : 5); that is, when
Jesus comes again for them, and they receive their glorified bodies. Because in the person of their Substitute
they have paid the full penalty demanded by the law on
account of sin, they are now free from all imputation
of sin through the first Adam, and receive the forgiveness of sins, and they are justified from all things, from
which they could not be justified by the law of Moses
(Acts 13 : 38, 39). And as those who are justified from
all things they stand before God as free from all imputation of sin as the Lord Jesus Christ Himself; for " as
He is, so are they in this world " (1 John 4 : 17): " and
they are complete in Him who is the head of all prin-
cipality and power " (Col. 2 : 10). But not only are they

justified in the person of the Lord Jesus Christ; they are also sanctified in Him (1 Cor. 1 : 2), and "by the will of God they have been sanctified by the offering of the body of Jesus Christ once for all " (Heb. 10 : 10); and by that one offering of Himself as a sacrifice for sin He "has perfected forever them that are sanctified" (Heb. 10 : 14). Thus, as to their standing before God in Christ, they are just as He is, complete in Him, justified, sanctified, and perfected forever, and so fitted and privileged to enter with boldness into the very presence of God, and worship Him in spirit and in truth (Heb. 10 : 19). And the assurance is given unto them in the Word of God that there is no condemnation to those that are in Christ Jesus (Rom. 8 : 1), and that nothing will be able to separate them from the love of God, which is in Christ Jesus our Lord (Rom. 8: 38, 39). And also that their life is hid with Christ in God (Col. 3 : 3), and, therefore, eternally secure.

God's Desire for Communion with Men.

This is a wonderful position for redeemed men to be placed in, but it is not all. When God created man for His own glory, in His own image and likeness, it seemed as if His heart was set upon having a race of beings with whom He could have more intimate fellowship than He ever had with any other created intelligencies; and thus, after man sinned, and justice required that he should be banished from Eden, 'and earn his bread by the sweat of his brow; and after the Flood had come and swept away the whole race for their sins, except Noah and his family, it seemed as if Jehovah was still longing to find in some of Adam's descendants a few in whom he could confide, and to whom He could reveal more of His character and purposes. God talked with Moses "as a man talketh with his friend," and Abraham was called "the friend of God." The tabernacle was built, and God's presence was manifested there by the Shekinah fire between the cherubim, over the mercy-seat, and in this way He dwelt in the midst of His chosen people. In the same manner also He dwelt in the temple which Solomon built at Jerusalem. In the tabernacle and in the temple He received the worship of His people, but only the high priest was permitted to enter once a year into the holiest of all, where His own immediate presence was signified by the Shekinah flame. Men were still kept at a distance, and God in His infinite love wanted to draw them nearer to Himself, and lift them into a higher place of blessing and privilege than any other created beings had yet reached. And this love that was in His heart towards the human race found expression in the words of the Lord Jesus Christ with which this chapter opened: "God so loved the world that He gave His only begotten Son, that whosoever believeth in Him should not perish, but have everlasting life."

Redeemed Men Forever Raised Above All Other Created Beings.

We have already seen something of the position into which redeemed men are brought, but there was a greater height to which God purposed raising men after the Atonement of Christ had made expiation for sin; and this purpose was a mystery kept secret since the world began (Rom. 16 : 25; but it was at length revealed through His servant, Paul (Eph. 3 : 3-11). It was a revelation of something new, the making of a new man, composed of Jews and Gentiles, saved during this dispensation; Christ Himself being the head of this new creation, already referred to, and each of the redeemed a member of His mystical body, indwelt by the same life as the head, and destined to be sharers of His glory. This is otherwise known as the Church (Eph. 1 : 22, 23), commenced at Pentecost, when believers were baptized by the Holy Spirit into "one body" (1 Cor. 12 : 13). The close and indissoluble character of this union is expressed by two other figures, one of which is that of a building, as follows: "Now, therefore, ye are no more strangers

and foreigners, but fellow-citizens with the saints, and
of the household of God: and are built upon the foundation of the apostles and prophets, Jesus Christ Himself
being the chief corner stone; in whom all the building
fitly framed together, groweth unto an holy temple in
the Lord: in whom ye also are builded together for an
habitation of God through the Spirit " (Eph. 2 : 19-22).
The other figure given to us of this union is that of the
husband and wife, as follows: " Wives, submit yourselves unto your own husbands as unto the Lord. For
the husband is the head of the wife, even as Christ is the
head of the Church; and he is the Saviour of the body.
Therefore, as the Church is subject unto Christ, so let
the wives be to their own husbands in everything. Husbands, love your wives as Christ also loved the Church,
and gave himself for it; that he might sanctify and
cleanse it with the washing of water by the Word, that
he might present it to himself a glorious church, not
having spot or wrinkle or any such thing; but that it
should be holy and without blemish. . . . For no man
ever yet hated his own flesh; but nourisheth and cher-
isheth it, even as the Lord the Church; for we are
members of his body, of his flesh, and of his bones
. . . This is a great mystery: but I speak concerning
Christ and the Church." (Eph. 5 : 22-32.)

It is no wonder that the angels should desire to look
into the revelation of such a wonderful mystery as this
(1 Peter 1 : 12); that men who had sinned and come
short of God's glory should be " justified freely by His
grace, through the redemption that is in Christ Jesus "
(Rom. 3 : 24), and raised to such a place of nearness to
the Godhead and of such security as the nature of their
union with Christ implies. This is the true "Ascent
of Man."

Equipment for Service while in the World.

The Lord Jesus Christ had promised His disciples
" the night in which He was betrayed, the very night
before He died," that He would not leave them com-

fortless. He would send them another Comforter, that
He might abide with them for ever; even the Spirit of
truth; "whom," said he, "the world cannot receive,
because it seeth Him not, neither knoweth Him, but ye
know Him, for He dwelleth with you, and shall be in
you" (John 14 : 17). And He said to them also, "But
the Comforter, who is the Holy Spirit, whom the Father
will send in my name; he shall teach you all things, and
bring all things to your remembrance, whatsoever I have
said unto you" (John 14 : 26). And again He said: "But
when the Comforter is come whom I will send from the
Father, the Spirit of truth which proceedeth from the
Father, He shall testify of me " (John 15 : 26). And a
little later He said: "Howbeit, when He, the Spirit of
truth, is come, he will guide you into all truth; for he
shall not speak from (R.V.) himself; but whatsoever he
shall hear that shall he speak; and he will show you things
to come " (John 16 : 13). After His resurrection, when
about to leave His disciples and ascend into heaven, He
told them to wait for the promise of the Father, "which,"
said He, "ye have heard of me: for John truly baptized
with water, but ye shall be baptized with the Holy
Ghost not many days hence. . . . But ye shall receive
power after that the Holy Ghost is come upon you;
and ye shall be witnesses unto me, both in Jerusalem,
and in all Judea, and in Samaria, and unto the uttermost
part of the earth " (Acts 1 : 5, 8). The fulfillment of
these promises took place on the day of Pentecost, as we
read in the second chapter of Acts, "And when the day
of Pentecost was fully come, they were all with one
accord in one place. And suddenly there came a sound
from heaven, as of a rushing, mighty wind, and it filled
all the house where they were sitting: and there appeared unto them cloven tongues, like as of fire, and it
sat upon each of them; and they were all filled with the
Holy Ghost, and began to speak with other tongues as
the Spirit gave them utterance" (Acts 2 : 1-4). When
this extraordinary occurrence was noised abroad, a multitude of Jews from every nation under heaven were

drawn together, and were confounded, because every man heard them speak in his own language. Peter then stood up with the other apostles, and he addressed the people, charging home upon them their guilt in the crucifixion of Christ: "Him being delivered by the determinate counsel and foreknowledge of God ye have taken, and by wicked hands have crucified and slain" (Acts 2 : 23). And he concluded his address with these words: "This Jesus hath God raised up, whereof we all are witnesses. Therefore, being by the right hand of God exalted, and having received of the Father the promise of the Holy Ghost, he hath shed forth this which ye now see and hear. For David is not ascended into the heavens; but he saith himself, The Lord said unto my Lord, Sit thou on my right hand until I make thy foes thy footstool. Therefore, let all the house of Israel know assuredly that God hath made that same Jesus both Lord and Christ" (Acts 2 : 32-36).

The Lord Jesus Christ Exalted as Head of the New Creation.

As a consequence, therefore, of the work of redemption, which He completed, Jesus has been exalted to the right hand of God the Father, who has made Him both Lord and Christ; and those who are really Christians now speak of Him as the Lord Jesus Christ, and not simply as Jesus, the name by which He was known during the days of His humiliation on earth, although that name alone is very precious to them. In Acts 5 : 30-32 His exaltation is again spoken of by Peter, who said: "The God of our fathers raised up Jesus, whom ye slew and hanged on a tree. Him hath God exalted with his right hand to be a Prince and a Saviour, for to give repentance unto Israel, and forgiveness of sins; and we are witnesses of these things; and so is also the Holy Ghost, whom God hath given to them that obey Him." And the same truth is repeated by Paul in his letter to the Philippians, where he says: "Wherefore

God also hath highly exalted Him, and given Him a
name which is above every name: that at the name of
Jesus every knee should bow, of things in heaven, and
things in earth, and things under the earth; and that
every tongue should confess that Jesus Christ is Lord,
to the glory of God the Father." This is a literal fulfillment in the person of Jesus, as the glorified man, of that
prediction in Isa. 45 : 21-23, which is made concerning
God, thus giving another proof that the Lord Jesus
Christ is God manifest in the flesh. "And there is no
God else beside me: a just God and a Saviour; there
is none else beside me. Look unto me and be ye saved,
all the ends of the earth; for I am God, and there is
none else. I have sworn by myself, the word is gone
out of my mouth in righteousness, and shall not return,
That unto me every knee shall bow and every tongue
shall swear."

Redeemed Sinners Exalted with Christ.

This is the extraordinary height of glory to which the
human race has been raised by virtue of the redemption
work of the Lord Jesus Christ, who, as the seed of the
woman, has "bruised the serpent's head" (Gen. 3 : 15),
and by His own death has destroyed "him that had the
power of death; that is, the devil" (Heb. 2 : 14). But
not only is He thus exalted Himself as the Head of the
new creation. It is clearly revealed that all the redeemed
from earth are also exalted, in the same manner, above
all other created beings in the universe, and made sons
of God, and heirs of God, through Christ, as we read
in Gal. 4 : 4-7. " But when the fulness of time was come,
God sent forth His Son, made of a woman, made under
the law, to redeem them that were under the law, that
we might receive the adoption of sons. And because ye
are sons, God hath sent forth the Spirit of His Son into
your hearts, crying, Abba, Father. Wherefore thou art
no more a servant, but a son; and if a son, then an heir
of God through Christ." And the same truth is taught
in Romans, where it is said, " For as many as are led

by the Spirit of God, they are the sons of God. For ye have not received the spirit of bondage again to fear; but ye have received the spirit of adoption, whereby we cry, Abba, Father. The Spirit himself beareth witness with our spirit, that we are the children of God; and if children, then heirs; heirs of God and joint heirs with Christ; if so be that we suffer with him, that we may be also glorified together " (Rom. 8 : 14-17).

This is more amazing still, that sinners of Adam's race who had been created for God's glory and failed to glorify Him, should themselves be glorified together with Christ, and should also be made partakers of the Divine nature, as it is expressly stated in 2 Peter 1 : 4. That the Lord Jesus Christ makes those whom He has redeemed sharers of His glory is plainly taught in Hebrews, where it is said, "What is man that thou art mindful of him ? or the son of man, that thou visitest him ? Thou madest him a little while inferior to the angels; thou crownedst him with glory and honour, and didst set him over the works of thy hands . . . But now we see not yet all things put under him. But we see Jesus, who was made a little lower than the angels, for the suffering of death, crowned with glory and honour, that he by the grace of God should taste death for every man. For it became him, for whom are all things and by whom are all things, in bringing many sons unto glory to make the captain of their salvation perfect through sufferings. For both he that sanctifieth and they that are sanctified are all of one, for which cause he is not ashamed to call them brethren " (Heb. 2 : 6-11). We are also informed that, "When Christ, who is our life, shall appear, then shall ye also appear with him in glory" (Col. 3: 3). And all this is in answer to the prayer of the Lord Jesus Christ to the Father the night on which He was betrayed as follows: "And the glory which thou gavest me I have given them; that they may be one even as we are one: I in them, and thou in me, that they may be made perfect in one; and that the world may know that thou hast sent me, and

hast loved them as thou hast loved me. Father, I will
that they also, whom thou hast given me, be with me
where I am; that they may behold my glory, which thou
hast given me: for thou lovedst me before the foundation of the world" (John 17 : 22-24).

Redeemed Men Left in the World as Witnesses for Christ.

Now, it would almost seem as if the best thing that
could happen to a man, who has been brought into such
a position as we have been considering, would be to be
taken at once to heaven, away from the temptations and
trials of earth. But the Lord Jesus Christ prayed for them
thus: "I have given them thy word, and the world hath
hated them, because they are not of the world, even as
I am not of the world. I pray not that thou shouldest
take them out of the world, but that thou shouldest keep
them from the evil one. They are not of the world, even
as I am not of the world. Sanctify them through thy
truth: thy word is truth. As thou hast sent me into the
world, even so have I also sent them into the world"
(John 17 : 14-18). It was not His purpose that they
should be taken away to heaven at once, as He had work
for them to do here, as He told them after His resurrection: "These are the words which I spake unto you,
while I was yet with you, that all things must be fulfilled, which were written in the law of Moses, and in
the prophets, and in the Psalms, concerning me. Then
opened He their understandings that they should understand the Scriptures, and said unto them, Thus it is
written, and thus it behoved Christ to suffer, and to rise
from the dead the third day: and that repentance and
remission of sins should be preached among all nations,
beginning at Jerusalem. And ye are witnesses of these
things. And behold, I send the promise of the Father
upon you, but tarry ye in the city of Jerusalem, until
ye be endued with power from on high" (Luke 24 :
44-49). And when He appeared to the eleven apostles

in the mountain in Galilee, where He had appointed, we
are told that "when they saw Him they worshipped
Him, but some doubted. And Jesus came and spake
unto them, saying: "All power is given unto me in
heaven and in earth. Go ye, therefore, and teach all
nations, baptizing them in the name of the Father, and
of the Son, and of the Holy Ghost; teaching them to
observe all things whatsoever I have commanded you;
and lo, I am with you alway, even unto the end of the
world" (Matt. 28 : 16-20). And on another occasion,
when they sat at meat, He appeared to them, and said:
"Go ye into all the world and preach the Gospel to
every creature. He that believeth and is baptized shall
be saved; but he that believeth not shall be damned"
(Mark 16 : 14-16). And again, as we have already seen
in this chapter, just before leaving them He said, "Ye
shall receive the power of the Holy Ghost coming upon
you; and ye shall be witnesses unto me, both in Jerusalem, and in all Judea, and in Samaria, and unto the
uttermost part of the earth. And when He had spoken
these things while they beheld, he was taken up, and a
cloud received him out of their sight" (Acts 1 : 8, 9).

These are the commissions which the Lord Jesus
Christ left for His disciples to execute as His witnesses,
and this is the power with which they were to be endued for the performance of the work committed to
them. And what was true of those to whom He then
spoke is equally applicable to all His redeemed people
throughout this dispensation. There is reason for thank-
fulness that in recent years the Church of God has
become more fully awakened to its responsibility to execute the trusts committed to it; and that many more
consecrated missionaries have gone to preach the Gospel
in heathen lands than at any other time since the days
of the apostles. And yet there is cause for shame that
most of the denominational missions are financially in
arrears; while there is but little difficulty in raising
large sums of money for political purposes ; and the
total amount spent upon missions in so-called Christian

countries is only a trifle compared with what is spent
yearly in liquor and tobacco. God could have commissioned angels to preach the Gospel, but He has not
chosen to do so. This work has been entrusted to those
who have been themselves redeemed, and can testify as
witnesses of the Lord Jesus Christ to what He has done
for themselves, and can, therefore, do for others. And
they are equipped for this service in the same manner
that He was during His earthly ministry. For even as
He, at His baptism in the Jordan, was filled with the
Holy Spirit, and in the power of the Spirit executed all His work, so has He made the bodies of all
His redeemed people temples of the Holy Spirit (1 Cor.
3 : 16 and 6 : 19), and commanded them to be filled with
the Spirit (Eph. 5 : 18), and promised that the Father
would give the Holy Spirit to them that ask Him
(Luke 11 : 13).

Redeemed Men Privileged to Suffer with Christ.

And there are certain great privileges allowed to the
redeemed during the time they are left in this world as
witnesses for Christ, foremost of which is that of suffering in fellowship with Him. When He was with His
disciples He said to them: "Think not that I am come to
send peace on earth: I am not come to send peace, but a
sword. For I am come to set a man at variance against
his father, and the daughter against her mother, and the
daughter-in-law against her mother-in-law, and a man's
foes shall be they of his own household. He that loveth
father or mother more than me is not worthy of me.
And he that taketh not his cross and followeth after me
is not worthy of me" (Matt. 10 : 34-37). Popularity
with the unconverted members of one's own household
is generally bought at the expense of compromise with
the world, in order to shun the cross, which unflinching
loyalty to the Word of God entails. It is not, therefore,
a bad sign if the ungodly members of a Christian's own
family speak evil of him. After the Lord Jesus Christ

had appeared to Saul of Tarsus on the way to Damascus the Lord spoke to Annanias in a vision, and commanded him to go and lay his hands upon him, so that he might receive his sight and be filled with the Holy Spirit. And He said to him at the same time: " I will show him how great things he must suffer for my name's sake" (Acts 9 : 16). After the eleven apostles had been imprisoned for preaching the Word and healing in the name of Jesus they were set at liberty after being beaten, and commanded not to speak in His name. "And they departed from the presence of the council, rejoicing that they were counted worthy to suffer shame for his name" (Acts 5 : 41). The secret of their rejoicing was that they were enabled to look away from their present sufferings to the glory that was in store for them as it is stated in Rom. 8 : 16-18, " The Spirit Himself beareth witness with our spirit that we are the children of God; and if children, then heirs—heirs of God, and joint heirs with Christ; if so be that we suffer with him that we may be also glorified together, for I reckon that the sufferings of this present time are not worthy to be compared with the glory that shall be revealed in us." But apart from the thought of reward in the coming glory there is a much higher motive for those who are called to fellowship with Christ in His sufferings, more especially when they are thus better fitted to minister to other members of the body of Christ. This is brought out fully in 2 Cor. 1 : 3-7: " Blessed be the God and Father of our Lord Jesus Christ, the Father of mercies, and the God of all comfort; who comforteth us in all our tribulation, that we may be able to comfort them which are in any trouble by the comfort wherewith we ourselves are comforted of God. For as the sufferings of Christ abound in us, so our consolation also aboundeth by Christ. And whether we be afflicted it is for your consolation and salvation, which is effectual in the enduring of the same sufferings which we also suffer: or whether we be comforted, it is for your consolation and salvation, and our hope of you is steadfast. knowing that as ye are partakers of the sufferings, so shall ye be also of the consolation." And if it is thus a great privilege to suffer for the sake of ministering blessing to other Christians, how much greater must be the privilege of suffering directly for the sake of Christ Himself as stated in Phil. 1 : 29, 30, "For unto you it is given in the behalf of Christ; not only to believe on Him, but also to suffer for his sake ; having the same conflict which ye saw in me, and now hear to be in me."

There is no kind of suffering to which a Christian is exposed that is harder to bear than misrepresentation and slander from others who profess to be Christians. When motives are misjudged, and actions misconstrued, and the tongue of slander busy in trying to blacken the private character of a man or the business in which he is engaged. When the basest ingratitude and the foulest calumny are experienced at the hands of those who should be the nearest and dearest friends, only those who have been tried in these ways know how hard it is to resist the natural feeling of indignation that is aroused, but cannot be indulged or expressed, because the sufferer is a Christian, and must bear patiently, but cannot help feeling keenly, even as the Lord Jesus Christ Himself felt the reproaches that were heaped upon Him, as we read in Psa.69 : 18-20, "Draw nigh unto my soul, and redeem it: deliver me, because of mine enemies. Thou hast known my reproach, and my shame, and my dishonour: mine adversaries are all before thee. Reproach hath broken my heart, and I am full of heaviness (or sore sick); and I looked for some to take pity, but there was none; and for comforters, but I found none." For those who suffer thus the Word of God says: "For this is thankworthy, if a man for conscience towards God endure grief, suffering wrongfully. For what glory is it, if, when ye be buffeted for your faults, ye shall take it patiently ? but if, when ye do well, and suffer for it, ye take it patiently, this is acceptable with God. For even hereunto were ye called, because Christ also suffered for us, leaving us an example, that ye should follow his steps" (1 Peter 2 : 19-21). It is stated in Heb. 1 : 10 that the Lord Jesus Christ was made perfect through sufferings; and again in Heb. 5 : 8, 9 it is said, "Though he were a Son, yet learned he obedience by the things which he suffered; and, being made perfect, he became the author of eternal salvation to them that obey him." The perfection of His character was absolute, for he was always holy, harmless and separate from sinners, and yet it is manifest that even He required a special training through suffering to be able, as a man, fully to sympathize with those who might be tried in the same way. And, therefore, we read, "For in that he hath suffered, being tempted, he is able to succour them that are tempted" (Heb. 1 : 18). And again, "For we have not an high priest which cannot be touched with a feeling of our infirmities; but was in all points tempted like as we are, yet without sin. Let us, therefore, come boldly to the throne of grace, that we may obtain mercy, and find grace to help in time of need" (Heb. 4 : 15, 16). And just as the Lord Jesus Christ Himself was made perfect through sufferings for His ministry on high as our Great High Priest; so it would seem as if it were His design that by the same means His redeemed people should be perfected for the ministry which they are called to engage in down here, as we read, "But the God of all grace, who hath called us unto His eternal glory by Christ Jesus, after that ye have suffered a while, make you perfect, stablish, strengthen, settle you" (1 Peter 5 : 10). Paul said, in writing to the Church at Colosse, "I Paul, . . . who now rejoice in my sufferings for you, and fill up that which is behind of the afflictions of Christ, in my flesh for his body's sake, which is the Church" (Col. 1 : 24). And again, in writing to the Church at Philippi, he said: "I count all things but loss for the excellency of the knowledge of Christ Jesus, my Lord; for whom I have suffered the loss of all things, and do count them but dung that I may win Christ, and be found in Him, not having mine own righteousness, which is of the law, but that which is through the faith of Christ, the righteousness which is of God by faith; that I may know him and the power of his resurrection, and the fellowship of his sufferings, being made conformable unto his death " (Phil. 3 : 8-10).

Redeemed Men to be Separated from Sin.

The redeemed are also left in the world as witnesses for the Lord Jesus Christ in their daily lives by separation from the ungodly like Him who was " holy, harmless, undefiled, and separate from sinners " (Heb. 6 : 26); and as they are commanded in 2 Cor. 6 : 14-18, " Be ye not unequally yoked together with unbelievers: for what fellowship hath righteousness with unrighteousness ? and what communion hath light with darkness ?   And what concord hath Christ with Belial ? or what part hath he that believeth with an infidel ?   And what agreement hath the temple of God with idols ? for ye are the temple of the living God; as God hath said,I will dwell in them and walk in them: and I will be their God, and they shall be my people.   Wherefore, come out from among them, and be ye separate, saith the Lord, and touch no unclean thing; and I will receive you, and will be a Father unto you, and ye shall be my sons and daughters, saith the Lord Almighty."   And they are reminded that, as temples of God, they are indwelt by the Holy Spirit just as the Lord Jesus Christ Himself was; and warned against the consequences of defiling that temple as follows: " Know ye not that ye are the temple of God, and that the Spirit of God dwelleth in you ?   If any man defile the temple of God him shall God destroy, for the temple of God is holy, which temple ye are " (1 Cor. 3 : 16, 17).   And again, " What! know ye not that your body is the temple of the Holy Ghost, which is in you, which ye have of God, and ye are not your own ?   For ye are bought with a price; therefore glorify God in your body " (1 Cor. 6 : 19, 20).   And they are commanded to be holy in 1 Peter 1: 15, 16 as follows: " But as he which hath called you is holy, so be ye holy in all manner of conversation; because it is written, Be ye holy, for I am holy." And again we read, "Abstain from all appearance of evil. And the very God of peace sanctify you wholly; and I pray God your whole spirit and soul and body be preserved blameless unto the coming of our Lord Jesus Christ. Faithful is he that calleth you, who also will do it" (1 Thess. 5 : 22-24).

Thus we see that those who are redeemed are witnesses for the Lord Jesus Christ in preaching the Gospel and ministry of the Word, in suffering with and for Him, and in living holy, separated lives; and, in order that they may have power thus to witness for Him, the command is given them to "be filled with the Spirit" (Eph. 5 : 18); and the Master Himself has also given the assurance: "If ye, then, being evil, know how to give good gifts to your children, how much more shall your heavenly Father give the Holy Spirit to them that ask Him ? (Luke 11 : 13). And they are exhorted to "present their bodies as living sacrifices, holy, acceptable to God, which is their reasonable service, and not to be conformed to this world" (Rom. 12 : 1, 2). And are told to "reckon themselves dead, indeed, unto sin and alive unto God, through Jesus Christ, our Lord" (Rom. 6 : 11).

There is, therefore, no doubt about the position which those redeemed by the precious blood of Christ should occupy in the world whilst left in it as His witnesses to continue the ministry, and the suffering, and the life in which He was Himself occupied whilst He was here. But those who die are said to fall asleep in Jesus, and to be "absent from the body, and present with the Lord; wherefore they labour that, whether present or absent, they may be accepted of Him" (2 Cor. 5: 8, 9). And so Paul wrote to the Philippians: "For me, to live is Christ and to die is gain. . . . For I am in a strait betwixt two, having a desire to depart, and to be with Christ, which is far better; nevertheless to abide in the flesh is more needful for you" (Phil. 1 : 21-24).

The Hope of the Redeemed.

But Christians are not told to look for death, because the Lord Jesus Christ has told them that He is coming again to take them to be with Himself where He is; and they are, therefore, told " to wait for the coming of his Son from heaven, whom he raised from the dead, even Jesus, which delivered them from the wrath to come " (1 Thess. 1 : 10). And the manner of His coming is thus spoken of: " But I would not have you to be ignorant, brethren, concerning them which are asleep, that ye sorrow not, even as others, which have no hope, for if we believe that Jesus died and rose again, even so, them also which sleep in Jesus will God bring with him. for this we say unto you by the word of the Lord, that we which are alive and remain unto the coming of the Lord shall not go before them which are asleep. For the Lord Himself shall descend from heaven with a shout, with the voice of the archangel, and with the trump of God; and the dead in Christ shall rise first, then we which are alive and remain shall be caught up together with them in the clouds, to meet the Lord in the air; and so shall we ever be with the Lord. Wherefore comfort one another with these words " (1 Thess. 4 : 13-18). This will be the fulfilment of the promise which Jesus gave to His disciples the night before He died on the cross: "Let not your heart be troubled; ye believe in God, believe also in me. In my Father's house are many mansions; if it were not so, I would have told you. I go to prepare a place for you. And if I go and prepare a place for you, I will come again and receive you unto myself; that where I am, there ye may be also " (John 14 : 1-3).

The Redeemed in Glory.

As we have already seen in a former chapter, there is a wonderful picture in Rev. 4 and 5 of all the redeemed from earth in glory, represented by four and twenty elders, sitting, clothed in white raiment; with crowns of gold on their heads, round about the throne of God. And they "cast their crowns before the throne, saying, Thou art worthy, O Lord, to receive glory and honour and power: for thou hast created all things, and for thy pleasure they are and were created" (Rev. 4 : 10, 11). And afterwards there was beheld "in the midst of the throne, and of the four living creatures and in the midst of the elders a Lamb as it had been slain. . . . And they sung a new song, saying, Thou art worthy to take the book, and to open the seals thereof; for thou wast slain, and hast redeemed us to God by thy blood, out of every kindred, and tongue, and people, and nation; and hast made us unto our God kings and priests; and we shall reign on the earth" (Rev. 5 : 6-10). And afterwards, we are informed in the same chapter, that ten thousand times ten thousand angels, and thousands of thousands said, "Worthy is the Lamb that was slain to receive power, and riches, and wisdom, and strength, and honour, and glory and blessing." And every creature which is in heaven, and on the earth and under the earth, and such as are in the sea, were heard saying, "Blessing, and honour, and glory, and power be unto him that sitteth upon the throne, and unto the Lamb, for ever and ever" (Rev. 5 : 11-14). From the Scriptures that have been read it is evident that the redeemed from earth who have been raised and glorified with Christ, and made unto God kings and priests, are coming back to reign on the earth, after the Lord Jesus Christ establishes His millennial kingdom.

The Whole Universe Interested in the Work of Redemption.

It is also clear from Rev. 5 that the whole universe of God, wherever intelligent created beings exist, are intensely interested in the work of redemption accomplished on this earth. As to what benefits they receive from that work we are not informed; but it is possible that by destroying Satan the Lord Jesus Christ has

removed a disturbing element from other worlds, as well
as from our own; and even if they are not directly made
partakers of the benefits of the Atoning Sacrifice offered
upon Calvary, they are so much interested that it calls
forth adoring worship from their hearts to the Lamb that
was slain.

Professor Smith's Failure to Understand about Rewards of the Redeemed.

Professor Goldwin Smith says, on page 104, that
" the doctrine of a future life with rewards and punishments pervades the New Testament, and is the sentiment
of the Founder of Christianity." That is certainly correct, and yet how far short that statement comes of
setting forth the exceeding glory of the position to which
the redeemed are raised in the universe of God by free
grace alone; and not as a reward for any merits of
theirs, as the Scriptures quoted in this chapter plainly
show. If such a position could be earned by a lifetime
of most arduous toil, it would surely be an object worthy
of the loftiest ambition; and none would grudge the
effort necessary to secure it. It seems to be despised just because men will not believe that the God of
all grace would offer them such wonderful blessing on
such easy terms. But the redeemed are not only glorified
with Christ by free grace alone, but rewards are offered
for faithful service. These are spoken of in 1 Cor. 3 :
13-15, " Every man's work shall be made manifest: for
the day shall declare it, because it shall be revealed by
fire; and the fire shall try every man's work, of what
sort it is. If any man's work abide which he hath built
thereupon, he shall receive a reward. If any man's work
shall be burned, he shall suffer loss; but he himself shall
be saved; yet so as by fire." There are also various
crowns spoken of as rewards for service. See, for instance, that referred to as a crown of rejoicing in 1 Thess.
2 : 19, " For what is our hope, or joy, or crown
of rejoicing ? Are not even ye in the presence of our

Lord Jesus Christ at His coming ?" In 2 Tim. 4 : 8 Paul speaks thus of a crown of righteousness which he expects to receive, " Henceforth there is laid up for me a crown of righteousness, which the Lord, the right- eous judge, will give me at that day; and not to me only, but unto all them also that love his appearing." In James 1 : 12 we read about a crown of life as follows : " Blessed is the man that endureth temptation; for when he is tried he shall receive the crown of life which the Lord hath promised to them that love him." And in 1 Peter 5 : 4 we read that the elders are to receive from the chief Shepherd crowns of glory that will not fade away if they are faithful in their office. These are doubt- less some of the crowns that are seen on the heads of the four and twenty elders in Rev. 4 : 10, and which they cast before the throne, saying, " Thou are worthy, O Lord, to receive glory, and honour, and power, for thou hast created all things, and for thy pleasure they are and were created."

Human Philosophy and Its Conflicting Theories.

The following remarks by Professor Goldwin Smith, on page 110, sound very strange after reading the Scrip- tures quoted in the early part of this chapter. He says: " The great thinkers of antiquity have the advantage (while they lacked our modern science) of studying the problem of existence, with minds free from ecclesias- tical or theological prepossessions. Plato believed in a life of future rewards and punishments. But there is no trace of this belief in Aristotle, Epiditus and Marcus Aurelius; and in Seneca there is a vague intimation that death is a transition to a higher life." Now, it may be asked in reference to this paragraph, What did the great thinking of these ancient philosophers amount to after all ? They were only guessing, and did not agree amongst themselves, and when they got through they were as much in the dark as before! No amount of

thinking can penetrate the veil that hides from the ken
of mortals here, the mysteries of a future state of existence; and if they choose to reject the revelation which
God has given in the written Word, and by the lips of
the Son of God Himself when as "the great Teacher
of humanity" He spake on earth, they cannot possibly
obtain reliable information on this subject in any
other way.

Again, on page 125, he says: "There is nothing that
can warrant us in looking for immortality as the certain
gift of unlimited benevolence invested with unlimited
power." This statement is quite correct if we add to it
the words, "Except the revelation given to us in the
Word of God." Nothing but unlimited benevolence
invested with unlimited power and, we might add, combined with infinite wisdom, could ever have devised and
carried out the work of redemption, in which God Himself has voluntarily taken the place of guilty sinners,
and, by a sacrifice of infinite value, made full expiation
for sin, and thus met all the claims of infinite justice,
so that He could be just, and at the same time justify
the ungodly who believe in Jesus. It is only on the
ground of Atonement made that sin can be put away
consistently with the holiness of God, all of whose attributes are infinite and perfect. But the possession of
immortality alone is, as we have seen in this chapter, but
a small thing compared with that "far more exceeding
and eternal weight of glory" (2 Cor. 4 : 17), which is
spoken of in 1 Peter 1 : 4 as "an inheritance, incorruptible and undefiled, and that fadeth not away, reserved
in heaven for you." This was the purpose of God in
redemption, as is proved by Gal. 4 : 4-7. "But when the
fulness of time was come, God sent forth His Son, made
of a woman, made under the law, to redeem them that
were under the law, that we might receive the adoption
of sons; and because ye are sons God hath sent forth
the Spirit of His Son into your hearts, crying, Abba.
Father. Wherefore thou art no more a servant, but a
son; and if a son, then an heir of God, through Christ."

No heathen philosophers ever imagined that men in a future state of existence could be elevated to such a place of blessing as this, of which we read again, "As it is written, Eye hath not seen, nor ear heard,. neither have entered into the heart of man, the things which God hath prepared for them that love Him. But God hath revealed them to us by His Spirit; for the Spirit searcheth all things; yea, the deep things of God" (1 Cor: 2 : 9, 10).

The Resurrection of the Body.

Professor Goldwin Smith in some of his remarks seems to be a good deal puzzled about the. resurrection of the body, and on page 125 he says: " Yet man shrinks from annihilation." The best way to learn all about the resurrection of the body is by reading 1 Cor. 15 : 35-57, " But some man will say, How are the dead raised up ? and with what body do they come ? Thou fool! That which thou sowest is not quickened except it die; and that which thou sowest, thou sowest not that body that shall be, but bare grain, it may chance of wheat, or of some other grain; but God giveth it a body as it hath pleased Him, and to every seed his own body. . . . So also is the resurrection of the dead. It is sown in corruption; it is raised in incorruption. It is sown in dishonour; it is raised in glory. It is sown in weakness; it is raised in power. It is sown a natural body; it is raised a spiritual body. And so it is written, The first man Adam was made a living soul ; the last Adam a quickening spirit. Howbeit that was not first which is spiritual, but that which is natural; and afterward that which is spiritual. The first man is of the earth, earthy; the second man is the Lord from heaven. As is the earthy, such are they also that are earthy; and as is the heavenly, such are they also that are heavenly. And as we have borne the image of the earthy, we shall also bear the image of the heavenly. . . . We (Christians) shall not all sleep, but we shall all be changed in a moment, in the twinkling of an eye, at the last trump; for the trumpet shall sound, and the dead shall be raised incorruptible, and we shall be changed. For this corruptible must put on incorruption, and this mortal must put on immortality; then shall be brought to pass the saying that is written, Death is swallowed up in victory. O Death, where is thy sting ? O grave, where is thy victory ? The sting of death is sin, and the strength of sin is the law. But thanks be to God, who giveth us the victory through our Lord Jesus Christ."

In these passages of Scripture the old and the new creations are compared and contrasted, with the first Adam as head of the first creation; and the Second Adam (or Christ) as head of the second. The first Adam is declared to have been made a living soul, and the Second Adam a quickening spirit. And the only means of transition out of the first creation into the second is by means of death and resurrection, as is taught in a former part of the same chapter, where we read: "And if Christ be not risen, then is our preaching vain, and your faith is also vain. Yea, and we are found false witnesses of God, because we have testified of God that he raised up Christ; whom he raised not up if so be the dead rise not. For if the dead rise not, then is not Christ raised; and if Christ be not raised your faith is vain; ye are yet in your sins. Then they also which are fallen asleep in Christ are perished. If in this life only we have hope in Christ, we are of all men most miserable. But now is Christ risen from the dead, and become the first fruits of them that slept. For since by man came death, by man came also the resurrection of the dead. For as in Adam all die, even so in Christ shall all (that is, all who are in Him) be made alive. But every man in his own order: Christ, the first fruits; afterward, they that are Christ's at his coming " (1 Cor. 15 : 14-23). All of which plainly teaches that in His work of redemption it was necessary that the Lord Jesus Christ should not only put away the sin of the world by the sacrifice of Himself when He died upon the cross, representing the seed of the first Adam, who were all under sentence of death; but also, that He should, as the Head of the new creation, rise again from the dead before any of the members of His mystical body could receive resurrection life through Him, who, as the Second Adam, is a quickening Spirit.

Conscience Warning Unbelievers of Judgment to Come.

On page 126 Professor · Goldwin Smith says that "there does seem to be a voice in every man which, if he will listen to it, tells him that his account is not closed with death." And again, on page 128, he says: "If death is to end all alike, for the righteous and the unrighteous, the Power that rules the universe cannot be just." But the great trouble is this, that men are not willing to admit that "There is none righteous; no, not one"; that "There is none that doeth good; no, not one"; that "All the world has become guilty before God"; and that "There is no difference, for all have sinned and come short of the glory of God" (Rom. 3 : 23). Yet this is the verdict which the Word of God pronounces against the whole human race; and it accords with the verdict rendered by men's own consciences, if they deal honestly with themselves. There is no man living who has never sinned against the light of his own conscience, and before that tribunal every man is held responsible who has not received the light of revelation through the Word of God. It is not a question of how much or how little any man has sinned. To commit one murder makes a man amenable to the same penalty of death as if he had committed a hundred murders, and to sin once against the light of either conscience or revelation makes a man a sinner just as fully as if he had sinned ten thousand times. A God of infinite justice and spotless purity cannot allow any taint of sin in His presence without punishment; and, therefore, He puts all on the same platform, and tells us "There is no difference, for all have sinned and come short of the glory of God." And it is only reasonable that all should be thus dealt with alike; for the man who is the offspring of refined and cultivated parents, and has been carefully nurtured from earliest childhood, deserves no credit for never having indulged in any of the gross vices which characterize the children of debauched and vicious parents. The Lord Jesus Christ said to the chief priests and elders of the Jews, " Verily, I say unto you, that the publicans and the harlots go into the kingdom of God before you. For John came unto you in the way of righteousness, and ye believed him not; but the publicans and the harlots believed him ; and ye when ye had seen it repented not afterward, that ye might believe him " (Matt. 21 : 31, 32). And thus it is still: the refined and intellectual and cultivated are generally too proud and self-righteous to believe the testimony of God's Word as to their own true condition as lost sinners, and thus to accept of that free salvation provided for. them " through the redemption that is in Christ Jesus," whilst the openly vicious and depraved, like John Bunyan and Richard Weaver, are conscience smitten by a sense of their own guilt, and gladly receive from the God of all grace that which He so freely offers to all upon the same principle of faith in the Lord Jesus Christ. And that voice in every man to which Professor Goldwin Smith refers is in full accord with the revelation that God has given in His Word.

It is, indeed, true that a man's account is not closed with death. " It is appointed to men once to die, but after this the judgment " (Heb. 9 : 27). " For God shall bring every work into judgment, with every secret thing, whether it be good or whether it be evil " (Eccles. 12 : 1). " Because he hath appointed a day in the which he will judge the world in righteousness by that man whom he hath ordained; whereof he hath given assurance to all men, in that he raised him from the dead " (Acts 17 : 31). " For if God spared not the angels that sinned, but cast them down to hell, and delivered them into chains of darkness, to be reserved unto judgment . . . the Lord knoweth how to deliver the godly out of temptations, and to reserve the unjust unto the day of judgment to be punished" (2 Peter 2 : 4, 9). And in Rev. 20 : 11-15 there is a description of the judgment of the dead who had rejected "that wonderful redemption, God's remedy for sin," as follows: "And I saw a great white throne, and him that sat on it, from whose face the earth and the heaven fled away; and there was found no place for them. And I saw the dead, small and great, stand before God; and the books were opened; and another book was opened, which is the book of life; and the dead were judged out of those things which were written in the books according to their works. And the sea gave up the dead which were in it; and death and Hades delivered up the dead which were in them: and they were judged, every man according to their works. And death and Hades were cast into the lake of fire. This is the second death. And whosoever was not found written in the book of life was cast into the lake of fire. And then in the following chapter we have a description of the characters of those who are cast into the lake of fire: " But the fearful, and unbelieving, and the abominable, and murderers, and whoremongers, and sorcerers, and idolators, and all liars shall have their part in the lake which burneth with fire and brimstone: which is the second death." For the unbelieving who are cast into the lake of fire one of the bitterest ingredients in their cup of misery will doubtless be the thought of their wilful refusal to believe in the revelation of Himself and His purposes that God had given in His Word, and especially respecting that wonderful redemption that was provided through the atoning sacrifice of the Lord Jesus Christ upon the cross.

Utter Failure of Man's Vain Philosophy.

On page 130 Professor Goldwin Smith says: " Supposing all proofs of personal immortality failed us, we should have to fall back on the Stoic idea of reabsorption in the universe"; and on page 132 he says that

" the estate of man upon this earth may in course of
time be vastly improved; but the sweeter life becomes
the more bitter death will be"; and again on page 131
he admits that " happiness seems to imply the sense of
security and permanence. It can hardly be predicated
of any human being, whose life is never safe, and at
most endures but for an hour." If anything were needed
to show the thoroughly unsatisfactory character of
human reasonings, apart from Divine revelation, regarding God and His purposes, and the origin and
destiny of man, these three extracts should be sufficient. They prove to us how utterly futile is the effort
to penetrate the mystery of human existence, here and
hereafter, without the teaching of the Holy Spirit, who
is now in this world, making the body of every true
Christian His temple; representing " the great Teacher
of humanity," who " spake as never man spake " before;
and guiding surely through the written Word into the
knowledge of all that God has revealed to us.

> "For ever with the Lord!" (1 Thess. 4 : 17)
>   Amen, so let it be;
> Life from the dead is in that word—
>   'Tis immortality.
>
> Here in the body pent,
>   Absent from Him I roam,
> Yet nightly pitch my moving tent
>   A day's march nearer home.
>
> My Father's house on high!
>   Home! to my soul how dear!
> I long to see thee, and I sigh
>   Within thee to appear.
>
> My thirsty spirit faints
>   To reach the home I love—
> The bright inheritance of saints,
>   Jerusalem above.

And though there intervene
  Rough roads and stormy skies,
Faith will not suffer aught to screen
  Thy glory from mine eyes.

There shall all clouds depart,
  The wilderness shall cease;
And sweetly shall each gladdened heart
  Enjoy eternal peace.

—*Montgomery.*

CONCLUSION.

PROFESSOR GOLDWIN SMITH professes to believe that there is a great Being who inhabits eternity and infinity; and he also admits that the phrase, " Nature's laws," presupposes a Lawgiver, who must be able to suspend the operation of the laws which He has given.

But he denies that this great Being has ever given any revelation of Himself and His purposes to the human race, and while, like Nicodemus, regarding Jesus as " the great Teacher of humanity," and speaking of His death as a "judicial murder," he rejects His claims to be recognized as the Son of God, the Messiah promised to the Jewish nation, or the Redeemer of mankind.

In view of his and many other conflicting theories advanced in these days by avowed infidels and so-called " higher critics " and " liberal theologians," it is of the utmost importance that honest enquirers after truth should be directed to the best means of satisfying their own minds as to whether God has really spoken to men or not. For until a man knows that God has spoken to him he cannot exercise faith in His Word. Instead, then, of commencing with the Old Testament, the simplest plan for such an one is first to consider carefully the evidence of the Life, Death, and Resurrection of the Lord Jesus Christ contained in the New Testament Scriptures. This is the most recent revelation that God has given, as well as the most wonderful; and it is brought to our knowledge by four independent histories, or Gospels, written at a time when many thousands of witnesses were living who knew as facts the things stated therein, and who were willing to seal their testimonies with their blood. It is a fact, moreover, that the things certified to in these histories have never been controvered by any reliable evidence, without which we must conclude that they are correct. Even confirmed infidels, like Professor Goldwin Smith, only try to raise doubts without producing any evidence in support of their assertions. The record given in the preceding pages of this book, from the Scriptures, of the Life, Death, and Resurrection of the Lord Jesus Christ prove that He was, as He claimed to be, the Son of God, who "spake as never man spake" before, and who, after offering Himself up as a sacrifice to atone for the sins of fallen men, rose from the dead and ascended into heaven, where He is now on the right hand of God the Father.

When a man is thoroughly satisfied that God has spoken in these last days by His Son, and especially when he has believed in the Lord Jesus Christ as his own personal Saviour, become a new creature in Him, and received the Holy Spirit as his indwelling Comforter and Teacher, it will be a very easy matter for him to see and to understand that the Old Testament Scriptures are inspired, which so plainly foretold, many centuries before the coming of Christ, so many events in connection with his history which actually happened. And if there are some things which he does not yet clearly understand, he will continue to wait patiently on God for further light in His own good time, remembering the words of Jesus: "Heaven and earth shall pass away, but my word shall not pass away" (Matt. 24 : 35), and steadfastly, like Abraham, believing God, even in direct opposition, if need be, to the evidence of his own senses and his own natural reason. This is the kind of faith that God expects from all His children, and those who can thus trust in Him will soon have reason to praise Him for the wonderful manner in which, by the teaching of the Holy Spirit, He will enable them to see Christ in the Old as well as in the New Testament, and to understand that both these records, although pertaining to different dispensations, are so closely connected with and dependent upon each other, that the teaching of one of them cannot be rightly comprehended without the aid of the other.

It should ever be borne in mind that the Scriptures have not been given to teach men scientific problems, but to reveal a Person, " in whom dwells all the fulness of the Godhead bodily." God, therefore, in speaking to men has always used language adapted to their own ideas of natural things. The heavenly bodies are spoken of as they appear to a person standing on the earth, and as with functions relative to the earth, just as we still continue to speak of the sun " rising," although well aware that it is not the sun but the earth that moves. It is only in modern times that the system of the universe has been understood, and infidels profess thus to find proofs that the Scriptures are geocentric, and not inspired by God, because the language used in such cases is not in accord with our present knowledge of astronomy and other sciences. It is easy in this manner to put stumbling-blocks in the way of those ignorant of the teaching of Scripture, and who have not yet experienced the new birth, but no true Christian will heed such frivolous objections.

God has certified to the inspiration of the Old Testament Scriptures by prophecies, many of which are referred to in this book, as literally fulfilled; but infidels and " higher critics " have vainly done their utmost to make it appear that some books must have been written at much later dates than generally believed, and often after the events predicted had occurred. Their object is only too obvious.

God has also certified to His revelations by miracles performed in the most public manner in the presence of many thousands of persons as recorded in both Old and New Testaments, but infidels and " liberal theologians " speak of such things as *incredibilities,* because they are contrary to the operation of natural laws. And yet Professor Goldwin Smith admits that the phrase, " Natural laws," presupposes a Law-giver, who is able to suspend the operation of the laws He has given; but with strange inconsistency he speaks of all miracles as being incredible, although just as real miracles are often performed at the present day in answer to the prayer of faith. The writer would mention one case especially of a girl, totally blind, having her sight restored at once in a crowded meeting in New York when he and several other persons from Toronto and other places in Canada were present. Jesus Christ is, indeed, still "the same yesterday and to-day and forever," and God still hears and answers the prayer of faith.

In fulfillment of many prophecies in the Old Testament Scriptures the Jewish race has been for the past two thousand years scattered amongst all other nations, and yet miraculously preserved as a separate people, awaiting the fulfillment of other prophecies, predicting their return in unbelief to Judea before the Second Coming of the Lord Jesus Christ as their Messiah, to reign gloriously at Jerusalem in His millennial kingdom. Their miraculous preservation, as a separate people, under such circumstances, for so many centuries, should be enough to silence those who try to make light of Old Testament prophecies, and who talk about miracles as "incredibilities."

Recent archaeological discoveries have confirmed the truth of early history as given in the Book of Genesis. The Assyrian legends are based upon the same facts as the history in Genesis ; but there is not the slightest reason to suppose that either of these accounts was borrowed from the other, and, therefore, no ground for the assertion of infidels that the Scripture history was of Babylonish origin, although Abram at the call of God went from Ur of the Chaldees, near Babylon, to Canaan. And besides, Berosus wrote of him as a man "skilful in the celestial science," showing that he had a knowledge of the true God, which was not derived from the myths and legends of those who had lapsed into idolatry, and thus corrupted the knowledge of the world's early history that their fathers had originally received from Noah and his sons, which was the same source from which Abram had received the history given in the first eleven chapters of Genesis. Later portions of Bible history have also been confirmed by many archaeological discoveries in Assyria, Babylonia and Egypt.

But no man who is really born of God requires any of these evidences to convince him that the Bible is a Divine Revelation. The miracle of his own regeneration, and the consciousness of a Divine Person dwelling within him, are more powerful arguments than all the sophistical reasonings of all the skeptical philosophers and theological professors in Christendom.

There are, however, many thousands of young men and women who at one time or another are seriously inclined to study the Scriptures with special reference to the question of their own eternal salvation; and it is impossible to form an estimate of the amount of mischief which has already been done to such persons by the plausible sophistries with which infidels and skeptical professors try to undermine faith in the Bible as being really the Word of God. To those who are honest enquirers after truth the advice is again given to read carefully the four Gospels and the Acts, and satisfy themselves as to the evidence that God has really spoken by His Son, and in the meantime to avoid reading or listening to skeptical arguments, which might hinder the investigation of this evidence with unbiased minds.

APPENDICES.

APPENDICES.

APPENDIX A.

ASSYRIAN LEGENDS.

THE antiquarian researches of the late Mr. George Smith and others in Assyria and Babylonia have led to the discovery of many important inscriptions buried in the ruins of ancient cities, which confirm Scripture history as recorded in the Book of Genesis. As is usually the case, infidels at first tried to make use of these discoveries by declaring that such records had been brought to the notice of the Hebrews who had been carried captive to Babylon, and that it was they who, during their captivity, had written the first five books of Moses, known as the Pentateuch, the historical books, and even the Psalms. It was from materials such as these, they alleged, that the Bible narratives of the Creation, the Fall, and the Flood, etc., were compiled, which were afterwards accepted as the writings of Moses. To the same authorship they also ascribed the historical books, and Professor Goldwin Smith goes so far as to suggest that the Psalms were also written by the Hebrew captives at the same time, because they bear marks of the *pensiveness of the Captivity!*

The object which infidel writers have in view when making these assertions is very obvious. If it could only be made to appear by any plausible kind of reasoning that all the most ancient books of the Old Testament Scriptures were compiled about the same time during the Babylonish captivity one of the strongest evidences of the truth of Christianity as a supernatural religion would be removed, and it would be a comparatively easy matter to set aside or explain away other books of the Old Testament Scriptures written in later ages. For, as Professor Smith himself puts it, if the Book of Genesis is not divinely inspired, there was no Fall, and if there was no Fall there was no need for redemption, and if there was no need for redemption there was no incarnation; and, therefore, the claim that the Lord Jesus was, as He professed to be, the Son of God, or God manifest in the flesh, is a delusion, and the story of His resurrection a fable, which is only on a par with those of ancient mythology.

One of the strongest arguments in favour of the truth of Scripture as a Divine revelation is the fact that so many different books in the Old Testament Scriptures were written by different persons, in different countries, at dates extending over many centuries, so that there was no possibility of collusion between them ; and that these books confirm each other as to the nature of those Divine revelations of Himself which God had given, and as to the miraculous manifestations by which the truth of those revelations had been attested. That these books were written at the times when they profess to have been written has been abundantly proved by the discoveries of archaeological science, which have unearthed from the ruins of ancient cities the names of persons and places mentioned in Genesis as existing in the time of Abraham, as, for instance, the names of Abram; of Arioch, King of Ellasar; Chedorlaomer, King of Elam, and Tidal, king of nations, referred to in Gen. 14 : 1, which have been found inscribed on some very ancient earthen tablets. In the same way legends have been discovered confirming in many respects the accounts given in the Bible narrative of Creation, the Fall, the Flood, the Tower of Babel, and the confusion of tongues. These legends evidently had their origin in the facts made known by the reliable traditions handed down from Adam to Abraham in the direct line of descent through Enoch, Methuselah, Noah, and Shem, and confirmed by many others living at the same time. But, as shown by the history of the Israelites in future ages, there was always a tendency on the part of mankind to depart from the worship and service of the one living and true God, and to lapse into idolatry. And thus it was with the great mass of Noah's descendants, who soon became idolators, and only preserved dim legendary ideas of those important events in connection with the early history of the human race; and these ideas were evidently mixed with much that was purely mythical. However, the discovery of such tablets and the positive evidence that they were inscribed about the time of Abraham are of immense importance as confirming the correctness of Scripture history given in the Book of Genesis.

It would seem that the hypothesis adopted by Professor Smith and other infidels is, that some of the Jewish captives in Babylon about 1,200 years after these tablets were inscribed became acquainted with their contents in some way not explained, and that, with the legends inscribed on them as a basis, they set to work and forged the first five books in the Bible and attributed the writing of them to Moses, and that in the same manner the historical books, and probably also the Books of Esther and Job and the Psalms, etc., were compiled by these wonderfully clever and *pensive* captives. If such a thing were possible what could be their object in perpetrating such a tremendous religious fraud? The absurdity of such a hypothesis is self-evident. It is impossible for any unprejudiced person to compare these legends, written 2,000 years before Christ, with the Scripture narrative without perceiving that the legends are derived from the same source as the reliable traditions afterwards committed to writing by Moses, and certified to by the Lord Jesus Christ as the Word of God; and that they are thus one of the strongest possible proofs of the truth of Scripture history.

To enable the reader to judge for himself as to the correctness of these statements, the following extracts are given from the translations by Mr. George Smith of the inscriptions found on Assyrian tablets, which contain legends regarding the subjects referred to in the first eleven chapters of Genesis. It must be remarked, however, that the earlier tablets, with their ancient Chal-

dean cunieform inscriptions, were, during the lapse of many centuries, broken into many thousands of fragments before being discovered by him over twenty years ago. Many of these have been lost or destroyed, so as to make their identification impossible, and this occasioned many breaks in the legends, which are shown just as they appear in the able and interesting work published by the discoverer, entitled "The Chaldean Account of Genesis." Breaks are shown as follows :
. . . .

Babylonian Legend of the Creation. Part of First Tablet.

1. When above were not raised the heavens;
2. And below on the earth a plant had not grown up:
3. the abyss also had not broken open their boundaries;
4. The chaos (or water) Tiamat (the sea) was the producing mother of the whole of them.
5. Those waters at the beginning were ordained; but
6. a tree had not grown, a flower had not unfolded,
7. When the gods had not sprung up any one of them;
8. A plant had not grown, and order did not exist;
9. Were made also the great gods,
10. the gods Lahmu and Lahamu they caused to come . . . . . .
11. and they grew . . . . . .
12. the gods Sar and Kisar were made . . . . .
13. a course of days and a long time passed . . . . .
14. the god Anu . . . . . .
15. the gods Sar and . . . . . .
16. . . . .

This tablet evidently represents the earth as "without form and void," as in Genesis 1 : 2.

Fifth Tablet.

1. It was delightful, all that was fixed by the great gods,

2. Stars, their appearance (in figures) of animals he arranged.

3. To fix the year through the observation of their constellations.

4. twelve months (or signs) of stars in three rows he arranged.

5. from the day when the year commences unto the close.

6. he marked the positions of the wandering stars (planets) to shine in their courses.

7. that they may not do injury, and may not trouble any one,

8. the positions of the gods Bel and Hea he fixed with him.

9. And he opened the great gates in the darkness shrouded

10. the fastenings were strong on the left and right.

11. In its mass (*i.e.* the lower chaos) he made a boiling,

12. the god Uru (the moon) he caused to rise out. the night he overshadowed.

13. to fix it also for the light of the night until the shining of the day.

14. That the month might not be broken and in its amount be regular.

15. At the beginning of the month, at the rising of the night,

16. his horns are breaking through to shine on the heaven,

17. On the seventh day to a circle he begins to swell,

18. and stretches towards the dawn further.

19. When the god Shamas (the sun) in the horizon of heaven, in the east,

20. . . . . . . formed beautifully and . . . .

21. . . . . to the orbit Shamas was perfected

22. . . . . the dawn Shamas should change

23. . . . . going on its path
24. . . . . giving judgment
25. . . . . to tame
26. . . . . a second time.
27. . . . .

Before this fifth tablet there are several others missing, which may have been destroyed. But this fifth one gives the legendary account of how God created the stars and the sun and the moon, after which there is a blank and then a fragment relating the creation of wild and domestic animals as follows:

Fragment of Tablet VII.

1. When the gods in their assembly had created
. . . . .

2. were delightful, the strong monsters . . . . .
3. they caused to be living creatures . . . . .
4. cattle of the field, beasts of the field, and creeping things of the field . . . . .
5. they fixed for the living creatures . . . . .
6. . . . . cattle and creeping things of the city they fixed . . . .
7. . . . . the assembly of the creeping things, the whole which were created . . . .
8. . . . . . . which in the assembly of my family
. . . . . .

9. . . . . . and the god Nin-si-ku (the lord of noble face) caused to be two . . .
10. . . . . . the assembly of the creeping things he caused to go . . . . . .
11. . . . . . . flesh beautiful ? . . . . . .
12. . . . . . . pure presence . . . .
13. . . . . . . pure presence . . . .
14. . . . . . . pure presence in the assembly
. . . . . .

15. . . . .

This corresponds with Genesis 1 : 24, 25, describing the creation of all living creatures and creeping things, after which it is stated that " God saw that it was good."

Many lines of the next tablet relating to the creation of man have been lost and many others are mutilated.

Fragment of Tablet VIII.

1. evil . . . . .
2. which is eaten by the stomach . . . .
3. in growing . . . . .
4. consumed . . . . .
5. extended, heavy . . . . .
6. firmly thou shalt speak . . . . .
7. And the support of mankind . . . . . thee.
8. Every day thy god thou shalt approach (or invoke).
9. Sacrifice, prayer of the mouth and instruments . . . . . .
10. to thy god in reverence thou shalt carry.
11. Whatever shall be suitable for divinity.
12. supplication, humility, and bowing of the face,
13. fire ? thou shalt give to him and thou shalt bring tribute.
14. and in the fear also of god thou shalt be holy.
15. In thy knowledge, and afterwards in the tablets (writing)
16. worship and goodness shall be raised ?
17. Sacrifice saving . . . .
18. and worship . . . .
19. the fear of god thou shalt not leave . . . .
20. the fear of the angels thou shalt live in . . . . .
21. With friend and enemy? speech thou shalt make? . . . . . .
22. under ? speech thou shalt make good . . . .
23. When thou shalt speak also he will give . . . .
24. When thou shalt trust also thou . . . .
25. to enemy ? also . . . .
26. . . . . thou shalt trust a friend . . . .
27. . . . . thy knowledge also.

This appears to be a speech by the Deity to the newly created man; and on the reverse side of the tablet is what appears to be a speech of the Deity to the newly

created woman, at the beginning of which many lines
are lost, and many of those remaining are much mutilated. It reads as follows:

1. Beautiful place also . . . . divide . . . .
2. in beauty and . . . . thy hand . . . .
3. and thou to the presence . . . . thou shalt
fix . . . . .
4. and not thy sentence . . . . thee to the end ?
5. in the presence of beauty and . . . . thou
shalt speak
6. of thy beauty and . . . . .
7. beautiful and . . . . to give drink ?
8. Circle I fill . . . . his enemies
9. his rising ? he seeks . . . . the man . . . .
10. with the lord of thy beauty thou shalt be faithful,
11. to do evil thou shalt not approach him
12. at thy illness . . . . to him
13. at thy distress . . . .

It is remarkable that on this tablet only one " God "
is mentioned, and it shows both the man and the woman
in a condition of purity and innocence, except where the
address to the woman breaks off, which proves that man
has already fallen.

In connection with the subject of the Fall of Man it
may be remarked that Mr. George Smith's book contains
a copy of an engraving on an Assyrian cylinder showing
a sacred tree with two attendant Cherubim, and a copy
from an early Babylonian cylinder of a sacred tree with
two human figures seated one on each side of it, and a
serpent in the background. The dragon referred to in
the following tablet is evidently identical with the serpent spoken of in Genesis.

The Fall of Man and the Curse. Result of Tablet VIII.

1. . . . . . .
2. . . . . . . the star . . . . .
3. may he take the tail and head . . . . .
4. because the dragon Tiamat had . . . . .

5. his punishment the planets possessing . . . .

6. by the stars of heaven themselves may they . . . :

7. like a sheep may the gods tremble all of them

8. may he bind Tiamat her prisons may he shut up and surround

9. Afterwards the people of remote ages

10. may she remove, not destroy . . . . for ever,

11. to the place he created he made strong.

12. Lord of the earth his name called out, the father Elu

13. in the ranks of the angels pronounced their curse

14. The god Hea heard and his liver was angry

15. because his man had corrupted his purity.

16. He like me also Hea may he punish him

17. the course of my issue all of them may he remove, and

18. all my seed may he destroy.

19. In the language of the fifty great gods

20. by his fifty names he called, and turned away in anger from him;

21. May he be conquered, and at once cut off.

22. Wisdom and knowledge hostilely may they injure him,

23. May they put at enmity also father and son, and may they plunder,

24. to king, ruler, and governor, may they bend their ear.

25. May they cause anger also to the lord of the gods Merodach.

26. His land may it bring forth but he not touch it;

27. his desire shall be cut off, and his will be unanswered.

28. the opening of his mouth no god shall take notice of;

29. his back shall be broken and not be healed;

30. at his urgent trouble no god shall receive him;

31. his heart shall be poured out and his mind shall be troubled;

32. to sin and wrong his face shall come . . . . .

33. . . . . . front . . . . .
34. . . . .

Mr. George Smith says that he believes the "Izdubar legends" give the history of the Biblical hero, Nimrod (Gen. 10 : 8-10); that he discovered them in 1872, and that they are principally of interest from their containing the Chaldean account of the Deluge. These legends are inscribed on twelve tablets, all of which are in fragments, and none complete; but it is fortunate that the most perfect tablet is the eleventh, which describes the Deluge.

The Story of the Flood. Tablet II.
Column 1.

1. Izdubar (Nimrod) after this manner also said to Hasisadra (Noah) afar off.
2. I consider the matter.
3. why thou repeatest not to me from thee,
4. and thou repeatest not to me from thee,
5. thy ceasing my heart to make war
6. presses ? of thee, I come up after thee.
7. . . . . how thou hast done, and in the assembly of the gods alive thou art placed
8. Hasisadra after this manner also said to Izdubar:
9. Be revealed to thee Izdubar the concealed story.
10. And the judgment of the gods be related to thee.
11. The city Surippak, the city where thou standest not . . . . placed,
12. that city is ancient . . . . the gods within it
13. . . . . . their servant, the great gods
14. . . . . . the god Anu,   .
15. . . . . . the god Bel,
16. . . . . . . the god Ninip.
17. and the god . . . . lord of Hades;
18. their will be revealed in the midst . . . . and
19. I his will was hearing, and he spake to me;
20. Surippakite, son of Ubaratutu,   ˌ
21. . . . . . make a ship after this . . . .
22. . . . . . I destroy ? the sinner and life . . . .

23. . . . . . cause to go in? the seed of life all of it to the midst of the ship,

24. The ship which thou shalt make,

25. 600 ? cubits shall be the measure of its length, and

26. 60 ? cubits the amount of its breadth and its height,

27. . . . . . into the deep launch it,

28. I perceived and said to Hea my lord:

29. The ship making which thou commandest me,

30. When I shall have made,

31. young and old will deride me,

32. Hea opened his mouth and spake and said to me his servant :

33. . . . . . thou shalt say unto them,

34. . . . . . he has turned from me and

35. . . . . . fixed over me

36. . . . . like caves . . . .

37. . . . . . above and below

38. . . . . . closed the ship . . . .

39. . . . . . the flood which I will send to you,

40. into it enter and the door of the ship turn,

41. Into the midst of it thy grain, thy furniture, and thy goods,

42. thy wealth, thy woman servants, thy female slaves, and the young men,

43. the beasts of the field, the animals of the field all, I will gather and

44. I will send to thee, and they shall be enclosed in thy door;

45. Adrahasis his mouth opened and spake, and

46. said to Hea his lord:

47. Any one the ship will not make . . . .

48. on the earth fixed . . . .

49. . . . . I may see also the ship . . . .

50. . . . . on the ground the ship . . . . .

51. the ship making which thou commandest me . . . .

52. which in . . . . .

Column 2.

1. strong . . . .
2. on the fifth day . . . .it
3. in its circuit 14 measures . . . .its frame
4. 14 measures it measured . . . .over it
5. I placed its roof, it . . . . I enclosed it
6. I rode in it on the sixth time; I examined its exterior on the seventh time.
7. its interior I examined on the eighth time.
8. Planks against the waters within it I placed
9. I saw rents and the wanting parts I added,
10. 3 measures of bitumen I poured over the outside
11. 3 measures of bitumen I poured over the inside
12. 3 . . . . men carrying its baskets, they constructed boxes
13. I placed in the boxes the offering they sacrificed.
14. Two measures of boxes I had distributed to the boatmen.
15. To . . . . were sacrificed oxen
16. . . . . . . dust and
17. . . . . . wine in receptacle of goats
18. I collected like the waters of a river, also
19. food like the dust of the earth also
20. I collected in boxes with my hand I placed
21. . . . . Shamas . . . . material of the ship completed
22. . . . . . . strong and
23. the reed oars of the ship I caused to bring above and below,
24. . . . . . . they went in two thirds of it
25. All I possessed the strength of it, all I possessed the strength of it silver,
26. all I possessed the strength of it gold,
27. all I possessed the strength of it, the seed of life, the whole
28. I caused to go up into the ship; all my male servants and my female servants

29. the beast of the field, the animal of the field the sons of the people all of them I caused to go up,

30. A flood Shamas made and

31. he spake saying in the night: I will cause it to rain heavily,

32. enter to the midst of the ship, and shut thy door.

33. that flood happened, of which

34. he spake saying in the night: I will cause it to rain (or it will rain) from heaven heavily.

35. In the day I celebrated his festival

36. the day of watching fear I had

37. I entered to the midst of the ship and shut my door,

38. To close the ship to Buzur-sadirabi the boatman

39. the palace I gave with its goods

40. Ragmu-seri-ina-namari

41. arose from the horizon of heaven extending and wide

42. Vul in the midst of it thundered, and

43. Nebo and Saru went in front,

44. the throne bearers went over mountains and plains,

45. the destroyer Nergal overturned,

46. Ninip went in front and cast down,

47. the spirits carried destruction,

48. in their glory they swept the earth

49. of Vul the flood reached to heaven

50. The bright earth to a waste was turned

Column 3.

1. The surface of the earth like . . . . it swept

2. it destroyed all life from the face of the earth
. . . .

3. the strong deluge over, the people reached to heaven,

4. Brother saw not his brother, they did not know the people. In heaven

5. the gods feared the tempest and

6. sought refuge; they ascended to the heaven of Anu.

7. The gods like dogs fixed in droves prostrate.

8. Spake Ishtar like a child,

9.uttered Rubat her speech:

10. All to corruption are turned and

11. then I in the presence of the gods prophesied evil.

12. As I prophesied in the presence of the gods evil,

13. to evil were devoted all my people and I prophesied

14. thus: I have begotten my people and

15. like the young of the fishes they fill the sea.

16. The gods concerning the spirits were weeping with her,

17. the gods in seats seated in lamentation,

18. covered were their lips for the coming evil.

19. Six days and nights

20. passed, the wind, deluge, and storm, overwhelmed

21. On the seventh day in its course was calmed the storm, and all the deluge

22. which had destroyed like an earthquake,

23. quieted. The sea he caused to dry, and the wind and deluge ended

24. I perceived the sea making a tossing;

25. and the whole of mankind turned to corruption,

26. like reeds the corpses floated,

27. I opened the window, and the light broke over my face,

28. it passed. I sat down and wept,

29. over my face flowed my tears,

30. I perceived the shore at the boundary of the sea,

31. for 12 measures the land rose

32. To the country of Nizir went the ship;

33. the mountain of Nizir stopped the ship, and to pass over it it was not able.

34. The first day and the second day the mountain of Nizir the same

35. The third day and the fourth day the mountain of Nizir the same

36. The fifth and sixth the mountain of Nizir the same

37. On the seventh day in the course of it,

38. I sent forth a dove and it left. The dove went and turned and

39. a resting place it did not find, and it returned,

40. I sent forth a swallow and it left. The swallow went and turned and

41. a resting place it did not find, and it returned.

42. I sent forth a raven and it left.

43. The raven went, and the decrease of the water it saw, and

44. it did eat, it swam, and wandered away, and did not return

45. I sent the animals forth to the four winds, I poured out a libation.

46. I built an altar on the peak of the mountain,

47. by seven herbs I cut.

48. at the bottom of them I placed reeds, pines, and simgar.

49. The gods collected at its savor, the gods collected at its good savor

50. the gods like flies over the sacrifice gathered

51. From of old; also Rubat in her course

52. The great brightness of Anu had created. When the glory

53. of those gods on the charm round my neck I would not leave;

Column 4.

1. in those days I desired that forever I might not leave them.

2. May the gods come to my altar,

3. may Elu not come to my altar,

4. for he did not consider and had made a deluge.

5. and my people he had consigned to the deep.

6. From of old also Elu in his course

7. saw the ship, and went Elu, with anger filled to the gods and spirits;

8. Let not any one come out alive, let not a man be saved from the deep.

9. Ninip his mouth opened, and spake and said to the warrior Elu:

10. Who then will ask Hea, the matter he has done ?

11. and Hea knew all things.

12. Hea his mouth opened and spake and said to the warrior Bel

13. "Thou prince of the gods warrior

14. when thou art angry a deluge thou makest;

15. the doer of sin did his sin, the doer of evil did his evil

16. the just prince, let him not be cut off; the faithful, let him not be destroyed.

17. Instead of thee making a deluge, may lions increase and men be reduced

18. instead of thee making a deluge, may leopards increase and men be reduced.

19. instead of thee making a deluge, may a famine happen and the country be destroyed.

20. instead of thee making a deluge, may pestilence increase and men be destroyed.

21. I did not peer into the judgment of the gods.

22. Adrahasis a dream they sent and the judgment of the gods he heard.

23. When his judgment was accomplished Bel went up to the midst of the ship

24. He took my hand and raised me up.

25. he caused to raise and to bring my wife to my side.

26. he made a bond, he established in a covenant, and gave this blessing.

27. in the presence of Hasisadra and the people thus:

28. When Hasisadra (Noah) and his wife, and the people, to be like the gods, are carried away;

29. then shall dwell Hasisadra in a remote place at the mouth of the rivers.

30. They took me and in a remote place at the mouth of the rivers they seated me.

It is unnecessary to continue this legend any farther, as enough has been given for the sake of comparison with the Scripture record. The balance of it is mainly taken up with conversations between Hasisadra (Noah) and his wife and the exploits of the hero Izdubar (Nimrod) and conversations between him and his boatman, Urhamsi. It is quite evident that this legend was originally founded upon the facts briefly stated in Genesis. The date of Nimrod or Izdubar is supposed to have been about B.C. 2250, and the time when the above legends were inscribed on the tablets is supposed to have been about B.C. 2000, so that about 250 years must have elapsed from the supposed visit of Izdubar to Hasisadra before the legend was reduced to writing, which, although originally founded on facts, became corrupted and enlarged by idolators. Mr. George Smith thinks that every tradition which has any foundation in fact springs up within a generation of the time when the circumstances happened, and says that he would not reject those events which may have happened because, in order to illustrate a current belief, or add to the romance of the story, the writer has introduced the supernatural.

Tower of Babel and Confusion of Tongues.

On having a fragment of one of the Assyrian tablets cleaned the same distinguished archaeologist, Mr. George Smith, was astonished to find that it contained a mutilated account confirming the Scripture record of this event as follows :

1. . . . . . them ? the father . . . .
2. . . . . . of him, his heart was evil,
3. . . . . . against the father of all the gods was wicked
4. . . . . . of him, his heart was evil,
5. . . . . . Babylon brought to subjection,
6. (Small) and great he confounded their speech

7. . . . . Babylon brought to subjection

8. (Small) and great he confounded their speech,

9. their strong place (tower) all the day they founded;

10. to their strong place in the night

11. entirely he made an end,

12. In his anger also word thus he poured out :

13. (to) scatter abroad he set his face

14. he gave this ? command their counsel was confused

15. . . . . . the course he broke

16. . . . . . fixed the sanctuary

It is really wonderful how God has so ordered events that these tablets should be discovered 4,000 years after they were written, and just at the time when infidels and "higher critics" had begun to fancy that they had succeeded in disproving the authenticity and inspiration of the Bible as a Divine revelation from God to man.

The reader is referred to remarks made in Chapter I., Page 21, under the heading of "Reliable Traditions Contrasted with Legends."

N.B.—Since the discovery of the above inscriptions by Mr. George Smith, over twenty years ago, other versions of them have been issued, in which most of the breaks have been filled in, but the author of this book has preferred to adhere to the original tablets as they were found by Mr. Smith, showing all the breaks, rather than to accept any version where these breaks might possibly be filled in to suit one-sided views.

APPENDIX. B.

DR. WORKMAN'S BOOK.

Under the title of "The Old Testament Vindicated"
a reply to Professor Goldwin Smith's essay on "The
Church and the Old Testament; or, Christianity's Millstone," has been published by Professor George Coulson
Workman, M.A., Ph.D., and endorsed in a highly eulo-
gistic introduction by Nathaniel Burwash, S.T.D., LL.D.,
Chancellor of Victoria University, Toronto.

This book has been commended to the public by very
flattering criticisms from many portions of the religious
and secular press, and from several theological professors in the leading denominations of this country
and the United States.

It is, therefore, with considerable diffidence that the
writer presumes to differ from its author as to some of
the statements which he, as one of the so-called "liberal
theologians," makes regarding the inspiration of the
Bible and kindred subjects.

The amazing assumption of superior scholarship on
the part of those who deny the verbal inspiration of the
Scriptures, and the repeated assertions that science has
proved this, that, and the other thing, without entering
into any explanations which people possessed of only
ordinary faculties and limited education can grasp, has
had the effect already of awing into submission many
simple-minded persons, who conclude too hastily that
great scholars would not speak so positively unless they
knew whereof they were speaking. And thus it has
happened that the rank and file in the various denominations have passively submitted to the introduction of
downright infidelity into their various seats of learning
in direct opposition to their doctrinal standards; and the
rising generation of preachers are being taught to reject

the verbal inspiration of the Bible as the Word of God, believed in thus by our fathers, and by all the most godly and spiritual minded men in ages past, who have been largely used in the preaching of the Gospel and the building up of the Church. The *great scholars* have now come to the front with the declaration that there is only *a Divine element* in the Bible, and that all those super-natural things revealed in it can be so explained away that unsanctified human reason will accept its spiritual teaching without believing that the Book itself is really the Word of God.

They seem to forget, however, that just as learned scholars as themselves still hold fast to the verbal inspir-ation of the Scriptures, and that the great majority, if not all, of those who are taking a leading part in evangelistic and missionary work hold fast to the same great truth, without which there would be but little blessing on their efforts to win souls for Christ.

It is nothing uncommon now to meet unconverted persons making no pretensions to either scholarship or scientific knowledge who openly deride the idea of the Scriptures being the Word of God, and talk loudly about what science has proved without being able to substan-tiate their assertions by facts. But when cornered in argument they are very apt to quote the opinions of such learned men as Professor Goldwin Smith, Professor Workman, or Professor Burwash.

A few quotations from Professor Workman's book will show the manner in which scholarship, or the as-sumption of superior scholarship, on the part of those known as " higher critics " or " liberal theologians," instead of spiritual discernment, is constantly paraded as the all-important requisite in the investigation of spiritual truths.

In the Preface (page 6) he says: " In former times *religious scholars have so magnified the influence of God* in the composition of the Scriptures as to see nothing but a Divine element in the Bible "; and again, " *Christian scholars now acknowledge a twofold element* in the Bible;

but, while they perceive two elements in it, they hold as firmly to the Divine element which faith recognizes as to the human element which reason sees."

On page 9 he says: "There is nothing about it that needs even to be modified but *an erroneous theory of the inspiration of its authors* and an irrational method of interpreting its books"; and on page 10 he adds: "The only thing about it that ought to be discarded is an old-fashioned way of viewing and treating its literature."

Professor Bonney, Canon of Manchester, in an address at Norwich, stated that: "The stories of the Flood and of the Tower of Babel are *incredible* in their present form. Some historical element may underlie many of the traditions in the first eleven chapters of that book, but this we cannot hope to recover." Regarding this assertion Professor Workman says, on page 23: "This statement indicates rather *a confused faith* than an intelligent abandonment of faith," whatever he may mean by that.

But Professor Goldwin Smith refers to the same statement by Canon Bonney, who is another of the "liberal theologians," and points to its legitimate conclusion as follows: "With the historical character of the chapters relating to the Creation Canon Bonney must resign his belief in the Fall of Adam; with his belief in the Fall of Adam he must surrender the doctrine of the Atonement, as connected with that event, and thus relieve conscience of the strain put upon it in struggling to reconcile vicarious punishment with our sense of justice. He will also have to lay aside his belief in the Serpent of the Temptation, and in the primeval personality of evil." To which Professor Workman, on page 24, makes the following extraordinary reply: "Professor Smith is too profound a student, general as well as special, not to know that *the account of the Fall in Genesis, which was once explained by theologians as literal history, is now explained by Christian scholars as religious allegory*—an allegory, like a parable, being a form of narrative employed by the sacred writers to inculcate spiritual truth. The second and third chapters of the book were constructed out of traditional materials, which are not only of Babylonian origin (see Appendix A), but are stamped with a Babylonian impress, as Professor Sayce, the eminent archaeologist, has shown. Hence, in primitive times, no doubt, some features of the story were regarded as literal facts, which at the present time are not so regarded."

On page 25 he says: "Inasmuch as the doctrine of a personal devil does not belong to Mosaism, and does not appear in the Old Testament before the time of the Exile, the *best* interpreters of Genesis do not hold that the story of the Fall teaches the primeval personality of Evil." This statement is absolutely untrue, as a personal devil is spoken of in the Book of Job, the oldest book in the Bible, generally believed to have been writen by Moses while among the Midianites, although infidel critics try to make it appear that it was written during the Captivity, without producing any reasonable proof for such a theory. That such a person as Job really lived is proved by Ezek. 14 : 14-20, and James 5 : 11, and the book may have been written by himself.

On page 26 Professor Workman says: "While Paul uses the familiar form of Genesis in introducing the doctrine of Atonement, and, in that sense, connects it with the Fall of Adam, the apostle really connects the doctrine with the entrance of sin as a moral fact into human nature. Consequently, we are not required by anything in the Bible to reconcile vicarious punishment with our sense of justice, because *the New Testament writers nowhere represent our Heavenly Father as punishing Christ for the sins of men.* They simply represent our Lord as in loving obedience to the will of His Father effecting the reconcilation of man to God." But the Lord Jesus Christ said plainly to those who claimed God as their Father and at the same time perverted His words: "Why do ye not understand my speech? . . . . ye are of your father, the devil, and the lusts of your father ye will do. He was a murderer from the beginning, and abode not in the truth, because there is no truth in him. When he speaketh a lie, he speaketh of his own, for he is a liar, and the father of it . . . He that is of God heareth God's words; ye, therefore, hear them not, because ye are not of God." No matter what critics and "liberal theologians" might think, it is quite certain that the Lord Jesus Christ believed and taught that there is a real, personal devil; and that those who would not believe God's words had no right to claim Him as their Father.

On page 27 he says that "Bishop Butler speaks of the sacrifice of Christ as a vicarious punishment, but he employs the words, not in the sense of an inflictive penalty, exacted or imposed by God, but in the sense of a providential appointment of every day's experience. In the daily course of natural providence, he says, it is appointed that innocent people should suffer for (on account of) the faults of the guilty. He further says that, as one person's sufferings contribute to the relief of another, so the sufferings of Christ *could contribute to* the redemption of the world." And then Professor Workman goes on to say: "Vicarious punishment, however, is an ambiguous, as well as an unscriptural, expression, which should never be applied to the redemptive work of Christ." In direct opposition to all which fine-spun theorizing the Word of God distinctly says: "But he was wounded for our transgressions, he was bruised for our iniquities; the chastisement of our peace was upon him; and with his stripes we are healed. All we like sheep have gone astray; we have turned every one to his own way; and the Lord hath laid upon him the iniquity of us all" (Isa. 53 : 5, 6). It is no wonder that infidelity is on the increase inside of the professing Church when such a fundamental, vital truth as the vicarious sacrifice of the Lord Jesus Christ, clearly taught in both Old and New Testaments is thus publicly denied by leading bishops and professors, whose teaching is in direct opposition to those doctrines which they have professed to believe.

On page 29 he says: "Assuming that Biblical inspiration is equivalent to dictation by the Holy Spirit (a theory which *no scholar holds*), he (*i.e.*, Goldwin Smith) shows that the Old Testament contains some things which are incompatible with such a view (a truism which *no scholar doubts*); and then he asks if these things are inspired (a supposition which *no scholar entertains*)." On the same page he speaks of Professor Goldwin Smith's article as perhaps "the most misleading, if not the most mischievous, critique of the ancient Scriptures that has ever been written *by a reverent, religious scholar*," and goes on to describe it as "simply an arraignment of an obsolete theory of the Old Testament. That is to say, he arraigns the well-known difficulties connected with *an old-fashioned view of Scripture*, which a recent but truly evangelical view removes."

On page 31 he says: "*Modern scholars* modify their views of the Bible." The extraordinary conceit about the value of scholarship in teaching the truth of Scripture as displayed and constantly repeated in this book must be simply nauseating to any godly, spiritual-minded man who knows "in whom he has believed," and who recognizes that it is the Holy Spirit alone who, through the Word, can guide into all truth. It is in striking contrast with the testimony and experience of that most honoured servant of God, George Müller, who, only a few months ago, went to his reward at the advanced age of ninety-three years.

Addressing a company of university students, Mr. Müller said: "Young gentlemen, I, too, have been a university student, and I am glad to meet you. I know you and your student life through and through. There isn't anything in the life you are now living or in the studies you are now studying that I do not know all about. Probably I know some things you do not know. . . . I have read all the Latin and Greek classics. I can talk Latin and Greek. I can speak nearly all the European languages. I can read Hebrew, Arabic, Syriac, and some other Oriental tongues. I have studied mathematics, philosophy, chemistry, and such things. So you see, young gentlemen, you have nothing to teach me in your departments of university study, and probably there are some things I could teach you." He then went on to tell them about his conversion and to preach Christ to them. If it had not been for this most important experience of the new birth his great learning would doubtless have qualified him for a first-class "higher critic," and he might have commanded a high salary as professor in any of our foremost theological colleges. But God had far higher work for him to do, and chose him as an honoured instrument to prove by a life of faith in His service, unparalleled in modern times, that He is indeed the same yesterday, to-day, and forever, a faithful, convenant-keeping God. Like the Apostle Paul, he counted all things but loss for the excellency of the knowledge of Christ Jesus, his Lord; and he only spoke of his scholastic attainments to point out their comparative worthlessness. One of the most marked traits in the life of that humble and distinguished servant of God was his reverence and esteem for the Scriptures, respecting which, not long ago, he wrote as follows: "I have been for sixty-eight years a lover of the Word of God, and that uninterruptedly. During that time I have read considerably more than one hundred times through the whole Bible with great delight. I have for many years read through the whole Old and New Testaments, with prayer and meditation, four times every year. I also state to the glory of God as His witness that in my inmost soul I believe all the books of the Old Testament, as well as the Gospels, Epistles, and the Revelation of the New Testament, are written by Divine inspiration."

Surely such a testimony as this to the verbal inspiration of the Bible must have infinitely more weight with any candid enquirer than all the theories of all the so-called and self-styled " higher critics " and " liberal theologians," whose opinions are only a rehash of the arguments of German and English skeptics since the days of Voltaire and Tom Paine. And there are many hundreds of other godly and spiritual men, who are also great scholars, that hold firmly to the Divine inspiration of the whole Word of God, notwithstanding the repeated confident assertions of Professor Workman as to what "the *best* Christian scholars and *modern* Christian scholars" hold and teach.

A few more extracts from this book will suffice to show the character of the teaching which young men studying for the ministry may expect to receive from Professors known as "liberal theologians." On page 35, writing in defence of one of the teachers of this school, Dr. Workman says: "The editor of *Lux Mundi* does not assume that myths are inspired. He simply regards traditional narratives, such as those presented in the earlier chapters of Genesis, as containing great inspirations of all things!" And again, on page 35, he says: "The Church does not need to insist, and certainly does not intend to insist, on the historical character of any account that is not demonstrably historical" (by which it is supposed that he means anything that is supernatural). Why he should assume to speak on behalf of the whole Church is not explained!

On page 26 he says that "*no scholar* of repute to-day accepts the dictation theory of inspiration because . . . he very properly speaks of verbal inspiration as being but a consecrated tradition"; and then he adds: "All such mechanical theories of the Bible have long since been discarded. The Holy Spirit did not dictate the words of Scripture, but inspired the spiritual ideas it contains. It might fairly be asked, "Where did this learned Professor get his information" on this subject, about which he writes so positively? Certainly not in the Bible itself. And there is no other way by which he could obtain it except by direct inspiration, which he surely does not claim on behalf of himself and other "liberal theologians."

On page 37, regarding the writers of the Scriptures, he says: "The Divine Spirit quickened their faculties in reference to spiritual, not temporal, things, Their inspiration thus consisted in their quickened insight into the ways of God, and their quickened foresight respecting His providential purposes." All of which is simple assertion on his part without one particle of Scripture to support it.

On page 38 he says: "Only the teaching in them which pertains to Divine redemption, and deals with those ideas which have to do with faith and conduct, has the guarantee of inspiration." And again, on page 39, he says: "It is only the moral truths and spiritual principles of the Bible that are divinely inspired." But, as this learned Professor has already discarded the doctrine of the vicarious sacrifice of Christ, it is as hard to understand what his theory of redemption is as it is to find out how much of the Bible he would admit to be really the Word of God.

On page 43, speaking of revelation, he says: "*Modern scholars* not only distinguish between revelation and Scripture, but they also distinguish between revelation and inspiration." And again, on page 44, he says in reference to Professor Goldwin Smith : "Though he rejects the Hebrew Scriptures as a supernatural revelation in the obsolete sense, which no *modern scholar* holds."

Upon the subject of Evolution, on page 48, he says: "We may safely assume the same sort of evolution for the ages before the Scriptures were produced, namely, a gradual ascent from fetichism and polytheism to the worship of a single God." Not at all. Such an assumption is entirely unwarrantable. It is disproved by facts in the whole history of the world, and specially in the history of the children of Israel. The tendency has always been to evolute downwards instead of upwards in this respect, from the worship of one God into idolatry and the worship of many gods.

On page 51, writing on the same subject, he says : "Revelations take place independently of the Bible. Being the outcome of a living, continuous agency, they are occurring all the time. God is always unveiling

Himself, and disclosing His secrets to the minds of devout men. Hence, there is a sense in which revelation can never be a finished product." In this way he might, perhaps, claim that his own unscriptural theories are inspired.

On the subject of Interpretation (page 51) he says: " Referring to an *old-fashioned method* of reading or studying the Scriptures," etc.; and then, on page 56, he says, "as if he believed *respectable scholarship* was still pursuing such a foolish course. It is a good while since the Song of Songs, which *all reputable scholars* now regard as a lyric poem, intended to display the triumph of pure affection over the temptations of wealth and rank, has been turned by intelligent interpreters into a crytogrammic description of the union of Christ with His Church."

Regarding the story of Jonah, he says, on page 60: " It is unwarrantable for men to claim that His (Jesus) reference to the story of Jonah proves that the incident is historical, or that He believed it to be historical." And again on page 61, he says: " We likewise have the best of reasons for believing that the story of Jonah is not literal but topical history." And on page 63 he says that " He (Jesus) leaves all questions of historical or literary criticism, such as the composite origin of the Pentateuch, the allegoric character of the account of the Fall, and the parabolic character of the Book of Isaiah to be settled by study and investigation." All contrary to plain Scripture, and only assertions on his part.

On the subject of History Professor Workman makes some references to the Assyrian legends, which the writer thinks are fully answered in the Appendix A to this book. It is sufficient to remark that in this, as in all other cases, the tendency with him is to adopt theories which throw doubt upon the inspiration of Scripture even when an opposite theory is much more reasonable.

On the subject of Science he says, on page 81 : " *Theologians once believed* that the whole universe was constructed piece by piece, that the first man was made directly from the dust of the ground, and that the first woman was built out of a rib taken from his side. They once believed, too, that the world was formed in six days of twenty-four hours each, and that the earth was just four thousand years old at the birth of Christ. Having obtained a better understanding of the literary construction of the story, as well as a clearer perception of the didactic purpose of the compiler, theologians now recognize that some features of the story are not to be treated literally, but topically; and they also recognize that the aim of the writer was not to explain how anything came into being," etc. But the learned Professor does not explain how it was that he and the other critics and liberal theologians found out the intentions of the writer of Genesis, which is a pity. In the last paragraph on the subject of Science he says, on page 86: "No competent instructor now finds anything in the story of creation to impugn since, technically speaking, the account is neither scientific nor unscientific, but non-scientific."

On the subject of Religion he concludes the chapter as follows on page 94: "It is owing to the influence of the Jewish, and not the Grecian or the Roman religion, that the human race has for upwards of two thousand years been steadily advancing to *universal brotherhood!!!*"

On the subject of Miracles, on page 126, the learned Professor says: "The account of the destruction of the Cities of the Plain is a graphic description of an ancient volcanic eruption, a kind of catastrophe to which the valley of the lower Jordan, from its geological structure, is said by Christian scientists to have been subject at one time." And he concludes the chapter by saying that "a miracle is not a suspension, much less a violation, of the laws of the universe, but something wonderful that has happened in the providence of God, or something remarkable that has been performed by the power of God in harmony with nature's laws." But Professor

Goldwin Smith's reasoning is much more consistent than this when he says that the term, "Laws of nature," presupposes a Law-giver, who has also the power to suspend the operation of those laws.

In the Introduction, which Professor Burwash, the Principal of Victoria College, has written, he says: "Dr. Workman's book is an able as well as a useful exposition of the new line of defending the Scriptures by a man of ripe scholarship in the department with which it deals"; and he concludes in the following words: "As such a work, having such an aim, I heartily commend the volume to the serious consideration, not only of the Methodist Church, but also of the Christian public, as a valuable contribution to the elucidation of the Old Testament."

When such a line of teaching is adopted by the Professors in our leading theological seminaries it is not much wonder that infidelity is rapidly on the increase. One traitor in the camp can do more mischief than a hundred open and avowed enemies on the outside. In this Laodicean age, when many of the leading denominations in Christendom are boasting of their wealth, and numbers, and scholarship, is it not only too true that the Lord Jesus Christ has taken His place on the outside of the whole scene of confusion, and is saying: "If any man hear my voice, and open the door, I will come in to him, and sup with him, and he with me?"

It is not surprising that some honest preachers should sound the alarm, as did the Rev. Dr. De Costa in an Episcopal church in New York recently.

"The time has come to think," said Mr. De Costa. "It is simply criminal to attempt to shut our eyes to the facts presented by the census, showing the spread of irreligion in the land. Millions of young men of three generations have gone down to unsanctified graves. Morally, denominationalism has not saved the people. It has not saved religion or morality. This morning Christianity is ignored by the masses of the people. Sectarianism has played a high game, and it has lost.

Even among its membership, if reports are true, there are men who reflect little or no credit upon its work.

"What is the prospect ? . . . One hundred years ago there were one million people out of the Church; to-day there are fifty million. How long is it going to take at this rate to convert the nation ?

"It is something pitiful to see the secretaries of church societies prepare figures to show an increase in the membership of their organizations, when the masses are drifting further away from the Gospel of our Lord and Saviour. You can count the gains on your fingers, while the census counts up the losses by millions. Blatant infidelity prevails throughout the land."

Nor is it surprising that such an avowed infidel as Professor Goldwin Smith should, after reading an account of Professor Workman's book, "The Old Testament Vindicated," publish the severe rebuke contained in the following letter :

To the Editor of The Globe :

"SIR,—Dr. Workman's new book has not yet come into my hands, but if your account of it is correct it must, as a reply to my argument, be a misdirection.

"My arguments have been pointed, not against the theories of rationalists like Dr. Workman, who abandon everything of orthodoxy except the names, but against the creed which Dr. Workman cannot deny is commonly taught in the churches, and is embodied in the ordination tests.

"Dr. Workman abandons, it seems, the historical authority of the Book of Genesis; he must then abandon the story of the Fall. If he abandons the story of the Fall, how can he maintain the doctrines of the redemption or the incarnation ?

"There is no use in trying to entangle me in controversies about the documentary origin of the books of the Old Testament. I have read Ewald, Kuenen, Renan and the rest, and have convinced myself that the subject is, and is likely to remain, in a highly hypothetical condition. The last guess is a Hebrew Homer, hidden be-

hind the figures of Elijah and Elisha. But all this is
entirely beside my mark.

"That there is much spirituality as well as historic-
ally valuable in some of the books of the Old Testament
no man of comprehensive intelligence will deny. How
much, we shall be better able to say when theological
sophistication on these subjects is at an end, when the
real facts are honestly admitted, and the superstitious use
of the Hebrew writings is frankly laid aside."

GOLDWIN SMITH.

There can be no compromise with infidelity upon the
Divine inspiration of the Bible without bringing dishonour upon the name of the Lord Jesus Christ, who,
as the Son of God, certified to the Old Testament Scriptures being the Word of God, and, therefore, divinely
inspired. It is altogether likely that Professor Workman's so-called vindication of the Old Testament will
do a thousand times more harm than Professor Goldwin
Smith's open attack upon it. Who can estimate the far-
reaching and mischievous effects of such teaching in one
of the principal theological and denominational colleges
of Canada? The attempt to vindicate the Old Testament by denying its inspiration, and using the stale
arguments of rationalistic critics, to explain away and set
aside all that is supernatural about it is, indeed, a novel
experiment, which must have a bad effect upon the
minds of young men who are not well established in the
knowledge of the truth, and are thus likely to be misled
by the confident assertions of any one who is reputed
to be a great scholar, and is in a responsible position.

An able booklet on "The Higher Criticism" has
recently been published by H. L. Hastings, of Boston,
editor of the *Christian*, from which the following extracts
are taken :

"It is not needful to go wild with panic over the
results of the Higher Criticism, or of any other criticism.
If these gentlemen throw away half or two-thirds of the

Bible, there will still be more left than most people are
likely to study carefully or practice faithfully; and
besides if half the books of the Bible can be thrown
overboard, it will save a large amount of labour for those
expositors who spend so much time trying to prove that
the book does not mean what it says, nor say what it
means; and there will be quite as much consistency
exhibited in rejecting the writing as there is in accepting it, and then perverting its sense.

*   *   *   *   *   *   *   *

"The sublime assurance with which some modern
critics announce their judgment concerning the origin,
authorship, and authenticity of the Holy Scriptures
implies the possession of great self-confidence, if not
absolute omniscience. They speak as if the questions
under consideration were definitely settled, and as if only
the ignorant, prejudiced, and bigoted could for a moment presume to question the soundness of their conclusions, or the accuracy of their assertions. Thus, questions of vast importance and wide-reaching interest are
decided with an assumption of infallibility or inerrancy
which ordinary mortals scarcely dare to claim. And all
this is done in the name of Higher Criticism, and exact
Biblical science, by men whose greatness is supposed
to be so manifest that the very mention of their names
should awe people into silence and submission."

*   *   *   *   *   *   *   *

In the *Methodist Review* for March-April, 1891, page
265, the late learned and lamented editor, J. W. Mendenhall, D.D., LL.D., while speaking of "The intrusion of
the hypothetical spirit in the investigation of Biblical
Doctrines, and of the origin of Biblical Literature," thus
illustrates the uncertainty of this scientific guess-work,
by which certain critics have endeavoured to determine
infallibly the origin and authorship of the various books
of the Old and New Testaments, until, where truth
ought to be found as transparent as sunlight, we find it

clouded and hidden in the thick network of rhetorical and fallacious theorizing.

Dr. Mendenhall gave a list of 747 theories applied to the various books of the Bible by the critics since 1850, and then concludes as follows :

" ' Of the 747 theories, 603 are defunct, and many of the remaining 144 are in the last stages of degeneracy and dissolution. It will assist the reader in estimating the work of the critics to remember that nearly one hundred theories die annually, many of them never advancing beyond infancy, and others being stricken with leprosy as for the first time they have taken hold of the horns of the altar of the Lord. We have by no means recorded all the inventions of the critics since Baur's day, but we have given enough to show that theory is the chief instrument of the critic. He does not always seek facts or truths, but is wedded to his hypothesis of the biblical question. Of the large number of theories here given no two of them agree, every one being distinct and separate from all the others. We have little doubt, if a correct enumeration of the theories that have been proclaimed during the last forty years could be obtained it would be found to *exceed two thousand*, for we suspended our examination long before the end had been reached. In these startling facts the orthodoxist finds abundant reason for refusing to follow the leadership of men whose chief business is to contradict truth, fact, history, and the fundamental principles of the Christian religion, with no stronger warrant than their own fancy or the limitations of their special education.'

" This, then," adds Mr. Hastings, " is a summary of the work of these learned critics, some of whom, smoke-dried and beer-sodden, handle the oracles of God with little reverence, and, instead of trembling at His words, which shall judge them at the last day, seem to have no more respect for the messages of those whom God has set ' over the nations, and over the kingdoms, to root out, and to pull down, and to destroy, and to throw down, to build, and to plant' (Jer. 1 : 10), than they have for an erotic song of a licentious pagan poet or some legend of heathen mythology.

*   *   *   *   *   *   *   *

" The whole story of the New Testament, and the proof of the Messiahship of Jesus of Nazareth, revolves around the expressions: ' Thus it is written,' and, ' That it might be fulfilled which was spoken by the prophets.' The Saviour in the concluding days of His ministry rebuked His disciples as being ' slow of heart to believe all that the prophets have spoken '; and the apostles, in proving the Messiahship of the son of Mary, reasoned out of the prophets and the Scriptures, ' saying none other things but those which Moses and the prophets did say should come to pass.' Christianity, therefore, stands or falls with the truth of sacred prophecy, and the apostle solemnly enjoins upon us to ' despise not prophesyings.'

*   *   *   *   *   *   *   *

" The Higher Critics despise and discredit prophecy by asserting that the men who claimed to be the messengers of God were really pretenders, forgers of fables, and writers of fictitious books; and hence they make constant efforts to bring down the dates of the books of the prophets and sacred writers to a period subsequent to the events to which they referred, thus endeavouring to prove that prophecy is a fable; that no man has ever been inspired of God to foretell future events; whence it follows that Christianity is a fraud, and Jesus of Nazareth was not the promised Messiah, the Son of God, the Saviour of the world, and that no prediction for the future can be accepted or depended upon.

*   *   *   *   *   *   *   *

" The assaults on Christianity at the present day are not open and above board; they are covered and insidious. The process of sapping and mining is going on. We are told that such an argument must be abandoned, but then we do not need it: that another position must be given up, but there are others that are so much stronger that it makes no difference. We are informed that 'all the learned believe' this, and that 'all the critics believe' that, and only a few belated, old-time bigots maintain the 'traditional view.'

"And yet there are men who had given thought and study to these questions before most of these Higher Critics were born, and who examined these difficulties when some of these learned gentlemen were in their swaddling clothes, and they are not at all certain that wisdom is likely to die with a lot of German Doctors who, over their pipes and beer, discuss and everlastingly settle these questions beyond the possibility of doubt or appeal, and make their conclusions the end of the law regarding this matter.

*   *   *   *   *   *   *   *

" But they must not ask us to depend on authority when we drop the Bible. We cannot make a *fetish* of the new books of the Higher Critics. They must give us evidence, and demonstration, and must bring this evidence down where the common people can read and understand it ; and if they will kindly agree among themselves, so that when one of them has settled everything no one else will come along next day and upset the whole, we shall be truly thankful. Especially would we be glad to have them tell us what they believe, and *why they believe it.* 'Tell me what you believe, I have doubts enough of my own.' is a saying attributed to Goethe. These gentlemen have spent time enough telling us what they do *not* believe; now will they inform us what they *do* believe, and also why they believe it ? They have showed us how to cut our cable: will they now tell us how to come to anchor, and where we are to find an anchorage ground ?

" Truth courts investigation. Candid men are not afraid to consider difficulties which occur in the Hebrew Scriptures; but when such difficulties are invented or exaggerated, they indicate the errancy of the critic rather than that of the Book he criticizes. Intelligent, careful, honest criticism is legitimate and welcome; but carping skepticism is not legitimate criticism.

"The phrase 'Higher Critic' is as indefinite as the term 'reptile,' which may be either a crocodile, a mud-turtle, a lizard, or a striped snake; or the word 'animal,' which may be a mouse, a mammoth, a pussy cat, or a Bengal tiger. So there are critics *and* critics, of every variety, from the mildest grade of perplexed doubters to the most outspoken type of skeptics and unbelievers. Names and brands signify little now; every parcel must be examined. Doubtless some of the Higher Critics are men of devout spirit and true faith, but they are in questionable company, and are sowing seed which may produce an unlooked-for harvest. They must not complain if men scrutinize or suspect them. Plain people are anxious to know just what the critics of the day are, and what they are doing. Are they Christians or infidels? Are they trying to pilot the old ship into port, or wreck it on the sandbar? Christians are quite willing that critics should scrape off barnacles, but they are not ready to have them scuttle the ship: and it seems to be time for those in whom faith is not utterly dead to watch the course of events, and stand for the defense of truths which are rashly assailed."

Since the above was in type the November number of "Watchword and Truth," published by Robert Cameron, of Boston, has been received, containing an article from the pen of Mr. A. Ben Oliel, the celebrated Hebrew scholar, and missionary to the Jews in Jerusalem.

Mr. Ben Oliel is a Sephardim Jew, and his family has always claimed descent from the house of David. He was educated for a Rabbi, and became a good Oriental scholar. When eighteen years of age he read a New Testament, which made a deep impression, and some time afterwards became convinced that Jesus was the Messiah. Since 1848 he has laboured as a missionary amongst the Jews in Spain, North Africa, Turkey and Palestine. In 1887 he was sent to Jaffa by the

British Society, who afterwards abandoned the work for want of funds, and Mr. F. Y. Edwards, the Treasurer of the Society, wrote thus respecting the missionary:

"I have the highest opinion of Mr. Ben Oliel as a scholar, Orientalist, linguist and Hebraist, and have always believed him to be both a gentleman and a true-hearted Christian."

Mr. Ben Oiiel has suffered much persecution since he went to Jerusalem without asking any one's permission, and without an appointment by any missionary society, over eight years ago; and he is now supported solely by the free-will offerings which the Lord leads His people to send to him.

Surely such a man as this, with his fifty years experience amongst Hebrew scholars and Jewish people, is better qualified to speak with authority about the books of the Old Testament than a few English Professors known as "liberal theologians," whose ideas have been borrowed from skeptical German doctors, and who yet presume to write and speak as if they represent the whole Christian Church. Mr. Ben Oliel writes as follows on the subject of "Higher Criticism and Common Sense":—

"One of the most commonly accepted theories of the so-called higher criticism in vogue in this generation of presumed superlative acumen in Biblical study, is that which attributes the composition of the book of the prophet Isaiah to several auhors, usually to two, and sometimes to three or more, on the ground mainly of differences of style and the use of peculiar phraseology in the latter chapters of the book. Other arguments are advanced betimes, and they all make my Jewish blood boil within me, and my Bible and Gospel-loving heart ache, when reading the works and writings of men, talented in other respects, but almost wholly destitute of any real grasp of the genius of the Hebrew tongue, which is a far higher attainment, and of far more practical importance, particularly in the study of its sublimely poetical books, than a mere knowledge of its grammatical construction, sitting in judgment, dissecting and mangling the sacred books of my fore-fathers—the incomparable, indubitably-inspired Bible—for the purpose of producing such fanciful assumptions as the theory referred to above, or, to say the least, with no better result than that.

"I shall confine these lines to that theory of plurality of authors in Isaiah by an appeal to common sense and the general experience of mankind, writers and authors included; and thereby prove and expose its utter absurdity and hollowness.

"Isaiah prophesied during the reigns of four Kings of Judah, extending to at least fifty years. We may reasonably suppose that he commenced to prophesy when he was twenty to twenty-five years of age, and more probably near thirty; and, if so, he must have lived to nearly eighty years—a long span of life.

"To demolish that theory I appeal to human experience all the world over. Is it not a fact that men change their style of writing as they grow in years? And, secondly, does not their style of writing change and differ with the subject matter of their discourse or composition and attendant circumstances and surroundings? Do people write a letter of condolence in the same style and phraseology as they write one of congratulation or felicitation to a dear friend? The change in style does not lead people to infer that some one else wrote it—some distinct and separate person. The signature settles that for them.

"And why should it be otherwise with a prophet, speaking and writing in his naturally acquired language, except when expressly dictated to? Why should he not, like everybody else, change his mode of writing—his phraseology and expressions—with age, with subject, with attending circumstances? Where is the logic, the common sense, of apportioning parts of the book of Isaiah to separate and distinct writers simply because the style is different, when the subject matter is so varied and so divergent? How could he possibly help it with the lapse of years and the change of his subject of discourse ? The chapters predicting happy times to come are naturally and necessarily clothed in correspondingly cheerful, joyous phraseology, very unlike those of gloomy events, full of sorrow and woe. How could such chapters as those which begin with ' Comfort ye, comfort ye my people,' ' Arise, shine, for thy light is come,' be expressed, dressed in the same terms as those foretelling dire calamities of Divine justice and deserving retribution near at hand ? It is simply absurd, illogical, opposed to common sense and human experience, all the world over and in all tongues to fancy that because the style is different, although the subject is different also, still it must be someone else that wrote it ? But, yet, this is what the higher criticism says! It is a glaring illustration of the hollow and frivolous assumptions of the higher critics—higher in their own conceit.

" By all means let us have all that true, conscientious, enlightened, painstaking scholarship can give us; all that the excavator and antiquarian can discover and produce in explanation and illustration of the Bible— the Oracles Divine; but, surely, modesty and reserve should characterize their writings when they cannot, cr fail to see the complete veracity and full reliability of all its parts, and wait for further and fuller light to dispel their doubts and illumine their vision.

" Light will in time dawn to verify, confirm and establish every part of the sacred volume, as it has so remarkably done in recent times by the labors of excavators in Bible lands. ' The Tell Amarna Tablets,' published by ' the Palestine Exploration Fund,' have thrown a flood of light on the conquest—of Canaan by Joshua and the Abiri—the. Hebrews. The Rev. John Urquart's articles on ' Modern Discovery,' published in The New York Observer, give a lucid and most instructive summary of late discoveries, well worth the attentive perusal of all Theologians and Biblical students.

" If the Lord sends me the means for the support

of an assistant in this Mission of faith and trust in Him, so as to be free from the minor cares of the work, I shall be glad to comply with the wishes of friends and give more time and attention to the defence of the inspired Scriptures from the mists of the higher critics, and their illustration by the ' stones crying out ' in these Bible lands in vindication of their reliability and Divine origin. At present I can seldom find leisure from constant Mission work to give due attention to such important subjects, which demand careful, prayerful consideration.

A. BEN OLIEL.

" Jerusalem, Palestine, August, 1898."

The greatest source of danger at the present time is the place that mere *scholarship* and natural intelligence is taking in the various theological institutions. Scholarship is useful in its own place, but it should be kept there, and not permitted to meddle with spiritual things, which can only be understood by spiritual men. If this course is not adopted, infidelity will continue to spread rapidly in these institutions, under the cloak of " higher criticism," or " liberal theology," until there will be a speedy fulfillment of New Testament predictions regarding the " last days," when " perilous times shall come " (2 Tim. 3 : 1-7), when there shall be " scoffers, walking after their own lusts, and saying where is the promise of His coming ?" etc. (2 Peter 3 : 3, 4), and when there " shall be false teachers, who privily shall bring in damnable heresies, even denying the Lord that bought them, and bring upon themselves swift destruction, and many shall follow their pernicious ways; by reason of whom the way of truth shall be evil spoken of " (2 Peter 2 : 1, 2).

Although a great scholar himself, Paul the Apostle never once mentioned scholarship as one of the qualifications for effective service in the Church of God. But he did tell Timothy that all Scripture was given by

inspiration of God (2 Tim. 3 : 16), and commanded him
to preach the Word (2 Tim. 4 : 2), and warned him that
the time would come when they would not endure sound
doctrine, but after their own lusts they should heap to
themselves teachers having, itching ears, and that they
should turn away their ears from the truth, and be turned
unto fables (2 Tim. 4 : 2-4). And Paul also warned the
Elders at Ephesus that after his departure grievous
wolves would enter in among them, not sparing the
flock (Acts 20 : 29). And he exhorted Timothy to commit the things he had heard of him among many witnesses to *faithful men*, who shall be able to teach others
also (2 Tim. 2 : 2).

The third chapter of Second Timothy commences
with solemn warning as to the perilous times that are
coming in the last days, and speaks of the men who
would be " ever learning, and never able to tome to the
knowledge of the truth. Now, as Jannes and Jambres
withstood Moses, so do these also resist the truth: men
of corrupt minds, reprobate concerning the faith " (2 Tim.
3 : 7, 8), and the chapter ends as follows:—" But continue thou in the things which thou hast learned and
been assured of, knowing of whom thou hast learned
them: and that from a child thou hast known the Holy
Scriptures, which are able to make thee wise unto salvation through faith which is in Christ Jesus. All Scripture is given by inspiration of God, and is profitable for
doctrine, for reproof, for correction, for instruction in
righteousness; that the man of God may be perfect,
throughly furnished unto all good works " (2 Tim. 3 :
14-17).

The reference to Jannes and Jambres withstanding
Moses will be understood by reading in Exodus 7 : 9-12,
where it is seen that the Egyptian magicians withstood
Moses by imitating the miracle which by the power of
God was wrought through Moses and Aaron in the pres-
ence of Pharaoh. And so has it always been ever since.
The Devil is constantly on the alert to deceive men by
imitating God's work. Although vanquished by the life,

death, and resurrection of the Lord Jesus Christ, and although his final overthrow and confinement in the lake of fire is thus assured; this enemy of God and of all righteousness still continues to exert a mighty influence in the affairs of men, but is liable to be defeated at any moment by the humblest and weakest Christian who uses the name of Jesus to repel his attacks. When he tempted Jesus for forty days in the wilderness he offered to give Him all the kingdoms of this world if He would fall down and worship him (Matt. 4 : 9), and three times over the Lord Jesus spoke of him as " the prince of this world " (John 12 : 31; 14 : 30: 16 : 11). In 2 Cor. 4 : 4 he is spoken of as the " god of this world "; and in Eph. 2 : 2 he is spoken of as " the prince of the power of the air, the spirit that now worketh in the children of disobedience." He cannot either create anything or foretell future events. These are attributes of God alone. But in other respects he is possessed of extraordinary powers, which he makes use of in resisting the purposes of God for blessing to the human race, and one of his most successful devices is to persuade men to reject the testimony of the Word of God and disbelieve in his own identity. The old-fashioned pictures representing him as a serpent, or with horns, and hoofs, and tail, are now cast aside; and he appears as an angel of light (2 Cor. 11 : 14), first suggesting doubts as to God having spoken to men at all through His Word, then denying the inspiration of the Bible and the vicarious sacrifice of Christ for the sins of fallen men; willing that Jesus should be regarded as a " great Teacher," but denying His divinity; and suggesting that the miracles He wrought and His own resurrection from the dead should be regarded as " incredibilities," because contrary to the operation of natural laws, for which he professes to have great respect, although he himself as a spiritual being has been able to assume various forms and to do many things contrary to the natural laws of this world, when it suited his purposes to do so.

During the earlier part of this half century, when the Gospel was being proclaimed in the power of the Holy Spirit, so that many persons under the mighty-power of God when convicted of sin were stricken down in public meetings, there was a great manifestation of satanic energy in various ways under the name of Spiritualism, and besides table rappings and table turnings there were many things done which could only be accounted for by the supernatural agency of Satan. For a time many were turned aside from the truth to believe the Devil's lie, but after it became generally admitted that he was the author of these proceedings, they became of no use to him, and the supernatural manifestations ceased.

During the past twenty or thirty years God has been manifesting His supernatural power in many thousands of cases, by healing the sick in answer to the prayer of faith, and thus proving that He is indeed the same yesterday, to-day and forever, and that He is just as able and willing to work miracles of healing now by the power of His Holy Spirit as when the Lord Jesus Christ was on earth. He is still "the Lord God of Elijah," and the same God who healed Miriam in answer to the prayer of Moses. The effect of these manifestations of divine power has been to confirm the faith of true Christians in the divinity of the Lord Jesus Christ and in the divine inspiration of the Scriptures. But Satan soon followed up this work of God with that monstrous development of the present day taking the name of "Christian Science," which is neither Christian nor scientific, denying as it does the personality of God, setting aside the Cross of Christ, and pretending to heal the sick by denying that either sickness or pain is real; but at the same time taking good care to charge fees for attendance on those whom they say are neither sick nor in pain. This horrible delusion has been the means of leading many thousands of souls astray; and the truth of God has been so confounded with the Devil's lie, that most persons do not understand the difference between the Scriptural doctrine of receiving freely, in answer to the prayer of faith, the healing of bodily ailments; and that miserable imitation of the Evil One which denies all foundation truths of Scripture, declares that there is no use in prayer, and under the false name of "Christian Science" extorts money from the ignorant under false pretences, by trying to make its dupes believe that there is really no such thing as either pain or sickness.

Throughout the latter half of the present century God has been impressing on the hearts of His own children as never before their indebtedness to all heathen lands to give them the Gospel, and thus to manifest their love for those who are perishing for lack of the water of life. And Satan has followed this up with the crowning abomination of this century, in the shape of the Parliament of Religions at the World's Fair in Chicago, where those who were supposed to be the most learned and distinguished amongst Mohammedans and Buddhists and other false and idolatrous religions of the world, met on the same platform with *learned* men and ministers professing to be Christians, and discussed the supposed merits of their various systems. As an imitation of that true Christian love that seeks the welfare of all mankind, this exhibition was certainly a masterpiece of Satan; and Dr. Workman assures us in his book that "it is owing to the Jewish, and not the Grecian or Roman religion, that the human race has, for upwards of two thousand years been steadily advancing towards "universal brotherhood"!

But a much more dangerous development of satanic energy is threatened in the near future than any of those abominations already referred to. During the past fifteen or twenty years God has been specially bringing before the minds of true Christians the necessity of yielding themselves up to Him in full consecration to be emptied and cleansed and filled with the Spirit, and the responsibility that rests upon them to endeavour to keep the "unity of the Spirit in the bond of peace" with all others who are true Christians, no matter by what other name they may be generally known. The spiritual union that has thus been brought about has evidently been of God, and the results are very blessed. Many thousands of genuine Christians have been drawn together in bonds of common sympathy, all fully believing in the divine inspiration of the Bible as the Word of God, all believing in the presence and power of the Holy Spirit as their indwelling Comforter and Teacher, and all looking for the speedy coming again of the Son of God from heaven. This movement has marvellously stimulated the work of missions in heathen lands, while God has been at the same time opening doors into which consecrated missionaries may enter in all parts of the world. Such a work as this could not long go on without attracting the attention and opposition of the great Adversary, and the great danger now is that, in imitation of the true Scriptural unity of the Spirit which God has thus established Satan may attempt to set up a union of merely nominal Christians with perhaps some who are really possessed of spiritual life, under the leadership of Professors and scholars known as " higher critics " and " liberal theologians," who would doubtless in a short time gain immense popularity by teaching that the Bible is not the Word of God, that Jesus did not " bear our sins in His own body on the tree," and that there is no such thing as a real personal Devil that we read about in Scripture. With such a liberal platform as this there would be nothing to hinder such an organization from becoming a most popular institution and gaining adherents amongst the unconverted church members in every denomination, and amongst infidels and skeptics of all classes. The membership would probably include a large proportion of the wealthiest and most intellectual people in some of the most fashionable churches, and the leadership in such an influential organization, supported by many of the principal papers of the secular and religious press, would give to those who are now known as skeptical Professors more weight than they at present enjoy in their several institutions of learning. They might promulgate their theories in a more authoritative manner than they have yet ventured upon in their various denominations, and be assured that they have the support of a large number of the fashionable and wealthy people in the propagation of their heresies. It would soon become apparent whether those who are longing for a restoration of "the old-time religion" would be forced to go out, or to take a back seat, and let the critics and "liberal theologians" rule the various institutions in which students for the ministry of the Word are being taught to forsake the *old-fashioned* way of believing that the Bible is really the Word of God, whose truths can only be understood by the teaching of the Holy Spirit" (1 Cor. 2 : 10-16). The establishment of such a union of those professing to be Christians would only be an imitation of the unity which God enjoins, and a hindrance to His work which no true Christian should countenance.

There is a Gospel Union extending through many of the United States, and composed of members of all denominations and of no denomination, whose platform reads as follows:—

"Members of the Gospel Union shall consist of those only who have accepted Jesus Christ as their personal Saviour, who serve Him by a separated and consecrated life, and who subscribe to the following:—'I believe in one God, who is revealed in Scripture as subsisting in three equal persons, Father, Son, and Holy Spirit; in the verbal inspiration of the Scriptures of the Old and New Testaments as originally given, in the substitutional atonement of the Lord Jesus Christ; in salvation only by faith in Him; in the eternal punishment of the unsaved; and in the personal and pre-millennial coming of our Lord.'"

The headquarters of this Gospel Union is at 415 Oak Street, Kansas City, Mo., U.S., and the General Director is Mr. George S. Fisher, who publishes an excellent monthly paper, "The Gospel Message," in connection with the work of the Gospel Union, containing reports from its missionaries in Morocco, South America, and in the Western States amongst the Indians, besides much valuable Scriptural teaching. No fees are required for membership, and its missionary work is carried on by faith in God for all needed supplies.

There is not the slightest danger of infidels, higher critics, and liberal theologians seeking admission into a Christian Union with such a platform as the Gospel Union, whose branches should be extended to every town and village throughout the world where the Anglo-Saxon tongue is spoken.

By all means let there be a Christian Union, but let it not be a miserable counterfeit, consisting mainly of "liberal theologians" and nominal Christians, who regard the Bible as a compilation of fables, with a "divine element" in it, and "containing great inspirations of all things." If there is to be a Christian Union at all, let it be a Gospel Union, composed only of true Christians who subscribe to the above Confession of Faith, and who accept the whole Bible, from cover to cover, as the Divinely Inspired Word of God, which solves the "Riddle of Existence," unfolds the wonders of Redemption, reveals the mystery of the church, and points forward to the speedy coming again of the Lord Jesus Christ, for whom His people wait, and, while waiting, work to hasten His Second Coming by sending the Gospel to every part of the habitable globe, and at the same time endeavour "to keep the unity of the Spirit in the bond of peace" with all others who are really born of God.

THE UNITY OF THE SPIRIT

—OR—

Failure of Brethrenism as a United Testimony.

WITH SOME REMARKS UPON

Holiness People and the Holiness Movement.

BY W. J. FENTON.

In Paper Covers, 10c.   In Cloth, 20c.

PRESS NOTICES.

A capital booklet, written by W. J. Fenton, and published in Toronto, Canada, has been received. It discusses the question in a calm and brotherly spirit, entirely free from the bitterness and bickering of sectarian strife, so common among those who write upon the subject, and shows how the remarkable movement inaugurated by J. N. Darby, B. W. Newton, George Muller and others, has utterly failed "as a united testimony." It would be well if the "Brethren" should heed the suggestions and warnings he gives; but there is no hope of this amid a people, who are on the whole the soundest in the faith, and most intelligent in the knowledge of our Lord Jesus Christ, "till He come."—*The late James H. Brookes, of St. Louis, in "Truth," for May, 1897.*

We have read this treatise with much interest, and we find its spirit and aim in every way excellent. The author has spoken the truth in love. In the fullest sympathy with much precious Gospel teaching to which "The Brethren" have borne testimony, he yet shows very clearly how that testimony has been hindered by their exclusiveness, arrogance and proneness to separation and division. . . . . Mr. Fenton emphasizes the need which Christians have of mutual forbearance on matters regarding which the Word of God gives no express directions, and urges on all the Lord's people the great duty of "endeavouring to keep the unity of the Spirit in the bond of peace." His work cannot fail to do good, and we trust it will have the large circulation it deserves.—*The "Faithful Witness" for April 2, 1897.*

OPINIONS OF PROMINENT BRETHREN.

A very prominent leader amongst the Brethren for thirty or forty years past, and still with them, wrote the author as follows in May, 1897:—" I read it with very great interest. I cannot now call to mind a sentence I do not most heartily endorse. It is a splendid setting forth of a painful subject. I trust the kindly spirit in which it is written will disarm the adversary. What you say about the Conferences, O how true ! . . . . you cannot ask an outside Christian without the risk of his being attacked in the most scathing denunciation, and all under the plea of faithfulness to truth. They seem to act as if no Christian had a conscience exercised but themselves."

Another Brother who was first a Methodist, then an " Exclusive," and afterwards amongst " Open Brethren," writes as follows:—" I am at present engaged reading your book on Brethren, and can most heartily endorse everything you have written. I wish it was read by all the Brethren. . . . . I can heartily commend your book, and trust it will have a large sale. I never met you, sir, but I cordially endorse your most excellent book, and I trust the Lord will abundantly bless and use you in His service."

And another Brother wrote the publishers on November 17th, 1898, as follows:—" Please send me by mail two copies of ' Failure of Brethrenism,' by W. J. Fenton; it corresponds with my views wonderfully, and although I am in fellowship with Brethren, their divisions and injustice, with their backbitings, are causing me to withdraw from them, and I am at a standstill to know where to go.

 **Trieste**

Trieste Publishing has a massive catalogue of classic book titles. Our aim is to provide readers with the highest quality reproductions of fiction and non-fiction literature that has stood the test of time. The many thousands of books in our collection have been sourced from libraries and private collections around the world.

The titles that Trieste Publishing has chosen to be part of the collection have been scanned to simulate the original. Our readers see the books the same way that their first readers did decades or a hundred or more years ago. Books from that period are often spoiled by imperfections that did not exist in the original. Imperfections could be in the form of blurred text, photographs, or missing pages. It is highly unlikely that this would occur with one of our books. Our extensive quality control ensures that the readers of Trieste Publishing's books will be delighted with their purchase. Our staff has thoroughly reviewed every page of all the books in the collection, repairing, or if necessary, rejecting titles that are not of the highest quality. This process ensures that the reader of one of Trieste Publishing's titles receives a volume that faithfully reproduces the original, and to the maximum degree possible, gives them the experience of owning the original work.

We pride ourselves on not only creating a pathway to an extensive reservoir of books of the finest quality, but also providing value to every one of our readers. Generally, Trieste books are purchased singly - on demand, however they may also be purchased in bulk. Readers interested in bulk purchases are invited to contact us directly to enquire about our tailored bulk rates. Email: customerservice@triestepublishing.com

You May Also Like

Legislative Honors to the Memory of President Lincoln. Message of Gov. Fenton to the Legislature, Communicating the Death of President Lincoln; pp. 1-117

Reuben E. Fenton

ISBN: 9780649629534
Paperback: 128 pages
Dimensions: 6.14 x 0.27 x 9.21 inches
Language: eng

The Twentieth Century New Testament: A Translation Into Modern English, in Three Parts, Part III, pp. 385-511

Fenton John Anthony Hort & Brooke Foss Westcott

ISBN: 9780649524600
Paperback: 152 pages
Dimensions: 6.0 x 0.33 x 9.0 inches
Language: eng

www.triestepublishing.com

You May Also Like

ISBN: 9780649507696
Paperback: 182 pages
Dimensions: 6.14 x 0.39 x 9.21 inches
Language: eng

Six Lectures on the Ante-Nicene Fathers

Fenton John Anthony Hort

ISBN: 9780649673087
Paperback: 274 pages
Dimensions: 6.14 x 0.57 x 9.21 inches
Language: eng

Poems: Tributes to Scarborough; Odes on Wellington & Napoleon; Haddon Hall; Ode on the Ruins of Conisbro' Castle Etc. Etc. Etc.

Ben. Fenton

www.triestepublishing.com

You May Also Like

ISBN: 9780649333158
Paperback: 84 pages
Dimensions: 6.14 x 0.17 x 9.21 inches
Language: eng

Report of the Department of Farms and Markets, pp. 5-71

Various

ISBN: 9780649324132
Paperback: 78 pages
Dimensions: 6.14 x 0.16 x 9.21 inches
Language: eng

Catalogue of the Episcopal Theological School in Cambridge Massachusetts, 1891-1892

Various

www.triestepublishing.com

You May Also Like

ISBN: 9780649352142
Paperback: 88 pages
Dimensions: 6.14 x 0.18 x 9.21 inches
Language: eng

Three Hundred Tested Recipes

Various

ISBN: 9780649419418
Paperback: 108 pages
Dimensions: 6.14 x 0.22 x 9.21 inches
Language: eng

A Basket of Fragments

Anonymous

Find more of our titles on our website. We have a selection of thousands of titles that will interest you. Please visit

www.triestepublishing.com